The Other Side of Silence

The Other Side of
SILENCE

Voices from the Partition of India

Urvashi Butalia

HURST & COMPANY, LONDON

2000

Published in the United Kingdom by
C. Hurst & Co. (Publishers) Ltd.
38 King Street, London WC2E 8JZ
under license from
Duke University Press,
Durham, North Carolina
© 2000 Duke University Press
Printed in the United States of America

ISBNS
1-85065-542-1 casebound
1-85065-533-2 paperback

We are grateful to Pantheon Books and to the author for
permission to use the quotation from *Corelli's Mandolin*, by Louis
de Bernières (New York: Pantheon Books, 1994). This work was
published in the United Kingdom as *Captain Corelli's Mandolin*
(London: Martin Secker & Warburg, 1994).

For my mother Subhadra
And my father Joginder
Who taught me about Partition
For Ranamama, my uncle
Who lives the Partition from day to day
And for my grandmother Dayawanti/Ayesha
Whose life Partition shaped
As it did her death

CONTENTS

Acknowledgments ix

1

BEGINNINGS 1

2

BLOOD 21

3

'FACTS' 53

4

WOMEN 85

5

'HONOUR' 137

6

CHILDREN 195

7

'MARGINS' 233

8

MEMORY 273

Glossary 295

Index 301

ACKNOWLEDGMENTS

More than at the thought of writing this book, I have balked at the thought of writing the acknowledgments. How will I thank the many friends who have held my hand and been more than just supportive throughout this exercise? How will I even remember them? And what will I do if I forget? It has been so many years since I embarked on this project. I did not know then that it would eventually turn into a book, but now that it has, I need to cast my mind back many years to remember the different ways in which this work has been influenced by my friends — although, of course, I must make the usual disclaimer that the mistakes are all mine.

My first thanks go to Peter Chappell and Satti Khanna whose film *A Division of Hearts* was what began this project for me. I owe a deep debt of gratitude to my friend, C. V. Subbarao; for me, the greatest tragedy is that Subba is no longer around to critique, argue, find fault with and support my work. I could not have carried on this exercise had it not been for my dear friend and onetime fellow traveller Sudesh Vaid who, when the burden of listening to stories of such tragedy began to seem particularly heavy, generously offered to come in and help. I have many families scattered all over the world. From the very beginning my London family, Olivia Bennett, Stephen Clues, Sarah Hobson, Aparna Jack, Naila Kabeer, Munni Kabir, Marion and Robert Molteno, Bunny Page, Anne Rodford, Parminder Vir and Paul Westlake have been a source of such deep support that it is difficult for me to find words to thank them. Not only have they provided so many homes away from home, they have put up with my endless encroachments on their lives, my demands on their time, and have good-humouredly allowed themselves to be coerced into reading 'just five pages of the introduction' at all hours of the morning and night, and especially before they were rushing to work. To them, my deepest thanks. In London, too, are other much-loved members of my family: Ian Jack, David Page and Ralph Russell have been particularly generous in providing feedback and gentle (and sometimes not so gentle) criticism and encouragement. To the editors at *Granta* I owe a debt of gratitude for having published part of my work in their special issue on India, for it was this experience that, in many ways, gave me the confidence to continue.

My London family is joined by my Hong Kong family: I am especially grateful to Geeta Chanda for all her cheering-on e-mails, and for keeping faith with my work, and to Nayan Chanda for his positive responses to it; to my friends in Arena, particularly and most especially, Lau Kin Chi, for sharing her work and believing in mine. I thank too my Pakistan family, Ferida, Firhana, Lala, Neelam and their parents, for providing warmth, hospitality and much needed support: Shukria. In Morocco, I am grateful to my friend Layla Chaouni and to Fatima Mernissi who locked me in a room and fed and looked after me while I wrote. Fatima would quiz me every evening as I presented her with yet another revised plan of the book, and I had to spend the day preparing for this 'exam'.

And at home: Where shall I begin? So many people have read bits of this work. Not a week went by while I was writing without one or other of my many wonderful friends calling and egging me on. When are you going to finish this? Why don't you just get on with it? Do you want someone to look at it? Had it not been for their encouragement, and sometimes their threats, I doubt I would have been able to let go of my manuscript. For their support, for their many readings of this and that, I am grateful to Gouri Chatterjee, Robi Chatterjee for several years of reproach at not getting on with the job, Ella Dutta, Beatrice Kachuk—for detailed feedback on my many attempts at making sense of this work, Anuradha Kapur, Arvind Kumar, Charles Lewis, Meenakshi and Sujit Mukerjee, Manjula Padmanabhan, Rajni Palriwala, Vinod Raina, Sanjeev Saith, Kumkum Sangari, Prabeen Singh, Radhika Singha, Drago Stambuck—for suggestions about the title which I did not take, Ramya Subrahmanian, Ravi Vasudevan. My thanks to my editor Udayan Mitra, and to my Indian publishers: David Davidar for his faith, his patience and his excellent advice on the details of my manuscript; and Zamir Ansari for believing in my work despite not being able to read it! At different times Subhadra Sanyal and Ram Narayan provided valuable research assistance; they unearthed new and constantly fascinating material and often pointed me in the right direction. To Shankar and Sanjay for giving up their weekends and typesetting in record time. From

India this book found its way to England and the United States, and for this I am grateful to my editors Michael Dwyer (who read it on a plane journey between Delhi and London) and Valerie Millholland, who decided to take it on. I am grateful also to the two anonymous readers who commented on it, and to Jean Brady for her reading and to Miriam Angress for all of her help. To Henry Aronson for providing a reading 'from outside', and, especially, to my friend, Claudio Nappo, for believing in me and in my work.

Three major debts remain. The first of these is to a small group of friends without whom I would not have been able to cope with this work. Not only have they read and re-read each page and chapter, but they have advised, criticized and been there for me at all times of the day and night. An acknowledgment is a poor thing: I do not know how I can thank them enough, but an acknowledgment is all I have, so I offer it, with a truly deep sense of gratitude to: Uma Chakravarti, Primila Lewis, Tanika and Sumit Sarkar and Harsh Sethi.

Equally, I offer thanks to the many people who agreed to speak to me, who gave of their time and trust. Had it not been for them, and their stories, this book would never have been written. Their names are too numerous to mention, and some may well not want them mentioned, but to them my sincere gratitude.

And finally, most importantly, my own family: my mother, father, Bela, my sister and editor extraordinary, Pankaj and Nilofer for coffee (much needed and without which I would have simply slept my way through the many years I have put in) and for the many discussions and readings, Rahul and Meera for the e-mail access at all times of day or night and for their general good humour, and my most beloved nieces and nephew Damini, Ishani and Vidur, without whom life with this book would have been unutterably dull. From across the border, Rana-mama, around whom so much of this work is woven, has been with me throughout, and I hope that one day I will be able to show this book to him and tell him how much it has meant to me, and from another world, my grandmother Dayawanti/Ayesha whose spirit has remained with me throughout this work.

Thank you

'The New History of Cephallonia' was proving to be a problem; it seemed to be impossible to write it without the intrusion of his own feelings and prejudices. Objectivity seemed to be quite unattainable, and he felt that his false starts must have wasted more paper than was normally used on the island in the space of a year. The voice that emerged in his account was intractably his own; it was never historical. It lacked grandeur and impartiality. It was not Olympian. He sat down and wrote: . . . 'This island betrays its own people in the mere act of existing,' he wrote, and then he crumpled the sheet of paper and flung it into the corner of the room. This would never do; why could he not write like a writer of histories? Why could he not write without passion? Without anger? Without the sense of betrayal and oppression? He picked up the sheet, already bent at the corners, that he had written first. It was the title page: 'The New History of Cephallonia'. He crossed out the first two words and substituted 'A Personal'. Now he could forget about leaving out the loaded objectives and the ancient historical grudges, now he could be vitriolic about the Romans, the Normans, the Venetians, the Turks, the British, and even the islanders themselves. He wrote . . .

—LOUIS DE BERNIÈRES, *Corelli's Mandolin*

Do you really think anyone will change with listening to your tapes? Yes, it's true that the experience will be caught, that will be there, that this kind of thing happened during Partition, there is a kind of suffering that people don't know or have forgotten about. And people don't know that it was only then that we got independence. So this may help in remembering that, but other than that I don't think this will make much difference to anyone.

Suppose the government plays some of your tapes. If you take fifty interviews, and they play one, and one person is such that he has had a bitter experience with the government — and this is entirely possible — and he criticizes the government. Do you think they will tolerate this? And there is one other thing. You keep these tapes, who knows what this is about? You will label these, saying this is about the Partition of India and Pakistan. You'll make a card, with a number, and it will say 'experience of the person who suffered during Partition' . . . The truth is that this experience has been with us for a long time. Do you think these tapes will make any difference to the next set of rulers?

—MANMOHAN SINGH, village Thamali

1
BEGINNINGS

The political partition of India caused one of the great human convulsions of history. Never before or since have so many people exchanged their homes and countries so quickly. In the space of a few months, about twelve million people moved between the new, truncated India and the two wings, East and West, of the newly created Pakistan. By far the largest proportion of these refugees—more than ten million of them—crossed the western border which divided the historic state of Punjab, Muslims travelling west to Pakistan, Hindus and Sikhs east to India. Slaughter sometimes accompanied and sometimes prompted their movement; many others died from malnutrition and contagious diseases. Estimates of the dead vary from 200,000 (the contemporary British figure) to two million (a later Indian estimate) but that somewhere around a million people died is now widely accepted. As always there was widespread sexual savagery: about 75,000 women are thought to have been abducted and raped by men of religions different from their own (and indeed sometimes by men of their own religion). Thousands of families were divided, homes destroyed, crops left to rot, villages abandoned. Astonishingly, and despite many warnings, the new governments of India and Pakistan were unprepared for the convulsion: they had not anticipated that the fear and uncertainty created by the drawing of borders based on headcounts of religious identity—so many Hindus versus so many Muslims—would force people to flee to what they considered 'safer' places, where they would be surrounded by their own kind. People travelled in buses, in cars, by train, but mostly on foot in great columns called kafilas, which could stretch for dozens of miles. The longest of them, said to comprise nearly 400,000 people, refugees travelling east to India from western Punjab, took as many as eight days to pass any given spot on its route.

This is the generality of Partition: it exists publicly in history books. The particular is harder to discover; it exists privately in the stories told and retold inside so many households in India and Pakistan. I grew up with them: like many Punjabis of my generation, I am from a family of Partition refugees. Memories of Partition, the horror and brutality of the time, the harkening back to an—often mythical—past where Hindus and Muslims and Sikhs lived together in relative peace and harmony, have formed the staple of stories I have lived with. My mother and father come from Lahore, a city loved and sentimentalized by its inhabitants, which lies only twenty miles inside the Pakistan border. My mother tells of the dangerous journeys she twice made back there to bring her younger brothers and sister to India. My father remembers fleeing Lahore to the sound of guns and crackling fire. I would listen to these stories with my brothers and sister and hardly take them in. We were middle-class Indians who had grown up in a period of relative calm and prosperity, when tolerance and 'secularism' seemed to be winning the argument. These stories—of loot, arson, rape, murder—came out of a different time. They meant little to me.

Then, in October 1984, Prime Minister Indira Gandhi was assassinated by her security guards, both Sikhs. For days afterwards Sikhs all over India were attacked in an orgy of violence and revenge. Many homes were destroyed and thousands died. In the outlying suburbs of Delhi more than three thousand were killed, often by being doused in kerosene and then set alight. They died horrible, macabre deaths. Black burn marks on the ground showed where their bodies had lain. The government—headed by Mrs Gandhi's son Rajiv—remained indifferent, but several citizens' groups came together to provide relief, food and shelter. I was among the hundreds of people who worked in these groups. Every day, while we were distributing food and blankets, compiling lists of the dead and missing, and helping with compensation claims, we listened to the stories of the people who had suffered. Often older people, who had come to Delhi as refugees in 1947, would remember that they had been through a similar terror before. 'We didn't think it could happen to us in our own country,' they would say. 'This is like Partition again.'

Here, across the River Jamuna, just a few miles from where I lived, ordinary, peaceable people had driven their neighbours from their homes and murdered them for no readily apparent reason than that they were of a different religious community. The stories of Partition no longer seemed quite so remote: people from the same country, the same town, the same village, could still be divided by the politics of their religious difference, and, once divided, could do terrible things to each other. Two years later, working on a film about Partition for a British television channel, I began to collect stories from its survivors. Many of the tales were horrific and of a kind that I had found hard to believe when I was younger and heard them second or third hand: women jumping into wells to drown themselves so as to avoid rape or forced religious conversion; fathers beheading their own children so they would avoid the same dishonourable fate. Now I was hearing them from witnesses whose bitterness, rage and hatred—which, once uncovered, could be frightening—told me they were speaking the truth.

Their stories affected me deeply. Nothing as cruel and bloody had happened in my own family so far as I knew, but I began to realize that Partition was not, even in my family, a closed chapter of history—that its simple, brutal political geography infused and divided us still. The divisions were there in everyday life, as were their contradictions: how many times have I heard my parents, my grandmother, speak with affection and longing of their Muslim friends in Lahore, and how many times with irrational prejudice about 'those Muslims'; how many times had I heard my mother speak with a sense of betrayal of her brother who had married a Muslim. It took the events of 1984 to make me understand how ever-present Partition was in our lives, too, to recognize that it could not so easily be put away inside the covers of history books. I could no longer pretend that this was a history that belonged to another time, to someone else.

*   *   *

I began, like any other researcher, by looking at what had been written about Partition. And there was no dearth of material. Yet, as I read my way through it, I found myself becoming increasingly dissatisfied, sometimes even angry. If the books I was reading were to be believed, the Partition of India was something that happened in August 1947. A series of events preceded it: these included the growing divide between the Congress and the Muslim League, the debates between Jinnah and Gandhi, Nehru, Patel, and a host of other developments on the 'political' front. And a series of events accompanied and followed it: violence, mass migration, refugeeism, rehabilitation. But the 'history' of Partition seemed to lie only in the political developments that had led up to it. These other aspects—what had happened to the millions of people who had to live through this time, what we might call the 'human dimensions' of this history—somehow seemed to have a 'lesser' status in it. Perhaps this was because they had to do with difficult things: loss and sharing, friendship and enmity, grief and joy, with a painful regret and nostalgia for loss of home, country and friends, and with an equally strong determination to create them afresh. These were difficult things to capture 'factually'. Yet, could it really be that they had no place in the history of Partition? Why then did they live on so vividly in individual and collective memory?

I looked at what the large political facts of this history seemed to be saying. If I was reading them right, it would seem that Partition was now over, done with, a thing of the past. Yet, all around us there was a different reality: partitions everywhere, communal tension, religious fundamentalism, continuing divisions on the basis of religion. In Delhi, Sikhs became targets of communal attacks in 1984; in Bhagalpur in Bihar, hundreds of Muslims were killed in one of India's worst communal riots in 1989; a few years later, the Babri Mosque was destroyed in Ayodhya by frenzied Hindu communalists (supported, openly and brazenly, by political parties such as the Bhartiya Janata Party, the Rashtriya Swayamsevak Sangh, the Vishwa Hindu Parishad and the Shiv Sena), and later, thousands of Muslims were again targeted in Surat, Ahmedabad and Bombay. In each of these instances, Partition stories and memories were used selectively by the aggressors: militant Hindus were mobilized using the one-sided argument that Muslims had killed Hindus at Partition, they had raped Hindu women, and so they must in turn be killed, and their women subjected to rape. And the patterns were there in individual life too: a Muslim and a Hindu in independent India could not easily choose to marry each other without worrying about whether one or the other of them would survive the wrath of their families or communities; if such a marriage broke up, or for some reason ended up in court, you could be sure that it would be accompanied by public announcements, for example on the part of the judiciary, about those who had accepted the two-nation theory and those who had not.

All of this seemed to emphasize that Partition could not so easily be put away, that its deep, personal meanings, its profound sense of rupture, the differences it engendered or strengthened, still lived on in so many people's lives. I began to realize that Partition was surely more than just a political divide, or a division of properties, of assets and liabilities. It was also, to use a phrase that survivors use repeatedly, a 'division of hearts'. It brought untold suffering, tragedy, trauma, pain and violence to communities who had hitherto lived together in some kind of social contract. It separated families across an arbitrarily drawn border, sometimes overnight, and made it practically impossible for people to know if their parents, sisters, brothers or children were alive or dead. A mother and daughter, separated in the violence of Partition, found each other fifty years later through the agency of a news magazine when, in search of stories to mark fifty years of independence for India, a reporter and a photographer went looking for families divided at Partition. A brother and a sister were brought together after fifty years at the border by the same news magazine. A father whose thirteen-year-old daughter was abducted from Pakistan by Hindu men made several trips to India to try to track her down. On one of these, he was arrested on charges of being a spy and jailed. His daughter was never returned to him.

*　*　*

These aspects of Partition—how families were divided, how friendships endured across borders, how people coped with the trauma, how they rebuilt their lives, what resources, both physical and mental, they drew upon, how their experience of dislocation and trauma shaped their lives, and indeed the cities and towns and villages they settled in—find little reflection in written history. Yet, increasingly after 1984, I began to feel that they were essential to our knowledge of Partition. What then, I asked myself, were the tools I had to have to begin this search, what were the 'sources' I could turn to? James Young, writing on holocaust memories and testimonies, poses the question: how can we know the holocaust except through the many ways in which it is handed down to us?[1] He answers it by suggesting that as much as through its 'his-

---

[1] James E. Young, *Writing and Rewriting the Holocaust: Narrative and the Consequences of Interpretation*, Bloomington, Indiana University Press, 1990, Introduction, pp. 1, 5.

tory', we know the holocaust through its literary, fictional, historical, political representations, and through its personal, testimonial representations, for it is not only the 'facts' of any event that are important, but equally, how people remember those facts, and how they represent them. The question might well be extended to Partition, for how do we know this event except through the ways in which it has been handed down to us: through fiction, memoirs, testimonies, through memories, individual and collective, through the communalism it unleashed and, only as one of these aspects, through the histories it has produced. Perhaps more than any other event in modern Indian history Partition lives on in family histories particularly in north India, where tales of the horror and brutality, the friendship and sharing, are told and retold between communities, families and individuals. A Punjabi refugee only has to meet another Punjabi refugee and immediately stories of 'that time', of home and country, are exchanged. Or, an Indian refugee only has to meet a Pakistani refugee for the same process to begin. This collection of memories, individual and collective, familial and historical, are what make up the reality of Partition. They illuminate what one might call the 'underside' of its history. They are the ways in which we can know this event. In many senses, they *are* the history of the event. It is to these, then, that I decided to turn.

The choice brought its own problems. Working with memory is never simple or unproblematic. I am deeply aware of the problems that attach to the method I have chosen. There has been considerable research to show that memory is not ever 'pure' or 'unmediated'. So much depends on who remembers, when, with whom, indeed to whom, and how. But to me, the way people choose to remember an event, a history, is at least as important as what one might call the 'facts' of that history, for after all, these latter are not self-evident givens; instead, they too are interpretations, as remembered or recorded by one individual or another. Let me try to explain this with an example. One of the commonest responses I encountered when I began work was people's (initial) reluctance to speak. What, they asked me, is the use of remembering, of excavating memories we have put behind us? Every time I was faced with this question, I came up with a question of my own: why, I wondered, were people so reluctant to remember this time? Surely this reluctance in itself pointed to something? Was it only to do with the horrific nature of events—sanitized into numbers and statistics in the pages of history books—or was it to do, at least in some instances, with people's own complicity in this history? There had been, at Partition, no 'good' people and no 'bad' ones; virtually every family had a history of being both victims and aggressors in the violence. And if this was so, surely that told us something about why people did not wish to remember it, publicly, except perhaps within their families where the 'ugly' parts of this history could be suppressed?

How then, we might ask, extending James Young's formulation, can we know Partition except in the ways in which it has been handed down to us: not only in the texts and memories it has produced but even through people's reluctance to remember it. In this kind of knowing then, what we know as 'facts' are not self-evident givens. So much of the existing history of Partition is made up of debates about these 'facts'—debates that balance one person's interpretation against another—that I do not plan to repeat these or indeed to go into them here. Thus, although Partition is the subject of this book, the reader will not find here a chronology of events leading up to Partition, or indeed the many 'political' negotiations that followed it. Nor will he or she find much about the major players of this history: Gandhi, Nehru, Patel, Jinnah, Liaquat Ali Khan, Mountbatten. Their absence from my work is deliberate. Instead, I focus on the stories of the smaller, often invisible, players: ordinary people, women, children, scheduled castes. I do this principally through interviews and oral narratives.

As I say this I know that I am entering a problematic terrain. Oral history is a deeply contested area in historical discourse. I have no wish to pose people's narratives, or even a notion of 'raw experience', against something that we might call history, for both are not unproblematic concepts. I am not a historian. History is not my subject. I have come to this work through a political—and personal—engagement with history, contemporary communalism, and a deep and abiding belief in feminism. All of these have led me to the realization that it is extremely important to be able to listen, to attempt to understand how and why religious difference, for example, has come to acquire the kind of resilience that it has. Why is it that so many second- and third-generation

9

Hindus and Sikhs after Partition have come to internalize notions of 'us' and 'them' when they have no reference to Partition—except through family and community memories? What is it about the selectivity of memory that, in this case, feelings of fear and hatred seem to have been nurtured, to have a greater resilience, while feelings of friendship and sharing are not allowed to surface? I am aware of the many pitfalls that are attendant on the method I have chosen: there is no way of knowing, for example, if the stories people choose to tell are 'true' or not, nor of knowing what they choose to suppress. How can we know that, four or five decades after the event, the stories are not simply rehearsed performances; or that they are told differently for different people, perhaps tailored to suit what the person thinks the interviewer wishes to hear? How do we reach beyond the stories into the silences they hide; how can we assume that speech, the breaking of silence, is in itself a good thing? There are a hundred such questions. But I am not making a claim for oral history as against what we understand as the disciplinary narratives of history; rather, I would like to ask if there is a way in which people's stories, notwithstanding all their problems, can somehow expand, stretch the definitions and boundaries of history and find a place in it. Is there some way in which history can make space for the small, the individual, voice?

Whatever its limitations, the oral narrative offers a different way of looking at history, a different perspective. Because such narratives often flow into each other in terms of temporal time, they blur the somewhat rigid timeframes within which history situates itself. Because people locate their memories by different dates, or different timeframes, than the events that mark the beginning and end of histories, their narratives flow above, below, through the disciplinary narratives of history. They offer us a way of turning the historical lens at a somewhat different angle, and to look at what this perspective offers. I do not want to argue here that oral narratives can replace what we see as history, only that they can offer a different and extremely important perspective on history, a perspective which, I believe, enriches history.

I have come to believe that there is no way we can begin to understand what Partition was about, unless we look at how people remember it. I do not wish here to carry out a literal exercise of first seeing how

people remember the history of Partition, and then attempting to pene-
trate their narrative for its underlying 'facts' to arrive at an approxima-
tion of some kind of 'truth'. Instead, I wish to look at the memories for
themselves—even if they are shifting, changing, unreliable. James Young
says: 'Whatever "fictions" emerge from the survivors' accounts are not
deviations from the "truth" but *are part of the truth in any particular version*
(my italics). The fictiveness in testimony does not involve disputes about
facts, but the inevitable variance in perceiving and representing these
facts, witness by witness, language by language, culture by culture.'[2] I can
find no more eloquent description of what I hope to do in this book.

* * *

Collecting material is sometimes the easiest part of putting a book together. The difficult decisions come when one wants to try to figure out
what to include and what to leave out. Over the many long years that I
have been working on this subject, I have interviewed perhaps seventy or
so people. While this number sounds quite substantial to me, it is neg-
ligible in terms of the number of people who were affected by Partition,
an indication of the fact that no single individual can tackle this project
in its entirety. While one part of this book is made up of my telling of
Partition stories, in the other parts people I have interviewed tell their
own stories. But of the number I spoke with, I have included only a fraction. This is not because the others are not worth reproducing. Indeed,
each story is rich in insights and unique in what it offers. But clearly
I could not have included them all, so in the end I have chosen to use
rather arbitrary criteria in my selection. I have included the stories that
meant the most to me, stories of people with whom I have formed real
friendships, or stories to which I keep returning again and again.

In presenting the interviews to the reader, I have taken the liberty of
narrativizing them—that is, I have removed the questions posed by the
interviewers, and have let the text run as one continuous narrative, although no chronological alterations have been made. And in a few cases
I have retained the interventions made by other people, particularly in
instances where they add to, or illuminate, certain aspects of the text.

[2] James E. Young, *Writing and Rewriting the Holocaust*, p. 32.

This shaping of the interviews to turn them into more 'readable' texts has been done quite consciously. I do not believe that the transcript of any interview can ever be an unmediated text. In transferring words to text, so much is lost: the particular inflection; the hesitation over certain thoughts and phrases, even certain feelings; the body language, which often tells a different story from the words; and indeed the conscious 'shaping' of the interview by the interviewer who is usually in a situation of power vis-à-vis the person being interviewed. Given this, I thought it pointless to pretend that the interviews could appear before the reader in some 'pure' form, and I have edited them into what I feel is a more readable form. The full text of each interview, and indeed of the ones I have not used here, will, I hope, be housed in a library or archive so that they can be used by others researching this area.

The fact that most of the interviews took place in family situations also meant that women were seldom alone when they spoke to us. Much of the time the interview had to be conducted in the nooks and crannies of time that were available to women between household tasks. Equally, if their husbands or sons were around, they tended to take over the interview, inadvertently or otherwise, making the women lapse into a sort of silence. This is not uncommon—many oral historians have written about the difficulty of speaking to and with women, of learning to listen differently, often of listening to the hidden nuance, the half-said thing, the silences which are sometimes more eloquent than speech. Listening to women is, I think, a different thing between women than it is between men and women.

When I reread the interviews now, it strikes me that there are some very clear differences between the speech of men and of women. Is there such a thing, then, as a gendered telling of Partition? I learnt to recognize this in the way women located, almost immediately, this major event in the minor keys of their lives. From the women I learned about the minutiae of their lives, while for the most part men spoke of the relations between communities, the broad political realities. Seldom was there an occasion when a man being interviewed would speak of a child lost or killed, while for a woman there was no way in which she could omit such a reference. This is a question I discuss further in the conclusion to this volume.

The process of identifying people to speak to was an almost random one. I first began to consciously speak to people when I was working on a film called *A Division of Hearts* made by two friends for Channel 4 Television in Britain. But once I had begun, almost everywhere I turned there was a story to be listened to. In Delhi particularly, you can be sure that almost every other Punjabi person over a certain age has a history of Partition somewhere in his or her family. I would often find myself stopping on roads to talk to people I thought looked the right age. Once, after talking to a family in Jangpura in Delhi, I came out to find an auto-rickshaw to take me home. The driver was dressed in the salvar-kurta that is typical of Pakistani Punjabis. I asked him where he was from. He responded with a question—one that is common when asking north Indians where they are from. Are you asking about now or earlier, he said. The word 'earlier' is only an approximate translation of the word that he actually used: 'pichche se', which refers to something that comes from an earlier time and has been left behind. I told him I was interested in where he was from 'earlier', not now. He said he was from Baluchistan, and had stayed on there for nearly ten years after Partition, in a small village where a community of Hindus lived peaceably, without any problems. Soon, we were in his house talking about his recollections of the time. One day, as I walked out of a take-away restaurant in south Delhi, clutching a roti and kebab, I was accosted by a beggar woman asking for money. She spoke in Punjabi, an unusual thing, for there are very few Punjabi beggars in the city. I asked her where she was from. She responded with the same question: now or earlier. I gave her the same answer and she told me she had come from a small village called Chak 53, that she had walked over with the large kafila of refugees and had ended up, by a circuitous route, on the streets of Delhi, begging. In this way, I moved from one person to another, one story to another, and collected stories, almost randomly. This is one reason why there is no clear pattern to the oral narratives in this book.

Some patterns will, however, be discernible to the reader. For example, many of the interviews I have used come from the same region—Rawalpindi district—and relate to incidents of violence that took place there in March 1947, just a few months before Partition. Often, in an attempt to recreate the communities that Partition destroyed, people moved en masse to one place, or were housed by the State in a particular place. When I began to track down Partition survivors, I was led, first of all, to survivors of the Rawalpindi violence who lived in a middle-class area in south Delhi. One person put me in touch with another, and then another and in this way I collected many stories. It is for this reason that the accounts of Rawalpindi survivors form a major part of my work.

Apart from all the methodological problems that attach to oral narratives, they are also very difficult to deal with in practical, structural terms. How do you structure a book that is primarily made up of such accounts? Should it contain just the texts of the interviews, should there be an accompanying commentary, should there be analysis and/or explanation, should the interviews be long or short, and so on. I have grappled with all of these questions. In the beginning, I thought it better to simply put together a book of oral accounts, without any explanation or commentary. Gradually, I came to believe otherwise: as a reader, and a publisher, I know that very few readers actually go through a collection of oral accounts unless they are very short, and I thought the things that people said in the interviews were too important to be either summarily cut short or just put together without any comment. Also, if I was shaping the interviews, I felt I needed to point to what, for me, was significant in those interviews. As I got more involved in the work, I found there was a great deal I wanted to say, in addition to what the people I spoke to had said. There were their stories, as they told them, and there was what I learnt and understood from those stories. I then began to think of a way of meshing the two together. The structure that you see in the book now, with excerpts from interviews forming a major part of the analytical chapters, was what emerged from this. Even so, there remained the problem of where and how to locate the full text of the interviews. I felt it important that, at least for the small number that I had selected, there be a place that was an integral part of the book. After much thought, I decided to place all interviews together in a separate section at the end of the book. But having once done that, the same problem re-presented itself: would people actually read them, or would they see them as simply adjuncts to the other chapters? It seemed likely that that was what would happen, and to me the interviews were far too important to be put aside as an appendix. Finally, I decided to move the interviews into the main text, and to supplement what I have said in each chapter with one or two interviews. Inasmuch as it was possible, I tried to relate the interview(s) to the chapter in which they have been included, but this was not possible each time. It is difficult, indeed it is too pat, to have at the end of each chapter an interview that perfectly fits the subject matter of that particular chapter. Had I had a list of chapters in mind before starting this work, I might have been able to consciously look for interviews that could directly relate to specific subjects. As it was, my interviews did not fit any particular pattern. Nonetheless, I have chosen to place them alongside each chapter because I believe they offer insights into all, and more, of the things I have discussed in this book, and are not only limited to the chapters they figure in. Sometimes, then, the interview begins the chapter, at others it ends it, and in one instance it provides the thread that weaves the chapter together. I think the reader may find it helpful to keep this in mind while reading the interviews.

While interviews form my primary sources, I have also looked at diaries, memoirs, newspaper reports and the kinds of documents that I feel are important for my work: letters written by different people, reports of enquiry commissions, pamphlets and, of course, books. From these I have reconstructed many different 'voices' of Partition: official, unofficial, informal, others. These include the voices of people telling stories, the voices through which they speak in memoirs, diaries, autobiographies, those that emerge from the official narratives, those that are evident in communal discourses, and, woven through all this, my own voice, reading, speaking, questing, hazarding explanations.

Together, these have made for a narrative in which my presence, as author and interpreter, is quite visible, some would say almost too visible. I make no apologies for this. I can only say that I have always had a deep suspicion of histories that are written as if the author were but a mere vehicle, histories that, to use Roland Barthes' phrase, 'seem to write themselves'. The absence of the 'I' in such histories helps perhaps to establish distance, even to create the illusion of objectivity, perhaps to establish factuality. I have no wish to pretend that these histories, these stories, are in any way an 'objective' rendering of Partition. I do not believe such a thing is possible. For the many years that this work has been with me, I have felt involved in it, intensely and emotionally, politically and academically. To pretend then, that this is a history that has 'written itself', so to speak, would have been dishonest.

In the process of working on Partition I have become, like every other researcher or writer who gets involved, obsessive about this work. For years, I have thought of little else. One of the things that troubled me enormously when I began was precisely the lack of what is known as objectivity in my work. There was no way I could deny a personal involvement; no way I could pretend that there wasn't an emotional entanglement; no way I could wipe out my politics. It has taken me several years to feel comfortable with this fact. If this account is read as history, it may well be thrown out the door. Perhaps then, the best way to read it is to add the word 'personal' to the history that I am attempting in this book. And to throw out, once and for all, any notions of objectivity or distance. This is a personal history that does not pretend to be objective.

There is also another reason that my voice moves in and out of these stories. Oral history is a methodological tool that many feminist historians have found enormously empowering. Looking at women's narratives and testimonies, and placing them alongside, or indeed against, the official discourses of history, has offered feminist historians a new and different way of looking at history. How does 'history' look when seen through the eyes of women? How does it evolve, in narratives and testimonies, when women talk to women? But while oral history has been empowering, it has also brought its own problems. After all, the telling is always only one-sided. How, further, can such historians ensure that the subjects of their interviews are not simply the 'raw material' on whose experiences they will build their theories? In some instances, oral historians, and particularly feminist oral historians, have attempted to return the results of their research to their subjects, in an attempt to not be exploitative. While such attempts establish sincerity of motive, they do little to change the equation of power that underlies the collection of oral testimonies: for long after your subjects have spoken to you, their voices will live on in your work, they may help to promote your career, and while they continue to figure where you are concerned, the subjects themselves will recede further and further into the background.

The always troubling awareness of this ambivalence has directed me to choose a methodology in which I make no pretence at being a shadow, in which I attempt to put the stories I have heard at centre stage, along with what I felt, and continue to feel, about them. Thus, women, their histories, and the methodologies they have created lie at the heart of this book, even though it is not 'only' about women. It is as a feminist, someone to whom the tools of feminist historiography are important, that I approach this work.

There is, however, a major lacuna in my work: it is one-sided; it relates only to one aspect of Partition—that is, the partition of Punjab. I have not looked at the east, at Bengal, at all. In the main this is because I do not have the language; also the partition of Bengal was so very different from that of Punjab that I would not have known where and how to begin. Equally, I have had no access to information, interviews or anything else from Pakistan (other than, of course, the story of my uncle—where there was a connection of blood, as well as one other interview that I have borrowed from the work of some friends). It is one of the tragedies of Partition that researchers working on this major event in the history of the subcontinent can only have access to both countries—India and Pakistan—if they belong to a third country. Not only are files and documents not easily available to researchers from either side, but, when attempting to interview people, the baggage of bitterness and pain makes it virtually impossible for someone from India to interview people from Pakistan—or indeed the other way round—about something as emotive as Partition. I have tried, on many occasions, to do this, but without success.

The interviews you will see in this book were conducted over a period of several years. When I began to talk to people, I had no fixed plan in mind: a book was not on the agenda and it was only gradually that the idea for one crystallized. I decided quite early on, however, that I would not follow a particular pattern in the interviews—that is, that there would be no fixed questionnaire, no chosen 'sample' of people, in terms of geography or class or any other category. I would simply ask people to speak about that time in their lives, and let the conversation take its own course, to flow in whichever direction seemed appropriate. This was a deliberate decision: if one is to do a proper collection of people's histories of Partition, no one individual can carry out such an enterprise. Any individual attempt then, such as mine is, remains limited. Given this, carefully constructed questionnaires, or thought-out samples, do not help to make the exercise any more complete. I decided, therefore, to follow whatever pattern the interviews dictated, and to locate people in whatever way seemed best. Thus I spoke to many people, over extended periods of time—sometimes, as in the case of Damyanti Sahgal, the interviews lasted several months.

In situations such as this, it is extremely difficult to be able to interview people alone. Most conversations took place in family situations: even though we may have been speaking to one person, the entire family —often several generations of it—would converge, and every now and again, someone or another would offer an explanation, or take on a question. Stories begun would be left incomplete, and when resumed, would move on to something else. Later, we might come back to the same story, or not at all. No neat chronologies marked the telling; there were no clear beginnings and endings. I began to understand how much, and how easily, the past flowed into the present, how remembering also meant reliving the past from within the context of the present. For so many people then, 1947 and 1984 flowed into each other and often it became difficult to disentangle what it was they were remembering: the memory of violence, the vulnerability of victimhood, elided the many years that had passed inbetween. At others, having begun to remember, to excavate memory, words would suddenly fail speech as memory encountered something too painful, often too frightening to allow it to enter speech. 'How can I describe this,' would come the anguished cry, 'there are no words to do so.' At such points, I chose not to push further, not to force the surfacing of memories into speech. Tellings begun thus would be left incomplete: I learnt to recognize this, the mixing of time past and time present, the incompleteness, often even contradictoriness, in the stories as part of the process of remembering, to oneself and to others. I recognized too the imbalance of power that oral historians have often spoken about as being inherent in such situations: for the most part I watched, listened, recorded while people laid their lives bare. When they turned around with a question to me: what do you think this will achieve, who do you think will listen to your tapes, will this really make a difference to anything, to our lives, the lives of others, I felt, immediately, the inadequacy of my answers. Did it matter to the people I was speaking to that I felt it important that the memory of Partition not be lost? That the history of Partition had ignored their experiences and stories, and mine was part of an exercise, tentatively begun, to restore these stories to history? That remembering, to me, was an essential part of forgetting? I had no easy answers to these questions.

A last word about the trajectory that has led me to this work. In the beginning, I began work alone. After some time, however, it became very difficult to continue thus. The kinds of stories I was hearing were so harrowing, so full of grief and anguish, that often I could not bear to listen to them. And I could not escape a sense of having the burden of the stories somehow shifted onto myself—it seemed almost as if, after their initial reluctance to speak, once people decided they would do so, they would do so almost cathartically, making you, as listener, the bearer of their burden. I remember coming out of a long interview with a family in Jangpura one day thinking that I would not be able to go on constantly listening to stories of such violence, such horror. It was at this point that a very dear friend of mine, Sudesh Vaid, stepped in—at my request—and with the two of us working together things became much easier. We were able to talk, to share some things, to laugh about others. Several of the interviews you see in this book were done by us jointly (this is why I often refer to the interviewers in the plural) and some were begun by me and then continued by both of us. At some point in the work, Sudesh dropped out. One of the key reasons she did so was because now *she* began to feel she could not cope with the kinds of stories we were hearing. By this time, I was too involved to drop the project and decided therefore to continue alone. It is one of my lasting regrets that Sudesh did not stay with this project: had she done so, it would have been a richer, and I firmly believe, a better—as well as a very different—work.

Whatever its limitations—and there are many—I now put this work before the reader in the hope that it will make some contribution, however small, to the writing of Partition histories, and that at some stage in the not too distant future, access to both sides becomes freely available to all of us. In 1997 India and Pakistan 'celebrated' fifty years of independence. At the time, I thought that the best way the two countries could mark this moment was to open the borders, even if only for a limited period (a year, perhaps two). I am convinced that, had this happened, there would have been hundreds and thousands of people wanting to go across to the 'other' country, to visit their old homes, to meet their old friends and relatives. But that moment is past: I think all we can hope for now is that there will be some opening up, sometime, for unless that happens and we are able to talk about Partition, I fear we may not be able to put it behind us.

2
BLOOD

Part I RANAMAMA

This story begins, as all stories inevitably do, with myself. For many years while this story has lived with me, I have thought and debated about how to tell it, indeed whether to tell it at all. At first it was painful and, I thought, too private to be told. Even though my uncle had said, time and again, that he did not mind my telling it, even though my mother knew I wanted to tell it, I still couldn't get rid of a sense of betrayal. I was convinced they didn't realize the implications of what they were saying. Perhaps then the simple thing to do would have been to show the story to them before I let it go. But when I thought of doing this I realized I did not want to. Because if I am to be honest, I had already decided the story had to be told. In many ways, as I began to see it, the telling unfolded not only my story, not only that of my family, but also, through their lives, many other stories, all of which were somewhere woven into a narrative of this strange thing we call a nation. This may sound very grandiose, and in the telling of this story—and all the others that follow—I don't mean to theorize about grand things. But I do want to ask questions: difficult, disturbing questions that have dogged me ever since I embarked on this journey.

For long, too, I have debated about how I would begin this story once the task of telling was upon me. There are so many beginnings, it was difficult to choose. Was it, for example, the stories of the trauma and pain of Partition, the violence that it brought, that I had heard all my life, that started me on this search? Was it the film I worked on for some friends which brought me in touch with Partition survivors and began this trajectory for me? Or was it 1984, the year that brought the aftermath of Indira Gandhi's assassination: the killing and maiming of thousands of Sikhs in Delhi, the violent upheaval and dislocation of their lives which recalled Partition with such clarity? Or was it all of these? I don't really know. Here, at any rate, is one beginning. Others, too, will surface somewhere in this narrative.

* * *

It was around 10 o'clock on a warm summer night in 1987 that I found myself standing in the veranda of a rather decrepit old house in a suburb of Lahore. A dusty bulb, hanging from a single plaited wire, cast a pale light on the cracked pistachio green walls. I was nervous, somewhat frightened, and also curious. The enormity of what I was about to do had only just begun to dawn on me. And predictably, I was tempted to turn around and run. But there was nowhere to run to. This was Lahore, it was night, women did not walk out into deserted streets—or indeed crowded ones—alone in search of nonexistent transport.

So I did what I had come to do. I rang the bell. A short while later, three women came to the barred window. I asked if this was the house of the person I was in search of. Yes, they said, but he wasn't there. He was away on 'tour' and expected home later that night. This was something I had not bargained for: had he been there I had somehow foolishly imagined he would know me instantly—despite the fact that he had never seen me before and was probably totally unaware of my existence. Vaguely I remember looking at the floor for inspiration, and noticing that engraved in it was the game of chopar that my mother had told us about—it was something, she said, that my grandfather had especially made for his wife, my grandmother. Gathering together my courage I said to the three assembled women: 'I'm looking for him because I am his niece, his sister's daughter, come from Delhi.'

Door bolts were drawn and I was invited in. The women were Rana's wife—my aunt—and her daughters—my cousins. To this day I am not sure if it was my imagination or if they were actually quite friendly. I remember being surprised because they seemed to know who I was— you must be Subhadra's daughter, they said, you look a bit like her. Look like her? But they had never even *seen* my mother. At the time, though, I was too nervous to ask. I was led into a large, luridly furnished living room: for an hour we made careful conversation and drank Coca Cola. Then my friend Firhana came to collect me: I knew her sister, Ferida, and was staying at their house.

This could well have been the end of the story. In a sense, not finding my uncle at home was almost a relief. I went away thinking well, this is it, I've done it. Now I can go home and forget about all of this. But that was easier said than done. History does not give you leave to forget so easily.

* * *

Crossing the border into Pakistan had been easier than I thought. Getting a visa was difficult, though, ironically, the visa office at the Pakistan High Commission ran two separate counters, one for people they called 'foreigners' and the other for Indians. At the latter crowds of people jostled and pushed, trying to get together all the necessary paperwork, while outside an old man, balding and half-bent at the waist, offered to take instant photos, using a small bucket of developer to get them ready. Once over the border, however, everything looked familiar at the airport — the same chaos, the same language, the same smells, the same clothes. What I was not prepared for, however, was the strong emotional pull that came with the crossing. I felt — there is no other word for it — a sense of having come home. And I kept asking myself why. I was born five years after Partition. What did I know of the history of pain and anguish that had dogged the lives of my parents and grandparents? Why should this place, which I had never seen before, seem more like home than Delhi, where I had lived practically all my life?

What was this strange trajectory of histories and stories that had made it seem so important for me to come here? Standing there, in the veranda of my uncle's house, I remember thinking, perhaps for the first time, that this was something unexpected. When I had begun my search, I wasn't sure what I would find. But I wasn't prepared for what I did find. This was something no history lesson had prepared me for: these people, strangers that I had met practically that instant, were treating me like family. But actually the frontier that divided us went so deep that everywhere you looked, in religion, in politics, in geography and history, it reared its ugly head and mocked these little attempts at overcoming the divide.

Ranamama, outside whose house I stood that night, is my mother's youngest brother. Like many north Indian families, ours too was divided at Partition. My mother, who was still single at the time, found herself on the Indian side of the border. Ranamama, her brother, chose to stay behind. According to my mother and her other siblings, his choice was a motivated one. He wanted access to the property my grandfather—who was no longer alive—owned. With all other family contenders out of the way, he could be sole owner of it. Because of this, and because of the near impossibility of keeping in touch after Partition, the family 'lost' contact with Ranamama. For forty years, no one communicated with him, heard from him or saw anything of him. Until, that is, I went to see him.

*   *   *

Ever since I can remember we had heard stories of Partition—from my grandmother (my father's mother) who lived with us, and from my parents who had both lived through it very differently. In the way that I had vaguely registered several of these stories, I had also registered Rana's. Not only had he stayed back but, worse, and I suspect this was what made him a persona non grata in our family, he had become a Muslim. My mother made two difficult and dangerous journeys, amidst the worst communal violence, to Lahore to fetch her family to India. The first time she brought her younger brother, Billo, and a sister, Savita. The second time she went to fetch her mother and Rana, the youngest (her father had long since died). But, she said, Rana refused to come, and he wasn't willing to let my grandmother go either. He denied that he wanted to hold on to her for the sake of my grandfather's property, which was in her name, and he promised to bring her to India soon. This never happened. Once the country was divided, it became virtually impossible for people of different communities to move freely in the 'other' country. Except for a few who were privileged and had access to people in power—a circumstance that ensured relatively smooth passage—most people were unable to go back to their homes, which had often been left behind in a hurry. There was deep suspicion on both sides, and any cross-border movement was watched and monitored by the police and intelligence. Rana and his family kept contact for some time, but found themselves constantly under surveillance, with their letters being opened, and questions being asked. After a while, they simply gave up trying to communicate. And for forty years it remained that way. Although Rana remained in my grandfather's house, no one spoke or wrote to him, no one heard from him in all these years. Sometime during this time, closer to 1947 than not, my family heard unconfirmed reports that my grandmother had died. But no one really knew. The sense of deep loss, of family, mother, home, gave way to bitterness and resentment, and finally to indifference. Perhaps it was this last that communicated itself to us when, as children, we listened to stories of Partition and the family's history.

*   *   *

At midnight, the phone rang in my friend Ferida's house. We were deep in conversation and gossip over cups of coffee and the salt/sweet tea the Pakistanis call kehwa. She listened somewhat distractedly to the phone for a minute—who could be calling at this time?—and handed it to me, suddenly excited, saying, 'It's your uncle.' As Ferida had answered the phone, a male voice at the other end had said, apparently without preamble, 'I believe my daughter is staying with you. Please call my daughter, I would like to speak to her.'

'Beti,' he said to me as I tentatively greeted him, 'what are you doing there? This is your home. You must come home at once and you must stay here. Give me your address and I'll come and pick you up.' No preamble, no greeting, just a direct, no-nonsense picking up of family ties. I was both touched and taken aback.

We talked, and argued. Finally I managed to dissuade him. It was late, he was tired. Why didn't we just meet in the morning? I'd get my friend to bring me over. 'I'll not settle for just meeting,' he told me, 'don't think you can get away from here. This is your home and this is where you must stay—with your family.'

Home? Family? I remember thinking these were strange words between two people who hardly knew each other. Ought I to go and stay with him? I was tempted, but I was also uncertain. How could I pack my bags and go off to stay with someone I didn't know, even if there was a family connection? The next morning I went, minus bags. He remarked on it instantly—where is your luggage? Later that evening he came with me to Ferida's house. I picked up my bags, and we went back together to his home.

I stayed with my uncle for a week. All the time I was aware of an underlying sense of betrayal: my mother had had no wish to re-open contact with her brother, whom she suspected of being mercenary and scheming. Why else, she asked, had he stayed back, held on to the property, and to the one person to whom it belonged: my grandmother? Over the years, her bitterness and resentment had only increased. But, given my own political trajectory, this visit meant too much to me to abandon. And once I had seen my uncle, and been addressed by him as 'daughter', it became even more difficult to opt out. So I stayed, in that big, rambling haveli, and for a week we talked. It was an intense and emotionally draining week. For a long time afterwards I found it difficult to talk about that parenthetical time in my life. I remember registering various presences: my aunt, my younger and older cousins, food, sleep—all somewhat vaguely. The only recollection that remains sharp and crystal clear is of the many conversations my uncle and I had.

Why had he not left with his brother and sisters at Partition, I asked him. 'Why *did* you stay back?' He replied that, like a lot of other people, he had never expected Partition to happen the way it had. 'Many of us thought, yes, there'll be change, but why should we have to move?' He hadn't thought political decisions could affect his life, and by the time he realized otherwise, it was too late, the point of no return had actually been reached. 'I was barely twenty. I'd had little education. What would I have done in India? I had no qualifications, no job, nothing to recommend me.' But he had family in India, surely one of them would have looked after him? 'No one really made an offer to take me on— except your mother. But she was single, and had already taken on the responsibility of two other siblings.'

And my grandmother? Why did he insist on her staying on, I asked, anxious to believe that there was a genuine, 'excusable' reason. He offered an explanation: I did not believe it. 'I was worried about your mother having to take on the burden of an old mother, just like I was worried when she offered to take me with her. So I thought, I'd do my share and look after her.'

My grandmother, Dayawanti, died in 1956. The first time anyone in our family learnt of this was when I visited Ranamama in 1987 and he told me. For years, we'd heard that she had been left behind in Pakistan, and we were dimly aware that rumour put her date of death variously at 1949, 1952, 1953, sometimes earlier. But she had lived till 1956. Nine years after Partition. At the time, seven of her eight children lived across the border in India, most of them in Delhi. Delhi is half an hour away from Lahore by air. None of them knew. Some things, I found, are difficult to forgive.

The way Ranamama described it, the choice to stay on was not really a choice at all. In fact, like many people, he thought he wasn't choosing, but was actually waiting to do so when things were decided for him. But what about the choice to convert? Was he now a believer? Had he been one then? What did religion mean to him — after all, the entire rationale for the creation of two countries out of one was said to have been religion. And, it was widely believed — with some truth — that large numbers of people were forced to convert to the 'other' religion. But Rana?

'No one forced me to do anything. But in a sense there wasn't really a choice. The only way I could have stayed on was by converting. And so, well, I did. I married a Muslim girl, changed my religion, and took a Muslim name.'

But did he really believe? Was the change born out of conviction as much as it was of convenience? It is difficult for me to put down Rana's response to this question truthfully. When I asked him if I could write what he had said, he said, 'Of course, write what you like. My life cannot get any worse.' But my own feeling is that he wasn't really aware of the kinds of implications this could have. So I did what I thought I had to: silenced those parts that needed to be kept silent. I make no excuses for this except that I could not, in the name of a myth called intellectual honesty, bring myself to expose or make Ranamama so vulnerable.

'One thing I'll tell you,' said Rana in answer to my question, 'I have not slept one night in these forty years without regretting my decision. Not one night.' I was chilled to the bone. How could he say this, what did he mean, how had he lived through these forty years, indeed how would he live through the next forty, if this was what he felt? 'You see, my child,' he said, repeating something that was to become a sort of refrain in the days we spent together, 'somehow a convert is never forgiven. Your past follows you, it hounds you. For me, it's worse because

I've continued to live in the same place. Even today, when I walk out to the market, I often hear people whispering, "Hindu, Hindu". No, you don't know what it is like. They never forgive you for being a convert.'

I was curious about why Ranamama had never tried to come to India to seek out his family. If he felt, so profoundly, the loss of a family, why did he not, like many others, try to locate his? Admittedly, in the beginning, it was difficult for people to cross the two borders, but there were times when things had eased, if only marginally. But he had an answer to that too: 'How could I? Where would I have gone? My family, my sisters knew where I was. I had no idea where they were. And then, who in India would have trusted an ex-Hindu turned Muslim who now wanted to seek out his Hindu relatives? And this is the only home I have known.'

And yet, home for him was defined in many different ways. Ever since television had made its appearance, Ranamama made sure he listened to the Indian news every day. When cricket was played between the two countries, he watched and secretly rooted for India. Often, when it was India playing another country, he sided with India. More recently, he sometimes watched Indian soaps on the small screen. And, although he had told me that his home in Lahore was the only home he had ever known, it was to India that he turned for a sense of home. There is a word in Punjabi that is enormously evocative and emotive for most Punjabis: watan. It's a difficult word to translate: it can mean home, country, land—all and any of them. When a Punjabi speaks of his or her watan, you know they are referring to something inexpressible, some longing for a sense of place, of belonging, of rootedness. For most Punjabis who were displaced as a result of Partition, their watan lay in the home they had left behind. For Ranamama, in a curious travesty of this, while he continued to live on in the family home in Pakistan, his watan became India, a country he had visited once only briefly.

His children and family found this bizarre. They could not understand these secret yearnings, these things that went on inside his head. They thought the stories he told were strange, as were the people he spoke about, his family—Hindus—from across the border. The two younger girls told me once, 'Apa, you are all right, you're just like us, but we thought, you know, that *they* were really awful.' And who could blame them? The only Hindus they had met were a couple of distant relatives who had once managed to visit, and who had behaved as orthodox Hindus often do, practising the 'untouchability' that Hindus customarily use with Muslims. They would insist on cooking their own food, not eating anything prepared by the family, and somehow making their hosts feel 'inferior'. Bir Bahadur Singh, one of the people I interviewed later in the course of my work on Partition, told me what he thought of the way Hindus and Sikhs treated Muslims:

> Such good relations we had that if there was any function that we had, then we used to call Musalmaans to our homes, they would eat in our houses, but we would not eat in theirs and this is a bad thing, which I realize now. If they would come to our houses we would have two utensils in one corner of the house, and we would tell them, pick these up and eat in them; they would then wash them and keep them aside and this was such a terrible thing. This was the reason Pakistan was created. If we went to their houses and took part in their weddings and ceremonies, they used to really respect and honour us. They would give us uncooked food, ghee, atta, dal, whatever sabzis they had, chicken and even mutton, all raw. And our dealings with them were so low that I am even ashamed to say it. A guest comes to our house and we say to him, bring those utensils and wash them, and if my mother or sister have to give him food, they will more or less throw the roti from such a distance, fearing that they may touch the dish and become polluted . . . We don't have such low dealings with our lower castes as Hindus and Sikhs did with Musalmaans.

*   *   *

As the years went by, Ranamama began to live an internal life, mostly in his head, that no one quite knew about, but everyone, particularly his family, was suspicious of. His children—especially his daughters and daughters-in-law—cared for him but they all feared what went on inside his head. For all the love his daughters gave him, it seemed to me there was very little that came from his sons. Their real interest was in the property he owned. Perhaps the one person who, in some sense, understood the dilemmas in his head was my mami, his wife. She decided quite early on, and sensibly I thought, that she would not allow her children to have the same kind of crisis of identity that Rana had had.

They were brought up as good Muslims, the girls remained in purdah, they studied at home from the mullah, they learnt to read the Koran. For the younger ones especially, who had no memory of or reference to Partition, Rana with his many stories of his family, his friends, his home, remained their father, and yet a stranger. In some ways, this distanced him further from the family and served to isolate him even more. In other ways, in a curious kind of paradox, his patriarchal authority was undermined, making him a much more humane father than one might normally find in a middle-class Punjabi household. But for several of his family members, he was only the inconvenient owner of the property, to be despatched as soon as possible.

I could not understand how he could have lived like this: was there anyone he could have spoken to? He told me no. How could he talk about what was so deep, so tortured? And to whom? There was no one, no one who could even begin to understand. Some things, he told me, are better left unsaid. But why then was he saying them to me? Who was I? One day, as we talked deep into the evening, stopping only for the odd bit of food, or a cup of tea, he told me about his life since Partition, I began to feel oppressed by him. 'Why,' I asked him, 'why are you talking to me like this? You don't even know me. If you'd met me in the marketplace, I would have just been another stranger. Yes, we speak the same language, we wear similar clothes, but apart from that . . .' He looked at me for a long moment and said, 'My child, this is the first time I am speaking to my own blood.'

I was shocked. I protested. 'What about your family? They are your blood, not me.'

'No', he said, 'for them I remain a stranger. You, you understand what it is I'm talking about. That is why you are here on this search. You know. Even if nothing else ever happens, I know that you have been sent here to lighten my load.'

And, in some ways I suppose this was true. I did understand, and I began to wonder. About how many people had been torn apart like this by the event we call Partition, by what is known as history. How many had had to live with their silences, how many had been able to talk, and why it was that we, who had studied modern Indian history in school, who knew there was something called the Partition of India that came simultaneously with Independence, had never learnt about this side of it? Why had these stories remained hidden? Was there no place for them in history?

*   *   *

That first time I returned to India from Pakistan, I brought back messages and letters and gifts from the entire family to various members on this side of the border. Ranamama sent a long letter, addressed to all his sisters (his one remaining brother was dead by then). Initially, my mother found it difficult to get over her bitterness and resentment, and to face the letter I had brought. Her sisters, all five of them, who had gathered in our house, sat in a row, curious, but also somewhat resentful. Then someone picked up the letter and began reading, and soon it was being passed from hand to hand, with memories being exchanged, tears being shed and peals of laughter ringing out as stories were recounted and shared.

Tell us, they demanded, tell us what the house looks like, is the guava tree still there, what's happened to the game of chopar, who lives at the back now . . . Hundreds of questions. I tried to answer them all—unsuccessfully. How could I tell them who was in which room or how the house had changed, when I hadn't seen the original house myself? Rana's letter was read and reread, touched, smelt, laughed and wept over. Suddenly my mother and my aunts had acquired a family across the border. We kept in touch after that, occasional letters did manage to arrive. I went back to Lahore several times and met him again. Once he wrote to my mother: 'I wish I could lock up Urvashi in a cage and keep her here.' And she told me I had made a real difference in his life. As he had, I think, to mine, for he set me on a path from which it has been difficult to withdraw.

But old resentments die hard. And there are many things that lie beneath the surface that we cannot even apprehend. Once, when I was going to visit him, my mother said to me: 'Ask him . . . ask him if he buried or cremated my mother.' I looked at her in shock. Religion has never meant much to her—she isn't an atheist but she has little patience with the trappings of religion.

'Why does it matter to you?' I said to her.

'Just ask him,' she said, implacable.

I asked him.

'How could she have stayed on here and kept her original name? I had to make her a convert. She was called Ayesha Bibi,' he said, 'I buried her.'

* * *

I often wonder what kind of silent twilight world my grandmother lived in for those nine years after Partition. Did she not wonder where her children had gone? Did she think they had all abandoned her? Did she even understand what had happened? Dayawanti, the merciful one, had indeed been fortunately named. Blessed with a large family — her surviving children numbered nine, six daughters and three sons — and a husband whose medical practice was enormously successful, she had good reason to be happy. Then, suddenly, tragedy struck and her husband took ill and died. As my mother tells it, Dayawanti retreated into some kind of shell from then on, although cooking and caring for the children would occasionally pull her out of this. Then, the second tragedy happened: her elder son, Vikram, died in an air crash on a practice flight and Dayawanti again sought solace in an inner world. When Partition came, the chances are that Dayawanti did not know what was happening. But the journey in and out of her twilight world must have left her with long moments of what one might call 'sanity'. What must she have wondered about her family? Who could she have asked? What must she have felt about her new identity? My mother has often described her mother as a 'kattar Hindu' — not a rabid, flame-spouting type, but a strong believer who derived comfort from her daily routine of prayer and fasting. What must it have cost her to convert overnight to a different faith, a different routine? Did it, I wonder, bring on an even more intense alienation, a further recoil into herself, or did it bring on the reverse, a kind of cold, clear sanity and understanding of the lie she had to live till she died? Who was with her these nine years? Will history be answerable for Dayawanti's life and death?

* * *

Twelve million people were displaced as a result of Partition. Nearly one million died. Some 75,000 women were raped, kidnapped, abducted, forcibly impregnated by men of the 'other' religion, thousands of families were split apart, homes burnt down and destroyed, villages abandoned. Refugee camps became part of the landscape of most major cities in the north, but, a half century later, there is still no memorial, no memory, no recall, except what is guarded, and now rapidly dying, in family history and collective memory.

Some of the tales I heard when I began my research seemed so fantastic that they were difficult to believe. We had heard time and again that in many villages on both sides of the border hundreds of women had jumped—or were forced to jump—into wells because they feared that they would be taken away, raped, abducted, forced to convert to the other religion. This seemed bizarre: could the pull of religion be so strong that people—more specifically women—would actually kill themselves? And then I met Bir Bahadur Singh's mother, Basant Kaur. Basant Kaur, a tall, strapping woman in her mid-sixties had been present in her village, Thoa Khalsa, in March 1947 when the decision was taken that women would jump into a well. She watched more than ninety women throw themselves into a well for fear of the Muslims. She too jumped in, but survived because there was not enough water in the well to drown them all. She said: 'It's like when you put rotis into a tandoor and if it is too full, the ones near the top, they don't cook, they have to be taken out. So the well filled up, and we could not drown . . . Those who died, died, and those who were alive, they pulled out . . .'

And Bir Bahadur Singh, her son, had watched his father kill his sister. He described the incident with pride in his voice, pride at his sister's courage and her 'martyrdom', for she could now be placed alongside other martyrs of the Sikh religion. The first time I had been alerted to family deaths, that is, men of families killing off their women and children, was when I had met an old man, Mangal Singh, in Amritsar during the course of making the film *A Division of Hearts*. Mangal Singh told me how he and his two brothers had taken the decision to kill—he used the word martyr—seventeen members of their family. 'We had to do this,' he told me, 'because otherwise they would have been converted.' Having done this 'duty', Mangal Singh crossed over into Amritsar where he began a new life. When I met him, he was the only one left of the three. He had a new family, a wife, children, grandchildren, all of whom had heard, and dismissed, his stories. Why do you want to know all this, he kept asking me, what is the use? I told him that I wanted to know how he had coped with the grief, the sense of loss, the guilt. He said: 'Hunger drives all sorrow and grief away. You understand? When you don't have anything, then what's the point of having sorrow and grief?'

* * *

Why do you want to know this? This is a question I have been asked again and again—by the people I have wanted to interview, or those to whom I have tried to present my work. Two or three times, having begun work on Partition, I gathered my courage and read a couple of papers in academic gatherings. I wanted to share some questions that had been bothering me: why, for example, had straight historical accounts not been able to really address this underside of the history of Partition, to gather together the experiences of people, to see what role they had played in shaping the India we know today? Was it that they knew they would have to deal with a story so riven with pain and grief, a story that was so close to many people—for in many ways, several of our families were Partition refugees—that some time had to elapse before this work actually began? I wanted to understand how to read the many stories I was now hearing: I knew, without being a historian, that I could not look at these unproblematically. Could I, for example, rely on the 'truth' of the stories I was hearing? How much could one trust memory after all these years? For many of those who chose to tell me their stories, I must have been just another listener, the experience perhaps just another telling. I knew that my being middle class, a woman, a Punjabi, perhaps half a Sikh, would have dictated the way people actually responded. What value then ought I to place on their memory, their recall? Often, what emerged from the interviews was so bitter, so full of rage, resentment, communal feeling, that it frightened me. What was I to do with such material? Was it incumbent on me, as a might-have-been historian, to try to be true to this material, or should I, as a secular Indian, actually exercise some care about what I made visible and what I did not? A question that has dogged me constantly has been: is it fair to make these interviews public if they relate (as mine do) to only one side of the story? Doesn't that sort of material lend itself to misuse by one side or another? To this day, I have not solved this dilemma: I am torn between the desire to be honest and to be careful. And all the time I was asked: why, why are you doing this? The question became important for another reason: the way borders were drawn between our two countries, it was virtually impossible for me to travel to Pakistan to do research, or even to carry out interviews. The result was that my work remained—and still does—very one-sided. I knew that this was not right. I didn't know—I still don't—what I should be doing. Ought I to have given up the work? There are no easy answers. But in the end, I decided that if this search meant so much to me, I simply had to go on with it. I could not abandon it.

* * *

For some years the border between Pakistan and India seemed to have become more permeable. As a result I was able to make several visits and to cement my relationship with Ranamama. Once, when his second-youngest daughter was getting married, I took my mother and her elder sister with me to visit him. There was a great deal of excitement as we planned the visit, for it was really like a visit to the unknown. They didn't know what their brother would look like, how he would react to them, what their home would look like, what their beloved city would have to offer them . . . At Lahore airport Rana came to fetch his sisters. The last time my mother and aunt had seen their brother was forty-one years ago, when he had been a young twenty-year-old: slim, tall and smart. The man who met them now was in his sixties, balding and greying. He wore an awami suit, the loose salvar and shirt made popular by Bhutto. I tried to imagine what he must have seen: two white-haired women: my aunt, in her seventies, and my mother, in her mid-sixties. The reunion was a tentative, difficult one, with everyone struggling to hold back tears. I stood aside, an outsider now. My friend, Lala, who came to the airport as well, tells me that she has never forgotten the look on their faces—she has no words to describe it. Everyone made small talk in the car until we reached home. Home—this was the house in which my mother and her brothers and sisters had grown up. They knew every stone, every nook and cranny of this place. But now, much of it was occupied by people they did not know. So they were forced to treat it politely, like any other house. My aunt was welcoming, warm, but also suspicious. What, she must have wondered, were these relatives from the other side doing here at the time of a family wedding? How she must have hoped that they would not embarrass her in front of her guests!

For the first two days Rana and his sisters skirted each other. They talked, but polite, strained, talk. On the third day somehow the flood-gates opened, and soon the three of them were locked in a room, crying, laughing, talking, remembering. Rana took his sisters on a proper tour of the house: they were able to go back into their old rooms, to find their favourite trees, to remember their parents and other siblings. I, who was the catalyst at the airport meeting, was now redundant. Earlier, I had told them that I would stay with Lala, and that's what I had done. But not without a sense of guilt. Now, I was glad I'd done that—they can talk now, I thought, without having me around.

But what I didn't reckon on was that while one family bonded, the other grew more distant. For Rana's own family, the arrival of the two sisters was, quite naturally, something to be concerned about. A girl was being married. What if the potential in-laws objected to Hindus in the family? What if the Hindus were there to reclaim their land? What if the Hindus did something to embarrass the family at the wedding? And, a further complication. My mother and my aunt are the older sisters. Custom demanded that they be given respect. This meant making space for them in the wedding rituals. Yet how could this be done? So, small silences began to build up between 'this' side of the family and 'that', and I was struck by how easy it was to recreate the borders we thought we'd just crossed.

* * *

Contact with Rana was maintained for some years. I managed, some-how, to go to Pakistan again and see him. But it wasn't easy. He began to worry that he was being watched by the police, and he gradually stopped writing. For a while my mother continued to send him letters and gifts, but slowly even that petered out. Several times, I sent him letters and messages with my friends until one brought back a message—try not to keep in touch, it makes things very difficult. This wasn't just something official, but also within the family, for his sons put pressure on him to break contact with his Indian family. And then, in any case, it became more and more difficult to travel from one country to the other.

It's been many years now since I have seen Rana. I no longer know if he is alive or dead. I *think* he is alive, I *want* him to be alive, no one has told me he isn't, so I shall have to go on believing that he is. And I keep telling myself, if something happened to him, surely someone would tell us. But I'm not even sure I believe myself when I say that. Years ago, when Rana answered my mother's question about whether he had buried or cremated my grandmother, I asked if he would take me to her grave. I still remember standing with him by his gate in the fading light of the evening, looking out onto the road and saying to him, 'Ranamama, I want to see my grandmother's grave. Please take me to see it.' It was the first time he answered me without looking at me: he scuffed the dust under his feet and said: 'No my child, not yet. I'm not ready yet.'

* * *

On the night of August 14, 1996 about a hundred Indians visited the India-Pakistan border at Wagah in the Punjab. They went there to fulfil a long-cherished objective by groups in the two countries. Indians and Pakistanis would stand, in roughly equal numbers, on each side of the border and sing songs for peace. They imagined that the border would be symbolized by a sentry post and that they would be able to see their counterparts on the other side. But they came back disappointed. The border was more complicated than they thought — there is middle ground — and also grander. The Indian side has an arch lit with neon lights and, in large letters, the inscription MERA BHARAT MAHAAN — India, my country, is great. The Pakistan side has a similar neon-lit arch with the words PAKISTAN ZINDABAD — Long Live Pakistan. People bring picnics here and eat and drink and enjoy themselves. Every evening, a ritual takes place which repeats, lest anyone forget, the aggression the two countries practise towards each other. As the flags are lowered, border security personnel of India and Pakistan rush towards each other, thrusting their faces at each other, then turn smartly and step away. The whole ritual is carried out with such precision that you wonder at how much they must have had to work together to establish their lines of difference. Farther down at Attari, during the day as people arrive at the border, coolies dressed in different colours—blue and red to differentiate them as 'ours' and 'theirs'—meet at the twelve-inch line that forms the boundary, passing heavy bags and sacks across from one head to another; the boundary is crossed as their heads touch, while their feet stay on either side.

The suffering and grief of Partition are not memorialized at the border, nor, publicly, anywhere else in India, Pakistan and Bangladesh. A million people may have died but they have no monuments. Stories are all that people have, stories that rarely breach the frontiers of family and religious community: people talking to their own blood.

Part II

SUBHADRA BUTALIA
'Children of the same parents, the same blood . . .'

Subhadra Butalia is my mother. She and I began talking, hesitantly, about Ranamama and Partition only after I had been to visit him, and later had taken her with me to her family home. I realized then how often, and with what regularity, we had heard stories of Lahore, the old family home, our grandparents, and how little we had absorbed about them. After Rana began to write, and particularly after my mother went back to Lahore, I was consumed with curiosity about how she had felt on seeing her brother again, on going back to her old home. If I had felt such a strong emotional pull going to Lahore, what must it have been like for her? Over the years, gradually, I managed to persuade her to describe her experiences, and I came up against another paradox. People of my parents' generation tell stories of Partition all the time: it preoccupies their minds, it fills their lives, it memorializes their pasts. Yet when you sit them down, formally, as if to interview them about these very stories, they are strangely reluctant to talk. I have thought a great deal about this and can only conclude that when retrieving memory becomes a self-conscious, self-reflexive exercise, people are perhaps more reluctant to commit themselves, unless they can be sure that what they are saying is 'accurate' or true. But this is not all. I think with my mother the wounds were so deep that it was doubly difficult to speak of them, the more so to me. Perhaps an impersonal stranger would have succeeded where I failed. At one point, talking about how she had felt at being forced to leave her mother in Lahore, she said: 'Who can describe the pain of having to leave a mother?' I realized, in that moment, how little I had thought about this aspect. The pain of parents having to leave children we understand, but that it can happen the other way round is something that is seldom considered. There is no way of knowing how many parents were lost to their children in the sweep of this history, no way of knowing how many of them were lost by accident and how many by design.

I have chosen to include this interview because in some ways it gives another side of the picture to Ranamama's story, but also because, in other ways, it is revealing of the silences within families and the difficulty of going beyond these. As important as the exercise of probing the silence is the question of how it is probed, who poses the questions and when, and indeed who takes the responsibility for what the silence unleashes. A friend of mine described how, after remaining silent for many years, her mother spoke about her memories of Partition to a persuasive researcher. For weeks after she had done so, she was unable to sleep, remembering the pain and anguish of the time. The researcher who had prompted her to speak was by then elsewhere, perhaps involved in another interview. Thus it is never a simple question of silence and speech, for speech is not always cathartic, not always liberating. In my work, I have tried as far as possible to speak to only those people who were willing to speak, and to take the responsibility for what that speech meant. There is no way of knowing if this is the right approach, but for me it was perhaps the only approach I could take.

There are other reasons why I felt it was important to include my mother's interview. In some ways, Rana spoke to her more frankly than he did to me: he did concede that one of the reasons he had stayed on in Pakistan was the house. It is tragic, and ironic, that the same house which, for Rana, represented a sort of freedom, an opening up of opportunity, at Partition became a millstone round his neck later. If he was to be believed, he, Rana, the person, was of little consequence for his sons. It was the house that counted. As he said to my mother: 'I am like a stranger, a man haunted in my own house by my own children.'

* * *

Subhadra Butalia:

In 1946 I was working in the State High School in Nabha. The school had a large compound and building. It was surrounded by a slum area. There were prostitutes, and there were some very poor Muslims who lived there. So on all four sides it was a Muslim-dominated area. At one stage, people began to talk of Partition and the discussion always was about whether it would happen or not. And I and the headmistress, Ranjit, and my mother and my brothers and sisters, we all lived together. We were always fearful, because the stories that were circulated made it sound as if whenever there would be trouble, when the fighting would begin, the girls' school would be the first to be attacked. And even our chowkidar and ayah were Muslims. So we used to be very scared, we'd wonder what we would do. We had sort of given instructions to everyone: we used to sleep outside, in the open maidan, and there were four walls forming the boundary. So the instructions were that if ever there was noise, and commotion, everyone should run directly inside.

Just across the road from the school there lived a prostitute. One day she had a fight with someone, a man from the army, and he shot her down . . . Two bullets he fired at night and then he ran, he jumped the wall, and then he shot himself and died. We were really scared, we all ran inside. And Munna, my sister, who was the youngest, she went mad and instead of going in she ran outside and hid. We were all frantic with worry: Munna, Munna, where is she? Who knew what was happening outside! Ranjit would not let me go outside. And I said how can I leave the girl alone? It was a real crisis. Then she heard us shouting and we brought her inside. In the morning we found out that it was nothing, it was this other story, he had killed the woman. When he had gone away to the army, he used to send this woman money. On his return he asked if she would marry him and she told him, go away, there are so many like you who come and fall at my feet. Something like that. But her mother, she used to cry out 'Allah' at night, and she said it in a really frightening way. It was because we had no male person with us. We were all women, so we used to feel really scared. The tension was extreme. And in this interim, I thought we should leave, go away from here. So the children thought they'd go to Lahore — we didn't know what would happen in Lahore. And Ranjit said don't go there, things there are very bad. And it was while we were in the process of discussing and deciding this that my brother came, the one who lived in Lahore. Rana. And he said that there was a lot of talk of Partition, so he thought the house should be sold off.

Let me tell you a bit about Rana. He is the sixth of my parents' nine children. When my father died he left us well provided for: there was enough in the form of future security (the house) so that even those relatives who came to our house to condole commented that the family would not want for anything. But something else was in store for us: Bikram, my eldest brother, was a college dropout. He decided to start a business, took money from my mother, but the venture failed. Still, the impact of the loss was not felt so much, and Bikram later joined the Royal Air Force. When he brought home news of his appointment he brought with him a beautiful Muslim girl,

Ameena. He said he would marry her the day he got his first salary. But this never happened. The day Bikram went to office to collect his first salary, the office was not yet open so he decided to take his small aircraft out for a brief flight. He crashed into some electric wires and died.

For some reason Rana's life was the most affected by Bikram's death. One of our uncles, a judge at the Lahore High Court, decreed that Rana should be sent to the village. So, at age twelve or thirteen, he was pulled out of school and sent off to Paragpur. He hated it. He wrote a letter home one day saying: 'Here I have to wash my own bedsheets, I don't want to stay here, if you don't call me back I will run away.' Shortly afterwards we heard that he had disappeared—but we did not know what to do, how to find him. My mother was by this time an epileptic, my elder sisters were married and had left home, I was barely twenty . . .

I don't remember how we discovered that Rana was with my aunt, my mother's sister. We tried to get him back, and he ran away again. He could not be traced for two years and we began to think we had lost another brother. I felt the loss more than anyone else . . . And then one morning my elder sister walked in with Rana. She had found him, waiting tables at a railway restaurant. The prodigal had come home. He had become a stranger to the family but he had also learnt the art of survival.

Later, when all of us moved to Nabha, Rana stayed on in Lahore. I took up a job in Nabha and kept my mother and my younger brother and sister with me. Rana stayed in the family home. How he maintained himself no one knows. Often he would ask me for small loans . . .

When the clouds of Partition began to weigh upon us I started worrying about the house in Lahore. This was our only security. I thought if someone grabbed the house in the confusion of Partition, we'd all be left with nothing. One day, I read an advertisement in the papers about a house in Saharanpur. The owner, a Muslim, wanted to migrate to Pakistan and offered to exchange his house for a similar house in Lahore. It sounded ideal. I began negotiations with him, and wrote to my uncle about this.

There was no reply from my uncle but a few days later Rana came to visit us. He was pleased that I had tried to arrange this exchange of property and said he wanted to take Mother with him to sort out some details on this. I agreed. I was happy that my efforts had succeeded. When she did not come back after many days, I began to worry. She was not well. So I went to Lahore to see her and find out.

There I learnt that my uncle had warned Rana against me, saying that I would grab the property. Rana had actually brought my mother back so that he could hold on to the Lahore house. When I asked him about this he said, 'I am an uneducated man. What will I do in India? How long will you support me? Soon you'll get married and then your family will be your priority. Here at least this house will give me shelter.'

I tried to argue with him. How would he continue to live here if Pakistan became a reality? Rana was quite clear. He said, religion is not more important than survival. He told me he had planned everything. 'You know the girl whose mother lives in the quarter next to Jatinder's house? I have known her a long time and she is willing to marry me if I convert to Islam.'

What about Mother? I asked him. He told me she was his mother too. He said he would become a Muslim, he'd marry this girl, Fawzia, and would keep Mother with him.

Who can describe the pain of having to leave one's mother? . . . I pleaded with Rana to let me take my mother and my younger brother. I felt I could not trust him any more. I thought, in his lust for property he might even kill my mother or my brother . . . There was so much tension. I was frightened. I did not want to stay in the house at night. But finally, I had to leave. I left my poor, ailing mother behind and I have never forgiven him for this cruelty. As I was leaving, I wept. He looked at me and said, 'You are unhappy because I am converting to Islam.' I just held his hand and cried. I told him to look after Mother. I told him it was immaterial to me whether he was a Hindu or a Muslim—after all our father was a very secular and forward-looking man. But the woman he was snatching away from me, she was ill and frail and needed care . . . I came away with a heavy heart. I hoped that one of my sisters would be able to persuade him to let Mother go. But that did not happen. How she lived, whether she was looked after, was she fed properly or starved . . . I never came to know any of this. In my heart I yearned for her. After my father had died, Mother had lived with me . . . She was a staunch Hindu, she would pray every evening . . . I wondered what her daily routine was like now . . .

Rana became Abdulla, and Fawzia became his wife. The house of our childhood was now the abode of a committed and converted Muslim family. Was he happy? Did he look after my mother? There was no way of finding out. Once or twice he wrote to my younger sister, Munna, but then, she had to ask him to stop. Her husband was in the defence forces and there would have been too many questions . . . As time passed and Rana began to feel more and more isolated, I think he began to miss us. But he never wrote to me. And then, years later, you established contact with him. He sent a letter through you. He wrote that he was the father of four sons and three daughters. He said, 'I have never forgiven myself for what I did in my youth. I can't retrace my steps. I have never been accepted here, not even by my own family . . .'

His letter made me uneasy. I wrote back. I told him I thought he was lucky—at least he had stayed on in the family house. 'Don't call me lucky, dear sister,' he said, 'do you know that ever since I have converted I have not had a single night's peaceful sleep. Every brick in this house seems to curse me. I rejected what was mine and I have not been accepted by the faith I adopted.'

When he took my mother away I had no idea that Rana had any dishonesty in his head. But I was very worried, I didn't know what to do. I thought I'd send the children to Suniti, my elder sister, in Mussoorie. So I wrote her a letter—saying this place is not safe and I am sending the children to you, keep them with you for some days and when things improve I'll bring them back. Thinking that now that they were taken care of, and I had some time, I thought I would join Miranda House and take up Russian. I had always wanted to study Russian. I stayed in the hostel. That was in July 1946. There was a lot of tension, and things were very bad, but I thought at least the children were safe. But Suniti sent the children back, saying we are here on holiday and I can't look after them. But then Ranjit told me don't worry, we are going to the village, we'll take the children with us, they'll be fine and you carry on with your Russian. So—because Ranjit was a very good friend—I continued with the Russian.

The first six months passed well, and then there were holidays and I went to Nabha. When I came back after the summer vacation, suddenly things became very bad. What happened was that there was this Principal, Rajaram, and with him we girls would get into his jeep and go off shopping, so he said let's go, it was Sunday so we decided to go out for a bit. But when we got out, things were so bad, there were bodies everywhere. We went from the University area up to Red Fort. I remember that. At Red Fort I saw that in a tonga, there were four girls and one man with a knife. The girls jumped out of the tonga and that man ran after them, I don't know what happened after that. The place was full of bodies. So Rajaram asked for the jeep to turn towards Rajpur Road. There was a police station there and he said let's go and inform the police. He went and informed the police, but they said we have no police force at all, we can do nothing. And then, I don't know for what reason, he went to the railway station, and the place was full of blood and all that. And then, he said I don't think we should go any farther, and we came back. He dropped us at the hostel.

In my room there was a Muslim girl whose name was Zahira Ilahi, I think she was Sir Syed Ahmed's niece, she was very well connected . . . There was a lot of loot and arson there in the University . . . There was a history professor, Quereshi; I remember seeing boys, I still remember, a boy holding his coat and tie. And I heard from people that he had some very valuable paintings etc., they looted all of that and took it away. We were told that . . . there was so much tension that we were all frightened. I think there were only some six or seven of us girls in the hostel. There was the warden, and she had a plump daughter, and we used to wonder how we could keep ourselves safe inside. One day we had just sat down to eat, and one man came running and he caught hold of Zahira by the hand and he said let's go. He didn't even wait and we were completely stunned as he dragged her out. Later we came to know that he was her brother and he had got to know that there was a mob which was going to attack the hostel or something like that. So he took the girl away, and all her stuff, big boxes and all that, remained behind. Later we heard that they were living in a place called Kota house. Then he took her to Hyderabad or somewhere and I lost track of Zahira. But the mob came, and they kept shouting, 'We want Zahira, we want Zahira, bring her out'. We were all locked in one room, and after that the warden rescued us all and sent us to Rajaram's house.

Since Zahira wasn't there, the mob realized she had escaped. After that we stayed at Rajaram's house for some days and I remember when people went from here, they took big boxes full of looted stuff. A couple of times they stopped, we were just girls standing outside and they even offered to sell us silks and all that in case we needed them for getting married.

Then, the girls all had to go to their own places, so they went off, all of them. But I had nowhere to go to. I couldn't understand where I should go, I had nowhere . . . you know, it was a very peculiar situation. So I thought a lot, I was a bit daring and I thought I'd go to Maharaj Nabha's office. I went there and said I used to work in Nabha, and I am stranded and I want to go to Nabha. So someone in his office said we have cars going every day and we'll send you in one. So they arranged for me to go in a car, in which a friend's mama was also there, and in that military car I went to Nabha. I had taken leave from there, I had got fed up with the Nabha job, I'd done it for six years, and nothing was firming up on the marriage prospects. There was tension, personal problems, so I thought I'd get out and increase my qualifications and try for something else. Then we came back, and near Ambala we stopped. It was night. I was really frightened, and I said to the gentleman, uncle can you drop me at the railway station? He said, no don't worry, we are all there and you are our responsibility . . .

It was 2:30 at night when we got to Nabha. He said to me at the school gate, if you want you can come home with me and I'll bring you here in the morning. I said no, it's okay, after all one's home is one's home. At this time of night I thought where will I go? So he just put me down at the gate and left. The chowkidar was called Jiwna. I began to shout Jiwna, Jiwna. There was nobody. I gently pushed the gate and it opened. I went in, and there was this huge place, completely empty, with not a single light. I saw that Jiwna's room was closed. It didn't dawn upon me that they had all gone to Pakistan. There used to be a woman called Saira, I called her too. No one. I walked to the house and found that it was locked. All these people had gone to the village. Ranjit had taken my sister and brother. Sudha, my sister, had got married. And I had put my other sister, Bhutcher, in a hostel in Jalandhar in Kanya Mahavidyalaya. So she had gone. Billo, my younger brother, had run away and gone to Lahore. I'm not sure where Munna and Mataji were. No, Rana had taken Mataji, but there was nobody. The whole house was empty and on this huge six- or seven-acre place . . . it was deep night and not a soul around. I was terrified. And I could not figure out what to do. I sat in the veranda for some time, but I was frightened to death, there was darkness on all sides. There were Muslims everywhere. Then I thought I have been foolish, I have taken a risk. Suddenly I remembered that behind the school we used to have a mashki. His name was . . . I can't remember. Then, I sort of crawled, clinging to the walls, and went to the back. I called him, and he got up, shocked, saying bibaji where are you, where have you come from? He jumped the wall and came in, and he opened the lock, and I went inside and he slept outside in the veranda. In the morning he took a cycle and went to Ranjit's village and she came. So I stayed there for some time.

During this time, I went to Lahore once, to ask Rana to send my mother back. I promised to look after her. That is when I saw the letter lying there, and I realized it was a letter saying Subhadra will eat up the property, don't let your mother go. And I realized it was no use now. I begged and pleaded that he should send Billo, who had run away to him. I thought if he has brought my mother for property, he will then kill my brother. So he did send Billo.

This was . . . before Partition. This was in 1947, this was a little before Partition. I went to Lahore twice. Both visits were before Partition but I don't remember exactly when. Like a fool I took a tonga from Lahore station to our home. Without any fear or anything. That was right in the midst of fights. The second time I begged and pleaded, saying how will you feed him, etc., and then I brought Billo. In the train he was in the other compartment. At some point someone came and said that the boy who is travelling with you, he's fallen out of the train. And I went mad, I ran, but he was perfectly safe. Then he went to Gurgaon to get a job, but of course he was a sort of a drifter . . . In this way the children sort of got settled. Then I had to go to Simla where your father was, I couldn't find any way. No trains were going there. And I kept on trying, then someone told me that there were taxis and you have to pay six-hundred rupees to get one seat. So I collected the money and I paid it and I got a taxi from Delhi to Simla. I left my stuff along with Zahira Ilahi's boxes—these were never found. I left them in the care of the hostel warden. We did find the trunks later, with the locks intact but with nothing inside them.

It's difficult for me to say how I felt when I saw him again after you took us back. When I saw him at the airport I thought he was not at all like the thin, lanky youngster that I had left behind forty years ago. He had put on weight and he looked so much like my father. Though Bikram was also just as tall—about six three—he was quite fair. Rana, as he stood before me, was a virtual image of my father. Memories flooded in, of my father, my childhood, my mother, the great betrayal . . . Yet, I found I did not hate my brother. I felt sorry for him. He looked to me like a fugitive caught in his own trap.

As I went and put my arms around him he whispered, 'Are you still angry with me?' I was weeping. We were children of the same parents, the same blood, yet today we were like strangers, inhabitants of two enemy countries. I thought it was not the conversion that mattered so much to me, but I could not forgive him for what he did to my mother.

He'd brought his car to take us home. We were driven to a place which had been my home for so many years. As we drove in, I looked at the house:

the same majestic look, but, as I peered through the dark to see, I found two things missing. My father's name no longer decorated the gate, and the big religious symbol 'Om' which had been drawn on the water tank above the house did not seem to be visible. We met Rana's family: his wife and three sons—the fourth was away. We made ourselves comfortable: it was the month of December, but the rooms were warm, with room heaters in each of them. Pakistan has a cheap supply of piped gas. It was only in the morning that I noticed that all the fruit trees were gone. Rana said he had had to get rid of them because of water shortages. But I felt a real sense of loss, an almost physical hurt. My father had loved his trees more than anything else. It seemed like a betrayal. I thought, we had lost so much in Partition—what did a few trees matter, yet to me at the time they seemed like a symbol of everything we had lost . . .

That day your friend Lala came and took me sightseeing in Lahore. So much had changed. I wanted to go to Hall Road to see my old college, but when we reached there, the college was not to be seen. It had been shifted. I visited many places I had known well, but nothing was the same: this wonderful cosmopolitan city had now become a Muslim one. Loudspeakers called the faithful to prayer . . . shops, streets, everything was different . . .

I had been in Pakistan and our house for a full day but I had not gone into the other rooms. I wanted very much to go into what had been my room but I did not have the courage. Just one look beyond the drawing room made me draw back. The rooms on the other side were full of dowry articles for the impending wedding. And no one seemed to be living in them. Perhaps they all lived on the first floor. At dinner, however, the whole family assembled and we had a delicious and pleasant meal.

A few days later, Rana came into our room. And he began to talk. He shut the door behind him. He said, 'if this house had not been there, I think we all would have been together. I would not have converted and lost every moment of peace in my life.' But surely, I asked, the conversion was his choice. Yes, but he said he had still not been accepted. 'For them I am still a Hindu. If a girl had not been getting married and my presence was necessary I might well have been in jail.' We were stunned. Then he told us that one of his sons had filed a case against him, accusing him of being a Hindu spy. 'I am like a stranger,' he said, 'a man haunted in my own house by my own children.' He told me time and again that he had come to one conclusion and that was that one should never change one's religion.

That was my last night in Pakistan. I remember when I sat down to eat the next morning, before we left, Rana pulled out a bowl of white butter from the refrigerator. 'I have not forgotten how you loved white butter. I bought it yesterday.' He put the bowl in front of me, and my eyes filled with tears. That was the last time Rana and I spoke.

I have not been able to decide whether Rana was telling the truth or not. Was his problem really one of conversion? But there are many people who have converted and stayed on—is religion so important after all? Or was he simply lying, choosing a method of survival he had resorted to many times earlier? I don't really know.

3
'FACTS'

Part I   DIVIDING LIVES

The plan to partition India was announced on June 3, 1947. For people who had been directly or indirectly involved in the many discussions and the protracted negotiations that preceded this decision, the announcement came as something of a relief. 'We were so tired and fed up with all the to-ing and fro-ing,' said Sankho Chaudhry, a political worker with the Congress at the time, 'that we were grateful some decision had been taken at last. We thought, well, here's a solution finally and now we can relax.' His sentiments were echoed by several others. 'At last,' said a couple who later become relief workers, 'the dithering and bickering was over and a new beginning could be made.'

The solution, however, wasn't really a solution, nor the beginning a beginning. And if political leaders and the State heaved a collective sigh of relief that things had finally been decided, hundreds of thousands of people were left with a sense of bewilderment. What did this really mean? In the months leading up to Partition, and indeed after the announcement of the Plan in June 1947, the offices of the All India Congress Committee (AICC) received large numbers of letters from people wanting to know what was happening. What will become of us, they asked. We believe India is to be partitioned: where will we go? *How* will we go? What will happen to our jobs? If we have to move, will we get our old jobs back in the new homeland? What will happen to our homes, our lands, if we have to move?

'Shri J. B. Kripalani,' said one letter dated May 14, 1947:

Your advice to the Punjab minorities [i.e., the Hindus and Sikhs who saw themselves as minorities] that those who cannot defend themselves may migrate is extremely shocking. That only indicates that the so-called mighty Congress has failed or cannot or does not desire to defend or protest the helpless minorities of Punjab, Bengal and Sind.

The Congress having made the Hindus defenceless by preaching the gospel of Ahimsa, now comes with the advice of migration. Can you please let us know, what areas have been allotted to the migrants. What provisions have been made so far to get them settled honourably. Where should they migrate. In what numbers and in what manner. What they are to do with their immovable property. Will you be please able to find jobs for every one, or some business for all. Are they to come like beggars, settle like beggars in your relief camps and depend and subsist upon cast away crumbs of your people in U.P., C.P., Bihar, Bombay etc.

We have been and are as respectable in our own land of five rivers as the Biharis, Madrasis and Bhaians of U.P. We fully realise that you have secured independence for your 7 Provinces at our cost and you care a hang for what may happen to the Bengalis or the Punjabis. If that is all that you can do for us, if you in no case can advise the Hindus to kill or fight the Mohammedans either in minority Provinces or in majority Provinces, and if you cannot protect us and we are to protect ourselves, then for God's sake keep off your hands from our affairs. No one of you should trouble your exhaulted [sic] feet to traverse our heated soil. We need no such advice. We cannot be saved by mere lip service. That gives us no material support. We need substantial help to defend ourselves and to maintain the integrity of your mother India.

We cannot migrate like nomads or gypsies. We shall fight to the last, and God willing shall succeed and survive. But—but if otherwise the fate of Rawalpindi awaits us then it is better—far better—far, far better to become Muslims than to remain Hindus and be beggars to peep for alms at your doors; and be scorned and laughed at by you and your descendants.

If you can't protect us we can't accept your advice. We are human beings just as you people are. Our lives are as precious and worth living as yours. We don't want to be *Butchers* for your magnanimity or elevation. We want to live and live honourably. If the Congress is impotent to protect us then dissolve Congress organisation in the Punjab and let the Hindus have their own course. We need no messages or sermons from high pedestals or from the skys that you soar in. Cowards that you are, cowardly that your gospel, and cowardly that you have stuck to it: we bid you adieu. We may perish or survive; we may live or die or live as Hindus or as whatever we may like, for Heaven's sake if you are not to render us any material help, please go off, keep off and do off.[1]

---

[1] AICC papers, Punjab, F. No. CL-9 (I)/1946. I have kept to the original text and spelling of this letter.

These questions—which remained largely unanswered—and the sense of profound betrayal this particular letter reflects, came from those who understood, or at least apprehended, what could happen. There were others—thousands, perhaps millions—who simply did not believe there would be change, or that it would be of so permanent a nature. Surely their lives could not be upturned that easily? 'Politicians, kings, leaders have always fought over power,' said Rajinder Singh, voicing something that was to be echoed by many people again and again, 'and kings and leaders may change, but when have the *people* ever had to change?' (*Raje, maharaje badalte rehete hain, par praja kab badli hai?*). He was wrong, though, as were many others. The people did change, and the change did not relate only to geographical location.

When things became particularly bad, he said,

> We realized it was time to leave. This whole area was going to go to Pakistan and we had to leave. The zamindars began to say, well, it is easy for you shopkeepers—all you have to do is take your weighing scales and stones and go off, but what about us, we have land here. How can we take that away? We can't carry our land on our heads. Shopkeepers can take up anywhere. And people kept telling themselves these kinds of things, saying, no, it won't happen, kings may change, but when does the public ever leave its place and go? When Ranjit Singh began to rule, did the public change? When the Sikhs came into power did they throw the Musalmaans out? Don't worry, they said, nothing will happen . . . this is how they used to reassure themselves. My father said . . . the story is over, finished. Even in the villages people don't look you in the eye.

Perhaps the most astonishing thing was that, despite the concern expressed by many people, neither the Indian nor the Pakistani governments—nor indeed the British—seemed to have anticipated that there would be such a major exchange of population; that, driven by fear, people would move to places where they could live among their own kind. By the time the Partition Plan was announced, the Punjab had already seen major violence: riots in Rawalpindi district in March 1947 had left thousands dead, and there had been widespread loot, arson, destruction and violence towards women, all of which were to become the hallmarks of Partition violence. Earlier, in 1946, there was violence in

Bengal, Noakhali, Bihar, Garh Mukteshwar, and both Hindus and Muslims had been at the receiving—and attacking—ends. Yet, it was only on August 17, two days after Partition, that the prime ministers of India and Pakistan met at Ambala and agreed to an exchange of population. By this time, according to Reports of the Ministry of Rehabilitation, more than 500,000 people had already moved across to India from Pakistan, and an equal number had moved the other way. Once it became clear that people would move, both governments were forced to accept this. But while refugees were allowed to move, they were prohibited from taking away their machinery, their vehicles, equipment in factories and other such assets. Not only would these slow their movement, but they would be useful for the country they were leaving behind.

For years afterwards—indeed well into the present day—people involved in Partition violence would ask themselves what it was that turned the interconnectedness of entire lifetimes, often generations, of shared, interdependent, albeit different lives, into feelings of enmity. 'I cannot explain it,' said Harjit, a Sikh who lives close to the border town of Attari, 'but one day our entire village took off to a nearby Muslim village on a killing spree. We simply went mad. And it has cost me fifty years of remorse, of sleepless nights—I cannot forget the faces of those we killed.' His feelings find an almost exact echo on the 'other side'—in those of Nasir Hussain, a farmer and an ex-army man: 'I still cannot understand what happened to me and other youngsters of my age at that time. It was a matter of two days and we were swept away by this wild wave of hatred . . . I cannot even remember how many men I actually killed. It was a phase, a state of mind over which we had no control. We did not even know what we were doing.' Like Harjit, he too is haunted by remorse for that moment of madness in his life.

The transformation of the 'other' from a human being to the enemy, a *thing* to be destroyed before it destroyed you, became the all-important imperative. Feelings, other than hate, indifference, loathing, had no place here. Later, they would come back to haunt those who had participated in the violence, or remained indifferent to its happening. A seventy-year-old professor recounted how, as a young volunteer with the RSS in Patiala, he remembered hearing the screams of a Muslim woman being raped and then killed in the nearby wholesale market. He had listened, and felt nothing because, he said, 'at the time, as members of the RSS, we were not allowed to feel for "them".' Fifty years later, he wept tears of mourning for the woman, and for his own indifference.

The irony of the 'solution' put forward by the leaders was nowhere more evident. Naively, they had imagined that if the warring factions (if warring factions they were) were to be separated, and a line drawn between them to mark their territorial separation, the problem would be solved. But wars and battles are notorious for crossing and not respecting boundaries. And the intricate intertwining of centuries can hardly be undone in one stroke. In what is perhaps the most tragic irony of all, the 'solution' actually became the beginning of the problem.

* * *

Once the Partition Plan was announced and accepted by both parties, a machinery had to be set in motion to implement it. Almost as if by tacit agreement, the most tricky question of all, the laying down of the boundary that was to change millions of lives, was put aside for a later date. Cyril Radcliffe, recruited to the task of deciding what the maps of Pakistan and India would look like, had not finished work when the transfer of power took place, and the two countries became independent. They were to learn the geographical limits of their territories later—and to dispute them for many years after. On July 18, 1947, shortly after the announcement of the Partition Plan, the Indian Independence Bill was passed by the British parliament and became law. By its provisions, ten expert committees were set up to deal with various aspects of Partition. These were:

1. Organization, Records and Government Personnel.
2. Assets and Liabilities.
3. Central Revenues.
4. Contracts.
5. Currency, Coinage and Exchange.
6. Economic Relations. (i)
7. Economic Relations. (ii)
8. Domicile.

9. Foreign Relations.

10. Armed Forces.[2]

Not one of these dealt with the dislocation and rupturing of people's lives. Despite the growing atmosphere of fear and mistrust, scant attention was paid to people's concerns for their safety and well being. Instead, political leaders naively continued to assert that things would be all right if people simply remained where they were. Early in August 1947, Gandhi regretted that people were leaving their homes and running away. This, he said, was 'not as it should be'. Later, in November of the same year, the AICC resolved to persuade people to return to their original homes. Appeal after appeal was issued to people, assuring them safety, asking them not to move.

These reassurances and exhortations fell on deaf ears. People knew that moving was now inevitable. They had seen what had happened in Rawalpindi, in Bihar, in Noakhali. When it did happen, the dimensions of the move were staggering. Never before or since, in human history, has there been such a mass exodus of people, and in so short a time. Just the mere scale was phenomenal. Twelve million people crossed the border in both directions. Between August and November 1947 — a bare three months — as many as 673 refugee trains moved approximately 2,800,000 refugees within India and across the border; in just one month, the Military Evacuation Organisation (MEO, made up of military personnel and set up, as the name suggests, to evacuate people) used some 10,00,000 [1,000,000] gallons of petrol to evacuate people in East Punjab. By the end of August, planes also began to be deployed though air travel was mainly limited to public servants and the rich. Even so, an average of six to seven planes flew every day between India and Pakistan carrying refugees from Sargodha, Lyallpur, Multan and Rawalpindi. This was in addition to the existing flights between Delhi, Karachi, Lahore, Quetta and Rawalpindi. By around the third week of November some 32,000 refugees had been flown in both directions. From Sind, for example, the most direct route to Bombay, where large numbers of people went, was by sea. By November 21, 133,000 people had been moved by steamer and

---

[2] *After Partition*, Modern India Series, Delhi, Publications Division, 1948, pp. 20–21.

country craft. This number, it seemed, could have been greater, but the port authorities at Karachi allowed the departure of only 2,000 people a day, as that was the maximum number they were able to handle.[3]

For the poor, and those who did not, or could not, get access to trains or road transport, the only way to leave to seek their new homeland was on foot, in massive human columns known as kafilas. These began to move roughly two weeks after Partition. Initially 30,000 to 40,000 strong, the kafilas grew, the largest consisting of some 400,000 people, an enormous, massive, foot column which, it is said, took as many as eight days to cross a given spot. Between September 18 and October 22, twenty-four kafilas of Hindus and Sikhs had moved from Lyallpur and Montgomery to India, taking with them some 849,000 people. It is believed that in all, a million people crossed the border on foot, travelling from West to East.[4]

Everywhere along the route, whether people were on foot, in trains, cars, or lorries, attackers lay in wait. As kafilas crossed each other, moving in opposite directions, people who looked exactly the same—for little in their appearance would, at first glance, tell whether they were Hindu or Muslim—and were burdened with poverty and grief, would suddenly turn in murderous attack on each other. Of the thousands of women who were raped and abducted, large numbers were picked up from the edges of kafilas. In the desperation of flight, the weak and vulnerable—the old and infirm, the physically disabled, children, women—often got left behind. Few had time for anyone other than themselves. In September, the elements lent a hand: unusually heavy rain led to floods and disrupted the lines of communication. Rail traffic had to be slowed down, it became difficult to travel by road, and in the kafilas, the rain led to illness and disease. The army had to be called in to repair roads and bridges, and the police and army were given the task of accompanying and protecting people travelling on foot and by road and rail.

But the police were no longer just the police—supposedly impartial people whose task was to protect law and order. Nor were the armed

---

[3] *After Partition,* pp. 50–55.

[4] *After Partition,* pp. 50–55, and U. Bhaskar Rao, *The Story of Rehabilitation,* Delhi, Department of Rehabilitation, 1967.

forces any longer just the armed forces—supposedly neutral forces intent only upon performing the task allotted to them. Partition shattered the myth of the neutrality and objectivity of such arms of the State conclusively. Sixty percent of the police force at the time of Partition was made up of Muslims. Non-Muslims travelling from Pakistan to India, and Muslims travelling from India to Pakistan, felt safe only if they were accompanied by police 'of their own kind'. But this was only possible in a limited sense, for the police and army too had to mark out their territorial jurisdiction. Refugees travelling within Pakistan towards the Indian border were accompanied by the Pakistani 'military' as they called them, and from a certain point, the Indians took over.

If the police force was largely made up of Muslims, in the army these numbers were reversed: Muslims made up only thirty percent, while non-Muslims comprised the rest. Once the decision to divide up the country had been taken, everything else had to be divided too. This included the army: not only stores and equipment such as vehicles, tanks, guns, ammunition depots, but also people. The forces were thus divided on a communal basis: Muslim soldiers to Pakistan, non-Muslims to India. Clause (f) of the general principles laid down by the Partition Council for the reconstitution of the armed forces read as follows:

> The Partition of the Forces will be in two stages. The first one will be a more or less rough and ready division of the existing Forces on a communal basis and the Plan should be prepared forthwith. The next phase will be to comb out the units themselves on the basis of voluntary transfers. However, there will be an exception—the Muslims from Pakistan now serving in the Indian Armed Forces will not have the option to join the Armed Forces of the Indian Union and similarly a non-Muslim from the rest of India now serving in the Armed forces would not have the option to join the Armed Forces of Pakistan.[5]

There was an element of choice, but this was denied to Muslims who were at the time in what became Pakistan, or Hindus and Sikhs who were at the time in what became India. It was an odd kind of logic. If

---

[5] Armed Forces Reconstruction Committee of the ten committees set up to deal with 'The Administrative Consequences of Partition'.

you'd been a Muslim, serving in the army at Lahore, you could not elect to join the Indian army, but if you had been a Hindu, serving in the army at Lahore, you had the choice to join the Indian or the Pakistani armies. Gurkhas stayed out of this: they formed seven percent of the Indian army and were somehow seen as separate, neutral—even though they came from a Hindu country, Nepal. The army of undivided India had ten Gurkha regiments: by an interim agreement arrived at between India, Nepal and Britain, six of these regiments remained in the Indian army, while four went over to the British army. For many who travelled from Pakistan to India and in the other direction at the time, the only safe escorts were the Gurkha regiments, seen somehow as more neutral than the Hindu or Muslim armies.

*   *   *

Looking back on it now, there are times at which the whole business seems absurd. Partitioning two lives is difficult enough. Partitioning millions is madness. So much had to be divided: drawing physical boundaries was no easy task. A network of roads and railways criss-crossed undivided Punjab: how could this be divided? Five rivers flowed through and provided water to the state: these would now have to be divided. A system of canals fed by these rivers irrigated many parts of Punjab: the Upper Bari Doab canal, for example, irrigated Lahore and Montgomery districts which came into West Punjab, but its headworks lay in East Punjab; the Depalpur canal which irrigated areas of West Punjab was controlled by the Ferozepur Weir which lay in East Punjab. Every administrative unit was divided, its employees being given the choice to move to India or Pakistan.

For those who did move, other problems arose: what would happen to their pensions, to things such as provident fund accounts, to loans taken from banks and employers? Opting for one or other country may have been relatively simple for some people (and not so for others) but when it came to the question of actually exercising that option, things were not that easy. An uncertain, disturbed situation meant that people sometimes had to wait, for days or even months, before they could move. What would happen to their jobs in this time of limbo? Who would pay their salaries? Education was disrupted, and endless arguments now took place about whether or not it was advisable to divide up universities. Away from the turmoil and ferment of home were a number of scholars: State scholars, studying for one thing or another abroad, and paid for, wholly or partially, by the State. Now they too had to opt for one of two countries. And there was no clarity about who would pay their stipends while the two countries got themselves organized. The departure of Muslim skilled labour from East Punjab left industries such as hosiery, metal works and railways crippled as Muslims formed the bulk of the workforce in these. Batala, for example, a centre for metal work, went into a decline following the departure of the Muslim workforce. Trade between the two sides of Punjab had to be restricted. Raw materials and chemical and machine goods that were earlier available from Karachi could now no longer be had, and new suppliers had to be found in Bombay. The textile industry, one of the key industries in Amritsar, now had to look for markets in the Indian interior. The shape of cities also changed: Lahore no longer remained the vibrant cultural centre it had once been. Amritsar, once in the heart of Punjab, and a thriving commercial city, now became the last city on the Grand Trunk Road before the border at Wagah.[6] In the rush to leave, everyone had left behind some kind of property: cash, jewellery, personal effects, deposits, securities, things in safes, old letters, account books . . . all sorts of things. Many people, believing they would return, had buried jewellery, money, gold in all sorts of places. How was all this to be recovered? The years following August 1947 were full of meetings and discussions between the two governments on who owed whom how much, and how what was owed—or owned—by those who had left was to be recovered. People who had money or goods deposited in banks had to apply to the Custodians of Evacuee Properties for permission to take these away; those who had National Savings Certificates, Defence Certificates and other similar securities could claim these at any post office in either dominion after which an elaborate process of verification had to be gone through before these could be realized. Even weapons had to be exchanged, the first such exchange taking place in Lahore in October 1956 and in Jalan-

---

[6] Navtej K. Purewal, 'Displaced Communities: Some Impacts of Partition on Poor Communities', in *International Journal of Punjab Studies*, Vol. 4, No. 1, Jan–June 1997, 129–46.

dhar on the same day. Four other exchanges took place, at the end of which, in February 1958, India had received 1200 weapons to be restored to their owners. Almost in tandem with this, in 1954, and up to May 1958, some 2200 searches for buried treasures were carried out in Pakistan, and about 1300 of these were successful, with Rs 69 lakhs worth of such treasures being recovered.[7] One of the enduring legacies of the Raj has been the administrative system and its reliance on 'files' — files that have notations, those that have been cleared, those that are pending . . . In 1947 as one administrative system transformed itself into two, it became necessary to duplicate all files.[8] At the time, though, duplication wasn't quite as simple as it is today. So, for several months, administrators who had opted for Pakistan had to be located inside Indian ministries copying by hand all the documents they wanted to take along with them. What would have happened, I have often wondered, if someone had fallen asleep over the copying or made mistakes in the notings? Of such details is history made.

* * *

On June 30, 1947, some three weeks after the Partition Plan had been announced, the Governor General of India constituted the Boundary Commissions for Punjab and Bengal. Each had four members, two Hindu and two Muslim, and both came to be chaired by Sir Cyril Radcliffe, a lawyer from England, said to be a man of 'great legal abilities, right personality and wide administrative experience'. The task of the Boundary Commissions was to demarcate the boundaries of India and Pakistan on 'the basis of ascertaining the contiguous majority areas of Muslims and non-Muslims,' and in doing so, to take into account 'other factors' — it was never clear quite what this last meant. With a bare five weeks in which to decide (Radcliffe arrived in India on July 8, 1947 and the award was announced on August 16, 1947) Radcliffe got down to the momentous task of deciding a boundary that would 'divide a province

[7] See Kirpal Singh, *The Partition of the Punjab*, Patiala, Publications Bureau, 1972.
[8] Kirpal Singh, *Select Documents on Partition of Punjab, 1947, India and Pakistan: Punjab, Haryana and Himachal—India and Punjab—Pakistan*, Delhi, National Bookshop, 1991, pp. 144–46.

of more than 35 million people, thousands of villages, towns and cities, a unified and integrated system of canals and communication networks, and 16 million Muslims, 15 million Hindus and 5 million Sikhs, who despite their religious differences, shared a common culture, language and history.'[9] Predictably, there were irreconcilable differences between the members, and the different political organizations each had their own interpretation of where the boundary should be laid. While the Muslims made their claim on the basis of demography, outlining the districts that they saw as contiguous for Muslims and non-Muslims, the Hindus staked their claim on the basis of 'other factors'—they wanted Lahore to become part of East Punjab because of its 'historical associations with Hindu and Sikh history', and because much of its commerce and industry was owned by non-Muslims. If the line of partition was, however, drawn on the basis of Muslim and non-Muslim majority districts, the Sikhs would be split down the middle. They then staked their claim on the basis of the fact that many of their most sacred religious shrines would fall in Pakistan if this principle was followed, and they asked for portions of certain Muslim majority districts on the basis of the fact that much of the land revenue was paid by them and they had extensive landholdings in these areas. Clearly, there was no reconciling these conflicting claims, and in the end, the decisions were left to Cyril Radcliffe.

Radcliffe's task was not an easy one. He had little time, no familiarity with the land or the people, and census statistics which were, by now, quite old and almost certainly outdated. Boundaries are usually demarcated along geographical features—rivers, mountains, etc. Where the two parties on either side of the boundary are at loggerheads, even geographical boundaries become suspect. (Rivers, for example, tend to change course, and this can become a cause for tension.) And religious contiguity does not, in any case, follow geographical patterns. The most sacred of Sikh shrines, Nankana Sahib, lay deep inside Western Punjab. Lahore was a city loved and owned equally by both communities, as was Amritsar, an important trading and religious centre, sacred to the Sikhs, but also loved by many Muslims. Gurdaspur district was said to have

[9] *After Partition*, pp. 28–29.

a Muslim majority, but economically, it was the Sikhs who dominated here. The line that eventually became the border had some shrines of Muslim saints dotting it. Yet, the hundreds of thousands who visited these included Sikhs, Hindus, Christians etc. Political considerations had dictated that the border follow contiguous areas. Geography dictated otherwise: the demands of politics fitted ill with the constraints of geography, but in the end, politics won over geography. Unable to follow natural divisions, Radcliffe was forced to draw what are called 'complex' boundaries which ran through villages, deserts, shrines — and people's lives. Equally, the constraints of geography fitted ill with the demands of economics and commerce. The Hindus and Sikhs made a case that was based on rather unlikely bedfellows: religious identity and economics. They emphasized the role they had played in the development of industry and commerce in Lahore: they owned the bulk of the banking system, insurance, factories, education. These, according to Justice Meher Chand Mahajan, one of the representatives of India on the Commission, were the 'other factors' the Boundary Commission needed to take into account. A mere focus on population was not enough.

In the end, predictably, the award satisfied no one. Indeed, there *was* no satisfactory way to make the division. The *Amrita Bazar Patrika* labelled it the 'departing kick of British imperialism at both the Hindus and Muslims', while *Dawn* called it 'territorial murder' and said 'Pakistan has been cheated by an unjust award, a biased decision, an act of shameful partiality by one who had been trusted to be fair because he was neutral'.[10] For his part, Cyril Radcliffe knew he had not made himself popular. He would never go back to India, he said, and wrote to his nephew: 'Nobody in India will love me for the award about the Punjab and Bengal and there will be roughly 80 million people with a grievance who will begin looking for me. I do not want them to find me. I have worked and travelled and sweated . . . oh, I have sweated the whole time.' Later — much later — he was asked in an interview whether he would have done differently had he had more time. And he said: 'Yes. On my arrival I told all political leaders that the time at my disposal was very short. But

[10] *After Partition*, p. 30.

all leaders like Jinnah, Nehru and Patel told me that they wanted a line before or on 15th August. So I drew them a line.'[11]

The political developments that preceded the drawing of Radcliffe's boundaries contributed to the growing hostility between the Hindus, Sikhs and Muslims. This did not only have to do with religion. Much more was at stake: jobs, livelihoods, property, homelands. A sort of competition developed for these, but significantly and differently, on religious lines: would a Muslim get x or y job, or a Hindu? Just as religion had conflicted with geography—how many Hindus or Muslims on this side of a river or mountain or desert—so also it clashed with things such as property and employment.

But while hostility may grow easily enough, instant boundaries are not that easy to lay down. Despite the boundary, people travelled back and forth. For some years, there was no passport system between Pakistan and India. Today, in a tragic travesty of this earlier 'openness', for Pakistanis and Indians to get visas to visit each other's countries is an extremely difficult, and often virtually impossible, enterprise. When they succeed, they must report to the other country's police when they arrive and before they leave, and they have permission only to visit three cities in either country!

Ironically, instant enmity and hostility were forced to rub shoulders with some sharing. The two countries were tied together in a relationship of fierce hatred and grudging interdependence. The departure of barbers, weavers, tailors, goldsmiths, and others en masse to Pakistan crippled certain aspects of life particularly in Delhi. In Pakistan, the departure of accounts clerks, bankers, lawyers and teachers dealt a similar blow, albeit at a different level, to life there. As a new country, Pakistan had no instant arrangements to print its currency: the mint was in India. Nor did it actually have a banknote to call its own. So, for about a year, Pakistani currency (Indian banknotes which were legal tender in Pakistan until it established its own) was printed in India, as was much government material and stationery, with the government press at Simla given over entirely to printing materials for Pakistan and a part

[11] Kirpal Singh, *Select Documents on Partition of Punjab*, p. 744 (author's interview with Cyril Radcliffe).

of the press at Aligarh given over for the same purpose. Pakistani officers (for currency) were trained in India for several weeks, and India loaned accountants to Pakistan to help out with accounting work. Until July 1948, when the State Bank of Pakistan was set up, the Reserve Bank of India continued to function for both countries. During this time, a new Pakistani banknote was designed and once it went into printing, Indian banknotes ceased to be legal tender. As with everything else, a string of disagreements accompanied these changes too, for Pakistan accused India of refusing to accept and encash Indian banknotes which were no longer of any use in Pakistan.

* * *

It can be argued that the conditions for Partition were obvious for all to see in Punjab. Although just short of a majority in numbers, non-Muslims (Hindus and Sikhs) were economically dominant. They owned the bulk of industry, agriculture and business and many were money-lenders. A very real fear of dominance and exploitation then lay behind the Muslim demand for separate electorates—your own representative in power, it was believed, would protect the interests of your community. Elsewhere in India, however, separate electorates had been granted to communities who were in a numerical minority. Here, in Punjab, if Census figures were to be believed, Muslims were in a slight majority, but their economic and social position vis-à-vis the Hindus and Sikhs was seen as a reason for granting them a separate electorate. Hindu and Sikh reaction to this in Punjab was, predictably, negative, with the Sikhs lobbying for similar treatment. Each of the contending claims had some justification, yet each meant injustice to the other.

But a demand for power, for a voice in the legislature, was one thing. How did this get transformed into a demand for a homeland, a separate *country*? How—and whence—did the *idea* of Partition come? As always, it is difficult to fix a point at which an idea becomes more than just an idea—Partition is no exception. In books on the subject, the idea is sometimes credited to Chaudhry Rahmat Ali, in others to the poet Mohammad Iqbal; it is also said that it was mooted by the Indian politician Lala Lajpat Rai, and it comes to be 'fixed' as an idea and attributed at this stage to Jinnah, after the Lahore resolution of 1940 (which is often also known as the Pakistan Resolution). Yet ideas never have such a simple history, or indeed geography. Recent research has shown that despite the growing tension between the Congress and the Muslim League, even after the so-called Lahore Resolution, Mohammed Ali Jinnah, widely seen as the architect of Pakistan, remained ambivalent on the idea of Pakistan, while the Congress was not as reluctant to accept it as has been believed.[12]

On the ground, too, there was evidence that religious differences were not so rigid. Historian Sumit Sarkar points out that the period preceding and leading up to Partition was marked by two seemingly contradictory processes—a number of protest movements on the ground in which Hindu-Muslim unity was a notable feature,[13] as well as a series of processes at the broader political level where the Congress and the Muslim League played a complicated game of alliance and separation. Through this, the British negotiated their careful moves, now encouraging one, now the other, their own approach varying as broader political developments on the home (the victory of Labour in the 1945 elections) and the international (the World War in 1939) fronts impinged upon it.

Whatever the origins of the idea, however, by 1946 it was clear that the departure of the British was now imminent. In England, a Labour government had been swept to power in July 1945, and shortly after the end of the Second World War, this government announced elections in India. Although a far cry from earlier promises of elections based on universal franchise, the Congress and Muslim League nonetheless took to these with gusto. They campaigned and won impressive victories with the League for the first time, making inroads into the all-important state of Punjab. Even so, a clear majority still remained outside its grasp because of a tactical alliance between the Unionist Party and the Congress and Akalis. This would be broken, in roughly a year's time, paving the way for the League's full control of Punjab, with the resignation of the Punjab Prime Minister, Khizir Hayat Khan Tiwana in June 1947. What

---

[12] See, for example, Aijaz Ahmed, 'Tryst with Destiny—Free but Divided', in *India! Special Issue on 50 Years of Independence*, published by *The Hindu*, August 1997.

[13] Sumit Sarkar: *Modern India 1885–1947*, Madras, Macmillan India, 1983, 'Introduction'.

was significant about this pattern of voting was its communal nature, which reflected the increasing communal tension on the ground. Strong revivalist movements such as the Arya Samaj, the Singh Sabha and others had already found fertile ground in Punjab. Now, other, newer actors entered the fray: the Rashtriya Swayamsevak Sangh, the Muslim League National Guards, the Akali Sena. All of these played no mean role in heightening tension between the different communities.

Other developments followed: in February 1947 British Prime Minister Clement Atlee announced that the British would transfer power in the Indian subcontinent by 'a date not later than June 1948'. The Muslim League now made a concerted bid to capture power in Punjab, and with the resignation of the Punjab premier, this became a reality. On March 8, 1947, even as Sikh majority villages in Rawalpindi were facing concerted attacks from Muslim mobs, the Congress Working Committee passed a resolution calling for a division of Punjab into two provinces.

There are many interpretations about how all these tangled strands tied in with Partition: the debates are well known, and have formed the stuff of much history writing about this time. I have no wish to enter these debates, to establish who was more to blame, the Congress or the Muslim League, or how the British manipulated their departure, or who was more communal, and so on. I am not a historian and have neither the capability nor indeed the interest to explore these questions. I am concerned instead with the consequences of Partition for people then, and its ramifications now, in their lives. My focus here is on the small actors and bit-part players, whose lives, as the lives of all people, were inextricably interwoven with broader political realities. How these realities touched on and transformed their lives is what my work is concerned with.

Whenever it took root however, the idea of *partition* was not new. India had already, for example, seen the partition of Bengal. But an internal partition, a dividing up of a province, is quite different from partitioning a *country*. Initial discussions in Punjab too included the possibility of partitioning the province, making a separation between East and West because Hindus and Sikhs dominated in one and Muslims in the other. All sorts of schemes were discussed — the separation of Ambala division from Punjab in order to make one community predominant; the amalgamation of Rawalpindi and Multan divisions (excluding Montgomery and Lyallpur districts) with the North West Frontier Province (NWFP) which would then ensure that Hindus and Sikhs were in a majority in what was left of Punjab.

Part of the problem, it seemed, was that the three communities were too evenly balanced. Moving one away from the province would change this balance—and perhaps solve the problem. But things are never this simple. Electoral victories and the assumption of power, albeit limited, had shown both parties how seductive power could be, and they now colluded in the confusion, the ad hocism and the rush to push things through. The original date of independence was advanced by Mountbatten, the man who was said to be 'in a hurry', and political leaders endorsed this speeded-up agenda, giving people little time to make thought-out decisions. As early as 1940 Nehru is reported to have said that Partition was preferable to any postponement of independence. Despite their reluctance to partition the country then, leaders, particularly within the Congress, began to see it as a necessary price for independence, and were complicit in the processes that led to the severing of what Sardar Patel described as a 'diseased limb'. The blood that was shed, however, was not only that of a limb cut off, but of thousands of lives.

To some extent, the seeds of the idea of Partition can be said to have lain within the economic and social differences that existed between Hindus/Sikhs and Muslims. Most Partition memories speak of pre-Partition days, when Hindus and Muslims and Sikhs lived in a state of—often mythical—harmony. Yet this harmony was built on concrete, material differences. At a more day-to-day level, there were other differences. Bir Bahadur Singh, to whom I spoke some years ago, described these eloquently:

> . . . if a Musalmaan was coming along the road, and we shook hands with him, and we had, say, a box of food or something in our hand, that would then become soiled and we would not eat it; if we are holding a dog in one hand and food in the other, there's nothing wrong with that food. But if a Musalmaan would come and shake hands our dadis and mothers would say, son, don't eat this food, it has become polluted. Such were the

dealings: how can it be that two people are living in the same village, and one treats the other with such respect and the other doesn't even give him the consideration due to a dog? How can this be? They would call our mothers and sisters didi, they would refer to us as brothers, sisters, fathers and when we needed them, they were always there to help. Yet when they came to our houses, we treated them so badly. This is really terrible. And this is the reason Pakistan was made.

*   *   *

These are some of the 'facts' of Partition. As facts, they recount only the minutiae of history, not its general, overarching patterns. These are well known and don't, in my view, need repetition here. It is the smaller actors that I am interested in, the bit-part players. Even as I look back to the history that we know of Partition, my purpose is not to question the veracity of its 'facts' but to question what I can best describe as the 'adequacy' of such facts: can we continue to think of the history of Partition only in terms of broad political negotiations? Where then do we place the kinds of 'facts' I have talked about here, and where the stories that lie beneath and behind them? Having spent a little more than a decade listening to people's memories, collecting their stories, the question before me is: given what these stories have told me, and what I, from my context and politics, have read into them, can 'that' history now serve? Carolyn Steedman describes what I think I am trying to do as a process of interpreting (or re-interpreting) 'facts'—a reworking of 'what has already happened, to give current events meaning'. The point, she says, 'doesn't lie there, back in the past, back in the lost time in which they [the events] happened; the only point lies in interpretation.'[14] I am concerned then with a different reality, a different interpretation.

Behind all the facts that I have described above, and those that don't figure in this telling, lie human beings, real flesh-and-blood figures whose lives were profoundly affected by Partition. Some have lived, as my uncle has, with a sense of permanent loss and regret, others have lived with the trauma of rape, and the conscious, perhaps slow and always difficult

[14] Carolyn Steedman, *Landscape for a Good Woman*, London, Virago, 1986, pp. 5–6.

process of the acceptance of so deep a violation as abduction; some with the knowledge that in the past they have killed . . . It is only when one is able to look behind and beyond the 'facts' of Partition, that these different, multi-layered histories begin to unfold. The stories that I recount in this book therefore, might be said to be of a different order of 'facts' from those that the tools of conventional history allow us to apprehend. For such tools, used as they are for dealing with documents, with reports, with speeches, are simply not adequate to unpick the seams behind which lie the silences I am trying to look at. There is no historical entry point, for example, that allows me to look for—and find—a story like my uncle's if all I have on hand are the tools of conventional history. No historical document can approximate his pain and anguish, none can reflect his trauma or even begin to understand his confusion and ambivalence. None that can see him and all or any of the other people you will meet in this book as human beings upon whose bodies and lives history has been played out. In most historical accounts of Partition, people are just numbers, or else they are that terrible word, 'informants', mere sources of information. For me, in my study of Partition, it is the people I spoke to who are an integral part of the history of Partition. In many ways, it is they whose lives *are* the history of Partition.

This book then attempts to interweave stories and histories. Let me try to illustrate this point with a story. One of the facts of Partition that I referred to earlier relates to the division of the Armed Forces. Properties, moveable and immoveable, were divided, and people were given the choice of joining the Pakistan army or staying with the Indian army. On the face of it, this is just information. But I was intrigued by it: what was it that guided people's decisions to go to one or the other side? Was it only religion? How was this division played out in life? Abdul Shudul, serving at the time at the lowest rung of the ladder in the army, had a choice in this matter like his other colleagues. He exercised it by staying in India. Appearing before a board of army officers—one from Pakistan and one from India—Abdul Shudul confirmed that he wanted to stay on in India. His home and family were there, and although there had been some rumblings of discontent in his village, Begumpur (which was fairly close to Delhi), he felt he had little to fear from his neighbours.

He had a good job, had just started a family, and it seemed much easier to stay on.

But then, his life took an unexpected turn. Concerned at the possibility of trouble, he sent his wife and two-month-old daughter away with his brother—who had decided to move to Pakistan. They were to go and stay with his in-laws, on the other side of Delhi, before the brother left for Pakistan. On the way, they met with trouble. They never made it to their destination, and instead found themselves in the refugee camp at Purana Qila, where people were housed, waiting—for the most part—to be sent to Pakistan. A week after they reached the camp, they left for Pakistan. Unaware of all this, Abdul Shudul set out one day to fetch his family back from his in-laws and got there to find they had never arrived. He then scoured the Purana Qila camp, and learnt that they had left for Pakistan a week ago. He feared they had all been killed: 'I knew that several trains to Pakistan had been stopped and the people in them murdered. I was sure this had happened to my family too.' Distraught, he came home, prepared now to live his life alone. Some weeks later, quite by chance, he found an address label inside one of the trunks his brother had kept at his home, and on it was the address of the place in Peshawar to which his brother had planned to go. Shudul prepared to go to Pakistan. 'At the time,' he said, 'there was no passport system, so it was not so difficult to go.' In October of 1947, he left for Pakistan.

His first stop there was at the army headquarters where he was fortunate to find one of his old officers from India, who promised him that he would have his old job back. 'Are you sure you want to stay in Pakistan?' he asked Shudul. 'Earlier you had chosen India.' But Shudul reassured him that he did want to be in Pakistan; now that his family was there, there was nothing to take him back to India. The officer said he would do all he could to help. The next few months were spent in sending letter after letter to the army headquarters in India, requesting that Shudul's file be sent to Pakistan so that he could be properly tranferred into the Pakistan army. The officer, a refugee himself, went out of his way to help other refugees. This wasn't, of course, liked by others who weren't refugees, and Shudul suspected that it was one of those clerks who perhaps blocked any replies from India. Or perhaps India simply could not be bothered to send them. His papers did not come. At the army headquarters in Pakistan, according to Shudul, it was generally believed that India was not at all keen to transfer the papers of those who had opted for Pakistan, and all kinds of blocks and obstructions were put in the way. He became an unwitting victim of the tussle for petty power between the two countries.

Meanwhile, he had managed to track down his brother and family. They came to fetch him, and he went for some time to Peshawar. 'But we were not happy,' he said, 'we knew no one. People did not mix much with refugees, and my wife kept saying let's go back to India. So I thought, since I'm not getting a job here, I may as well go back to India and get my old job back.' In February 1948 they returned. Their home in Begumpur was now occupied by a Hindu refugee. They applied to get it back. Shudul went back to his old office and asked if he could have his job back. It took him several months of making applications, but finally, nine months later, he rejoined the army. And shortly afterwards his house was vacated by the people living there. 'Actually, they had been asked to vacate, but they themselves were waiting to get a house. So they requested me for a little time, they promised they would return the house and ensure that I was actually installed in it when they moved out, and sure enough, they did.' Today Abdul Shudul continues to live in his old home in Begumpur with three generations of his family, almost the only Muslim family in that village. 'The people have changed,' he said, 'most of the old ones have gone. But still, we have never had any trouble here.'

In his narrative, nation and country seemed to have meant little to Shudul. The important thing was to be where there was work and family. If that took him to Pakistan, he would go, and if that brought him back to India then that was what he would do. I asked him, time and again, why he had chosen to return to India, what life was like in Pakistan, hoping perhaps for some insight into feelings of nationhood and homelands. But his answer was no-nonsense, direct: 'I came back because there seemed to be no chance of getting my old job back there. The Indian government just wasn't sending my files. And my wife thought, let's just go back to our old home, *at least we have a place to live* [my italics]. So we did.'

It is stories such as Abdul Shudul's which lie behind the 'facts' of Partition, and it is stories such as these that enable us to look beyond what the facts reveal. For armed forces personnel to opt for one or the other country was not such a simple decision after all, and opting was not the end of the story. It was only the beginning.

My uncle's story. Abdul Shudul's life. The stories you will encounter later in this book—for me, it is these experiences, the perceptions they contain, the feelings they reveal, that make up the meaning of Partition. From where I stand today—a woman of the post-Partition generation, born to refugee parents, a feminist, a middle-class Indian committed to the ideals of secularism and democracy, it is these perceptions and histories that allow me to go back and arrive at a different view, a different interpretation. This is what Partition looks like, to me, when you put people—instead of grand politics—at its centre. In what follows I explore this further by looking at the histories of three of the most marginalized groups of actors in Indian history: women, children, and Harijans, the lowest of the low in Hindu society.

Which nagar? Which side? Which direction?

In 1990 Sudesh and I began to speak to Rajinder Singh, a three-wheeler scooter driver in Delhi. We boarded his scooter, to get from one part of the city to another. Somewhere along the way, because he looked the right age, we asked him where he was from. He suggested that we come to his home and he would tell us his story. The story took us to Gandhi Nagar, a resettlement area on the outskirts of Delhi where Rajinder Singh and his family lived in a small house set deep in a narrow, crowded lane. As with all the families we visited, they welcomed us into their homes as if we belonged there. The several sessions during which we interviewed him and his brother, Manmohan Singh, were interspersed with long conversations with neighbours, who dropped in and out, curious to see what was happening, and who had their own stories to tell. Stories were begun, only to be left halfway as people interrupted; sometimes a sudden thought would break the narrative as Rajinder or Manmohan asked themselves if they should be telling us this. As always in family situations, we seldom got to speak to the wives, except in snatched moments when we were able to get them alone. Initially concerned at this, we later decided not to attempt to speak to men and women at the same time, but to do so separately.

Partition meant many different things to different people. For Rajinder Singh, his most powerful memory is not of the event itself but of something that took place a few years earlier when, as a young boy, he ran away from home to join a group of street singers and prostitutes in Hira Mandi in Lahore. Four years after his disappearance, his father managed to track him down and went to the kotha to fetch him back. The young Rajinder watched from the roof of the kotha as his father walked through the marketplace, he listened to the jibes and taunts directed at the old man, and then saw him being deliberately tripped by a flower seller at the foot of the stairs of his 'home'. As he fell, Rajinder's father's turban came loose and rolled off, the ultimate loss of honour for a Sikh. Broken, the old man gathered up his turban and walked slowly away. Torn between his wish to stay on in a place which he loved and his compassion for his father, Rajinder followed him to the railway station, and thence to his home where he then began a job in a utensil factory in Daska.

It was there that he first came across evidence of the divisions that became much more visible after Partition. The factory owner, a Hindu, employed Sikhs, Hindus and Muslims and, as Partition drew closer, fights began to break out between them. Rajinder has no special feelings of enmity or hatred towards his Muslim co-workers. He tells his story — of which I reproduce only a part here — with a matter-of-factness and realism which runs through all descriptions. Like many people who did not have a 'profession', Rajinder turned his hand to different things after he crossed over to India: he worked in a halvai shop in Amritsar, later set up his own halvai shop, drove a tonga for a while, and when we met him, was driving a scooter which he owned. I have chosen to include a section of Rajinder's interview here because he describes how people from his family and his village came away on foot, in a kafila that grew as more and more people joined it. Up to a certain distance the kafila was ac-companied, and presumably protected, by the Pakistani army, and then the Indian army took over. He said he had never really told this story to anyone before. His grandchildren were too young, and his children too busy making their own lives to be bothered to listen. Yet, as we sat and spoke, family members came in again and again and asked us to replay this or that incident, as if listening to his voice on tape somehow in-vested it with a greater authority. Rajinder's narrative here recounts how unprepared people were to move, how they had to be convinced to do so, and, once they did, the enormous hardship and suffering they faced on the way. He tells the story of a woman who gave birth to a girl (she was born by the river Dek, he told me later, and all her life she was called Deko), of an old man who offered her support because he had left his own granddaughter behind. We are not told whether the granddaughter was abducted, killed or given away, but the help offered to the pregnant woman now seems almost a sort of penance. I find Rajinder's account moving, for its sense of inexorable, slow, tortuous movement as people headed, as he said, from a life shattered by forces beyond their control, into an unknown future. In his words, 'Our hearts were full of fear —

where were we headed? Where would we end up?' — a question that runs through virtually every Partition narrative that I have heard.

*   *   *

Rajinder Singh:

My bua's older son's in-laws lived in a village called Richade. My brother went there with my bua's younger son. He thought, we have to go out this way anyway, so let's go little by little so that everyone does not get killed all at once. We sort of knew we would have to die anyway, so we thought that if we spread ourselves out then we could perhaps see if one or the other could be saved. I went to fetch my wife . . . but I was worried that my brother would get left behind. So we all came to a place called Baba Lakhan, we came there and people from that village stopped there. I said to them, there are so few of you, why don't you also include people from this village. There are many Sikhs, include them and our kafila will grow large and become strong. As it is there are only a few people from this one village, why not increase the size of the kafila? In this way we kept progressing and others joining up and the kafila kept growing. We went to another village and found that everyone there was sleeping comfortably. It was about nine at night. They were all asleep, they had no worry about anything. When we went and told them, they said, no, can these sorts of things ever happen? I said to them if they have not happened before, they have happened today. If you think these kinds of things will not happen, you are mistaken, they are happening. So some of the older people started to pay attention. They asked, are you speaking the truth? I said, yes, go outside and look, go to Baba Lakhan. There are many people there, waiting . . . When we came back to Baba Lakhan we found people from two more villages had collected there. Now there were some thousand people or so . . . earlier there had only been four or five hundred . . . Hindus, Sikhs . . . Whatever people could pick up, big things and small, they put clothes on top of those they were wearing, and threw a khes or sheet over their shoulders. They picked up whatever they could and then they joined the kafila. Who could take along heavy things? And the kafila began to move. The next village on the way was Katiana. There, there was a marriage, a Musalmaan's wedding, and there were a lot of fireworks and things going on. We thought there was firing and guns, so we stopped the kafila some distance away from the village. Some people said they would go and find out . . . as they were leaving people said to them, you should be careful, don't go openly. It shouldn't happen that you have gone to find out and you just get killed yourself . . . they went and looked and they heard music and realized it was a wedding!

Gradually, daylight came. This was the first night, and then it became morning and as the sun rose, it began to rain. It rained so much and our clothes became so heavy . . . we could not even lift them. Our clothes got more and more wet, and people just left them there. Our stomachs were empty, we were hungry, our clothes were wet and sodden, our hearts were full of fear—where were we headed? Where would we end up? Our hearts were full of grief: what will happen? Where will we go? It's like when you started from home today, you knew you were going to Gandhi Nagar. We did not even know this. Which nagar, which side, which direction . . . we had no desire to eat, nor was there anything to eat. After all, when we left our homes, we did not carry our atta with us, we did not take the rotis from our tavas. We did not think that we will take atta and knead it and cook it. We just left, as we were, empty-handed. Then some people fell ill—some fell ill from grief, some got diarrhoea, some had fever . . . so many people had left all of a sudden, they could not all be healthy and stay well. Some were ill from before, some fell ill from sorrow, and then there was rain and then the sun. The heat and cold made people's bodies shrivel up, and from all these changes people fell ill. And what with all this, it was afternoon in Batiana before we knew it.

There was one woman who was pregnant and about to give birth. The whole kafila began moving, but she was already a little upset and she said, you people go on ahead, I am prepared to die. In any case, I have no one to call my own. The hardship I have to face, I will bear, don't worry about me . . . the baba who was with me, I said to him, baba, it is given to some people to do good. Your granddaughter was with you and you decided to come with me. I kept telling you why bother . . . but look at this poor woman, she is about to give birth, she is a young woman, and here she is lying in the road . . . let us try to do good. We are all full of grief, we are all weeping. He said, what is it? I said, look at that girl, she has no brother or father, and she is alone, her man has been killed and she is about to give birth. There were some other women sitting with her, and when the kafila began to move, they too started to move. So my baba said, girl sit on my horse, and wherever we find someone who can help, we will take you there. But perhaps from fear, she gave birth right there, to a daughter. Out of fear. No one had a knife or anything, you know the instruments you need to cut the cord. There was one man, and he had a kind of sword, we asked him, baba, this is the thing, please help us. So he gave it to us and the women cut the cord, and we stopped the kafila for about three quarters of an hour. We said to them, you are leaving your honour behind to go to the houses of unknown people. Even if you get a little late, how does it matter? On the way there was a village called Pasroor. We had the Baluchi military with us. They put us in a school there. They said, anyone who tries to get out of here, out of these four walls, we will cut him down. The school had a four-foot-high wall. They tried to be strict but we had nothing to eat or drink . . . so people went, they broke into a shop and they brought some sacks of mungphalis, peanuts, so we roasted those and ate them. After all, what else could we do? Someone got this much and someone got that much. Then someone else jumped the wall and got to the sugarcane fields nearby to steal sugarcane. The military people killed some of them—in front of us they killed a Jat. His family had a cart, they had loaded things on to it and brought it, so they set fire to it and used it for the last rites of their man who was killed . . .

After Narowar, the Madrasi military joined the kafila . . . they told the Baluchis to go away, that their duty had finished and they should go away . . . the two militaries confronted each other. One said, it is our duty, while the other said, your duty is over, you should go away . . . the wells had medicine and poison in them, there were dead people in there, there was no water to drink, we were hungry and thirsty . . . nothing to eat, nothing to drink. Then our military brought two trucks to Narowar and they were filled with atta. They spread a tarpaulin and handed out atta to people, saying take as much as you want. They gave us corn, they kept giving it to us saying eat, destroy their fields. The Madrasi military really helped us. Everyone was grief stricken. Someone's mother had died, someone's father had gone, someone's daughter had been abducted . . . then we moved on. You know you feel some fear of a dead body, but at the time, we had no fear at all . . . From there we came to the bridge on the Ravi. There they told us, this is the limit of our duty, we are now going back to help the kafila that has come from Daska. We saw a trainload of Hindus had been killed and in Dera Baba Nanak, a trainload of Musalmaans who had come from the direction of Ludhiana had been killed . . . they killed each other's people. We saw bodies of Musalmaans, utensils lying in the mud, clothes . . . some people buried under others, and disease and illness all around. When we got to Dera Baba Nanak they said to us, you have come home. But we thought, our home was over there. We have left it behind. How can this be home?

4

WOMEN

DAMYANTI SAHGAL *'A lot of stories to tell . . .'*

I first met Damyanti Sahgal in 1989. At the time she was eighty years old—a diminutive, energetic woman with mischief and humour lurking constantly in her eyes. It was her niece, Lina Dhingra, who introduced me to Damyanti. 'Talk to my aunt,' she said one day when I was talking to her about my work on Partition, 'she has a lot of stories to tell.' Damyanti, however, wasn't too enthusiastic. 'Why do you want to talk to me?' she said, 'I have nothing to say. Just a few foolish stories here and there.' I persisted, saying I'd be happy to listen to her stories, foolish or otherwise—and eventually, reluctantly, she relented.

Having decided to speak, Damyanti fell into the project with gusto. She brushed aside my suggestions that I should go to see her in her home and said instead that she would come to mine. 'So that,' she said, 'you can give me some coffee and lunch and I can have some fun.' Fun we did have—this was the first and only time an entire interview was conducted in my home. Normally, we had tried as far as possible to meet people in environments they were comfortable in and much of the time, these happened to be their homes. Later I realized that Damyanti's insistence on meeting in my house came from an essential sense of homelessness that had stayed with her since Partition, such that there wasn't any home that she would call her own. 'Unless,' as she told me, 'you count my little cottage in Hardwar.'

On the first day we were to meet, Damyanti arrived with her sister Kamla Buldoon Dhingra and her niece Lina. With me was my friend—and at that time fellow traveller—Sudesh Vaid. This long interview was conducted over many sessions spanning several months. Often, as with many interviews, most of which were collective rather than individual, the whole thing would turn into a conversation with everybody pitching in. There was a point at which, in Damyanti's interview, her sister began to question her on why she had not done this or that, another at which Kamla took over and began to speak, one at which various people walked into the room and the story Damyanti was telling us was left incomplete, and so on.

The interview that you see here, however, has few of these elements. It has been constructed as — or more correctly edited into — a continuous narrative. While I have not altered the chronology of the interview, I have, quite consciously, and deliberately, in this as in other interviews that follow, removed the questions Sudesh and I posed, as well as the interruptions and small bits of incidental dialogue and conversation. At two points, however, I have kept the conversations between Damyanti and Kamla because I feel they are particularly significant in what they point to, and presenting them as conversation as they happened is the only way, I feel, of capturing what those moments were about.

When I reread the transcript of Damyanti's interview now (of which the reader will see only a part at this stage of the text), it seems to me to fall into four broad, and somewhat overlapping, divisions. The first has to do with Damyanti's description of herself, her life before Partition and her flight, alone and virtually penniless, from what became Pakistan to India. This is the part you will see here. In the second part, which appears later, she speaks of her slow, and initially somewhat reluctant, involvement in what came to be known as social work, and in the third and fourth parts, which follow at the end of this particular chapter, of the actual work, which consisted mainly of the 'recovery', 'rescue' and 'rehabilitation' of abducted and raped women in Pakistan. None of these parts is clearly demarcated and each flows into the other. The third and fourth parts essentially continue the story of the second, and in some ways the description becomes quite linear, assuming the stages of the actual work: first rescue, then recovery, then rehabilitation. The first and second parts seem to have more danger attached to them, the third is somewhat 'safer', although we find out soon enough that both for the women and for the social workers, rehabilitation is fraught with its own dangers. Throughout the narrative Damyanti describes a tension between herself as a social worker, a servant, if you like, of the newly formed nation-state — and in a broader sense, an instrument of her private God, her thakur — and herself as a woman who feels for other women. Just as many of the women resist their rescue, so also Damyanti makes her own private rebellion in her work. But, interestingly, she sees no contradiction between the two. The fact that she has more success with her particular rebellion has (as becomes clear in her encounters with a senior official of Pakistan and later, the Deputy Magistrate who is to certify the ages of the women she is in charge of) surely to do with her class and the access that provides her.

To me, Damyanti's interview was one of the most important of the ones that Sudesh and I did. Over the months that we spoke together, we became friends. She insisted we call her Danti, and said we could add 'masi' or 'auntie' if we felt better. At the time we met, and for some considerable time before and indeed after, Damyanti divided her life between Delhi, where she stayed usually in her sister Kamla's flat, and Hardwar where she had a small cottage, or room. Gradually, she began to spend more and more time in Hardwar and at one point, she refused to come back to Delhi altogether, preferring to live—and die—alone in Hardwar.

Damyanti's story was important for other reasons too. Partition rendered many thousands of women alone in the way that it did Damyanti. It ruptured their lives, often at the point of marriage, doing away, usually permanently, with 'normal' life practices such as marriage. Krishna Sobti, a well-known writer and someone who has lived through Partition herself, speaks movingly of a whole generation of women whose lives, she says, were destroyed by Partition.[1] In refugee families all available hands had to be pulled into the process of reconstruction, of rebuilding broken homes. Girls and young women were drawn into different kinds of work—domestic, professional, other. By the time things became more 'normal' their presences had already become somewhat shadowy. In some instances families had become so dependent on the labour of women that the women's own desires and aspirations had to be pushed into the background. In other cases, women had simply been abandoned by their families, or forgotten about. From her account of her life, Damyanti was one such woman. Virtually homeless, she was pulled into social work by her aunt, Premvati Thapar. But she had little or no contact with her immediate family. Nor, if she is to be believed, were they particularly interested to know where she was. And once into social work, long years of her life were given to it. There is, however, an irony here. That very 'rejection' by her family, the very real fact of her

---

[1] Krishna Sobti, personal interview.

aloneness, allowed Damyanti to move into the public world and make something of her life. Just as a whole generation of women were destroyed by Partition, so also Partition provided an opportunity for many to move into the public sphere in a hitherto unprecedented way.

I have often wondered how Damyanti must have felt about her aloneness. In an earlier part of her interview, she speaks about her desire to look attractive, to marry . . . but by the time Partition had happened, all this had been put aside. By her own description, she was too old to marry (she was close to forty at the time), but not, I think, too old to dream. Nonetheless, she took the work on, and my sense of it is that she took it on without a driving sort of 'commitment'. She did it because she was pushed into it, and, quite simply, because it was there.

I found Damyanti's interview important for several other reasons. According to her, it was the first time she was actually talking about all she had been through, the first time, she said, that anybody had *asked* her, the first time she was remembering with and to someone. Even for her sister and niece, the experiences she recounted were new. At one point Kamla asked Damyanti why she had never told these stories before. Listening to them, I found it difficult to believe that even in the closest of relationships in families, people could be so ignorant of—and indifferent to—what was going on in the life of someone so close to them. Damyanti, I think, understood this proximity of love and indifference much better than any of us, having seen and lived through Partition in the way she had. It was because of this, I feel, that she chose to live much of her life—especially the latter part—alone. In many ways, she was very close, often even like a parent, to many of the people she worked with. But at another level she remained separate, and alone.

It was because of this that I came increasingly to feel that in her narration of the stories of abducted women, her telling of how they had been basically rendered alone by history, Damyanti was really describing her own life. Despite the fact that at some point, contact was remade with her family, Damyanti remained essentially alone. For some time before her death, she had been ailing—she was, at this time, in Hardwar. But despite the entreaties of her sister and niece, she refused to return to Delhi where she could have access to better health care. When she died, she was, as in life, alone. Later, one of her 'sons'—a young man who had been orphaned during Partition and to whom she had been like a mother—went to fetch her body and to perform the last rites.

There is another reason why I find Damyanti's narrative so significant. She worked for many years in the Indian State's recovery and relief operation. She travelled, usually accompanied by Pakistani policemen, who were often hostile not only to her, but to the whole idea of the operation, into the interior areas of Pakistan to locate abducted women. In interviewing her, I learnt more about the nature of the relief and recovery operation and about the women who were recovered through it than I have found in any book. I found her insights and descriptions particularly valuable in retrieving the history of such violence—rape, forcible abduction and marriage, and a further violence of the kind perpetrated by the State in its relief and recovery operation. In looking into this, the researcher is faced with a difficult dilemma: how can she recover the voices of women who experienced such violence? *Ought* she to attempt to locate women who have been through such violence, to get them to speak? For me, Damyanti's description of the anguish abducted women went through thus becomes doubly important.

For all of these reasons, I have deliberately chosen Damyanti's narrative as the thread that weaves together this long chapter on the histories of women's abduction and rape during Partition.

* * *

Damyanti Sahgal:

At the time of partition I was in my village, Kotra, just thirty miles from Lahore, near Raiwind station on the road to Multan. Everything we owned was there. We had a factory. Because I didn't get married, I stayed with my father. I had no mother. I was my father's companion, whatever happened . . . my father thought that because he had all his property there, his workers would help him out of whatever trouble there was. So much faith . . . my uncle P. N. Thapar was a commissioner of Lahore division at that time. He sent a man to say that in Jandiala the Sikhs had held a conference, they'd met in a gurudwara and taken oaths that they would avenge Rawalpindi on the Musalmaans, and had sworn that on such and such day—I don't remember the day—they would begin the wholesale slaughter of Musalmaans. So my uncle Thapar sent this message that you should go away from here because I have a confidential report that in Jandiala village, near Amritsar, Sikhs have met in the gurudwara and have taken oaths that on such and such day we will put an end to Musalmaans. This will have repercussions. Musalmaans will kill Hindus. They said, whatever has happened with our women in Pindi, we will not let that go unavenged . . . My father said, well, this Thapar is a coward . . . how can we leave everything and just go? I have so many men, they will protect me. There'll be some noise for a few days and then everything will come back to normal. So he refused to go. Then a second message came . . . my uncle said your father is stubborn, so you should go. At the most he will be killed, but you, you will be gutted . . . and this is very difficult for us to tolerate. You will be gutted . . . so you should leave.

Father didn't agree . . . the workers in his factory were mixed: Jats, Hindus, but on the whole it was a Muslim village so most of the workers were Musalmaans . . . at the time they were respectful and humble. They seemed safe . . .

When I tried to persuade my father he said, well if you feel scared you go. I said but bauji, he said, no bibi, if you feel scared you go. But where do I go? Then I came to Lahore. I remember asking what I should do, where I should go, my father was refusing to go. And they said the safest Hindu area is—now what is it called? Kamla, what is that, just north of Beasa . . . my brain forgets very fast. Oh yes, Kulu, Kulu Manali that whole area.

Partition had started. I went alone, and there was rioting in Amritsar . . . I went alone. We used to have a small boy with us, I don't remember what his name was, Dipu or Tipu, a small boy. Bauji said you take this servant with you and money . . . whatever, some two or three hundred, whatever was in the house he handed to me. I don't exactly remember. And he said once you get there, in Kulu, Dr Devi Chand told me that they have a house there and that I should go there. You'll be safe there and when all the disturbances finish you can come back . . . So I took the servant and some rupees, some two or three hundred, I don't know how much, perhaps it was only a hundred. When we came close to Amritsar, we found that they had started stopping trains, killing people in them, but we were lucky. Everyone said put your windows up, they are cutting down people.

Train, train. Everyone was full of fear . . . they kept saying put your windows up, put your windows up, Amritsar is coming and they're cutting people down there. We put our windows up . . . God knows what they were doing outside, we were too frightened even to look, we kept praying our train would not stop at the station. And from there our train passed straight through . . . we had heard that killing and looting had begun there, that the Musalmaans had also risen up in arms, so also the Sikhs. Anyway, we went from there and I went straight to Kulu, and stayed there some time in Devi Chand Vohra's house. The small boy, the servant, was also with me. After this I left the house and went to—what was it Kamla, your nagar? I went there too, and to Manali, I roamed about a lot in this whole area, I had to stay in rest houses. In rest houses they have some specific days—they let you stay for eight to ten days. On arrival, when I got there, I used to sign, the chaprasi would bring the book, the visitor's book and then, they would come and say now your time is up and you must leave, and we had to pay the rest house, after that. After a short while in their house they sent me to Nagar, that's what I remember. When I left, when I ran away I went with just one or two dhotis. Yes, my father had said that once I arrived I should take a house on rent, and then send him a telegram or letter and he would come then. He said, I don't want to come like this with you. I'm an old man, where will you carry me around? I'm not willing to go like this, but once you manage to arrange something let me know and I'll come. But what was there to arrange?

First of all, I went to Dharamsala. That little boy realized that I had no money left, some ten days or a month he stayed with me. Then there was no money even to feed myself, let alone him. So he thought she has nothing left, and he quietly ran away. Towards Kangra, I don't know where he went. The next day I kept calling for him, Dipu, Dipu, but he was nowhere to be seen. He had run off. Then in the rest house the chowkidar asked me for money, I told him I had no money, but that I'm from an important family and I can sign and put my name down . . . I've run away from my home and can't go back there. It was in the newspapers and on the radio that there was looting and killing going on there. I don't know where my relatives are, but the moment I get news of anyone from the family, I'll get you money. From there I went to Nagar and came back—which place was it, I don't remember. It was another place. Here there was killing . . . there were Gujars and they started killing Musalmaans. The Jansanghis used to kill, they would drink and kill. Hindus can't do this, they're afraid. Young boys would drink a lot and then they would come and kill Musalmaans. There was one young boy, small, but strong and handsome like a Pathan. I was at Dr Devi Chand's house at that time. I was standing there when they began crying and shouting, 'They're going to kill him, they're going to kill him' and people began to plead, 'Don't kill him, don't kill him, he's so young . . .' and they replied, 'Well, we're telling him you become a Hindu and . . . if he becomes Hindu we will leave him, otherwise we'll not leave him.' We tried to persuade him, we said, child, become a Hindu. But he roared: 'I WILL NOT BECOME A HINDU, THEY CAN CUT MY THROAT BUT I WILL NOT BECOME A HINDU!' Such courage, I'll have my throat cut. They took him away screaming, I don't know whether they killed him or not. Things were bad then, bodies used to be found lying around, the Beas had risen so much . . . there was so much rain. I have never seen rain like that, the river broke its bounds, bodies would flow down the river . . . I had no money, no clothes, only rags. Somehow I managed to buy a thali and I would scrape together some atta and cook on the thali itself . . . things were bad . . .

One evening, I was walking on the banks of the river . . . I had a mala in my hand, no money in my pocket . . . you see, at one point I had become almost an ascetic, when I was in Kotra, when I decided that I didn't want to marry, I have been married to my god, my thakur, I loved only him, and it was because of that that I was putting an end to one kind of life. So the mala used to be in my hands and his name on my lips . . .

Earlier, of course, I used to be very fond of dressing up, of looking after my figure, my sisters were fair and I was dark, but I used to be proud of my figure and I was always measuring myself with a tape measure, so much from here, so much from there . . . and all those things you know, eating grapes to make the breasts grow larger, and this should be like this and this like that, so I used to examine myself, up from here, in from there, so much outwards, so much inwards . . . curly hair was fashionable and we thought that putting some kinds of leaves in the hair made it curly! So I used to put those leaves and hide. Then someone said you're doing the wrong thing, you should put beri leaves, and then someone said you should put kerosene oil . . . And I can't tell you for how long I put kerosene in my hair . . . I thought it would keep it from going white. Of course the hair became what it had to become, but I'm just telling you . . . nails, waist . . . and then, when God blessed me . . . why and how I don't know, but after that I simply spent time in Hardwar, on the banks of the Jumna. I used to always think of my god. And then they said my father thought something had happened to my brain, and I used to roam about alone praying, and it was in this condition that Partition happened . . .

In the resthouse, there was an old chowkidar. I had not eaten for a day or two; after all, one can only eat if there is money. Just then, an officer came. He asked the chowkidar who was in the next room. The chowkidar said I don't really know, I don't understand, there's a woman—at that time I was healthy, red cheeks—she keeps the room closed, she doesn't eat or drink anything, she's been in there for two days or so, she doesn't come out or eat anything. Then the officer knocked on my door and said I'm the officer from here and am on duty here, where have you come from? I told him how I was there. He said, what are the arrangements for your food and drink? I kept quiet . . . what could I say? . . . Perhaps my eyes filled with tears, he felt very bad and said you come with me, you can't stay here like this, this is not right . . . and he got me food and drink.

One day that old chaprasi came, the chowkidar, he said, 'I'll tell you a story. The Englishman here, the deputy commissioner'—I don't remember what name he took—'he stayed in this rest house. I used to be his chaprasi. He came in one night and said to me, chaprasi, take off my shoes . . . I have shoes on my feet, take them off. And today . . . I'll tell you a story . . . note it down with pen and paper . . . you know your baba Gandhi, he's given us a lot of trouble, a lot of trouble. That old man, he doesn't even stop for breath, he keeps telling us get out, get out. After all, where will we go? Here we are very happy. Baba, we'll leave because we have to, we'll leave, but not before we have taught him a lesson. We'll leave such a state of affairs that brother will fight brother, sister will fight sister, there will be killing and arson and rape, we'll leave such a state of affairs behind that he will not be able to control it, and he will raise his hands and plead with god to send us back . . . send them back. And then what will happen . . . his own men, his own people will hurl abuses at him, they will give him trouble, they will say look at this mess you have got us into. And he pulled out a paper and said, see, take it down, see today's date. I'm telling you we will go, we're not likely to stay now, but we'll teach him a lesson before going. This will happen, that will happen and everyone will say, Oh god, send them back . . .'

* * *

KAMLA: What stories these are, you've never told us these stories . . .

DAMYANTI: You don't know, Kamla, you don't know anything because you were in England . . .

KAMLA: No, I mean, we haven't had much time to talk . . . an hour here, an hour there . . . you used to come for short visits . . .

DAMYANTI: And after this, I had another life altogether, and things kept changing . . .

KAMLA: I know, we've never asked you how you came away . . .

DAMYANTI: I came alone.

KAMLA: No, I mean we thought . . .

DAMYANTI: Never, never . . .

KAMLA: We took it for granted because we came from England. We knew that everyone had come, no one asked how . . . we took it for granted . . .

DAMYANTI: Kamla, no one was there to help . . .

KAMLA: No, I mean you came and you went from ashrams . . . one didn't know, the others came together . . .

DAMYANTI: You know . . .

KAMLA: The others came together, we thought you must have come with them all . . .

* * *

I felt I had no one in the world. I didn't really know where anyone was. I was in the mountains, alone, without money. What could I do? One day, I saw two young men by the banks of the river, they were talking softly to each other. I tried to listen . . . They were saying, our office is going to open, we don't have leave . . . from Nagar there is the place where they've taken electricity. Kamla, what is the name of this place? It will come back. They were worrying, it had been so many days, they had to report for their jobs. I pricked up my ears. They said there's one place, one passage through the mountains from where the police goes. It's some pass, not Khyber Pass, but something . . . it goes through the mountains, we'll go through there. The river was full. I approached them and asked them, very gently, are you planning to go? They said, yes, our office is opening, we have to get back, otherwise action will be taken against us. We'll go through the mountains. I said, take me along. They said no, sorry, the way is very dangerous, sometimes it is narrow, we may have to stop a night or two, and it will be difficult to reach. I said I must go, but they were adamant.

They fixed with each other to meet at a particular time the next morning. In the morning, the place where the mountains opened up, I arrived there and sat down. After all, what did I have to lose? Whatever I had I was wearing. I told myself that I would simply follow them, how could they stop me. Yes, before that I went to the jungle people. I asked if there were forest rest-houses on the way and if they could book me in. They said those places were dangerous, there was still killing and looting going on there. I pleaded with them, I said somehow, if you can send me to Simla by road, there I have people. But they refused. They said we can give you money. But I refused to take it even though they kept saying you are like our sister, our mother, we know you're from a good family, but I refused. So I decided to go to the mountain . . . and when they came, the two young men, they were shocked. They said what are you doing here, on this path? We've explained to you again and again that you can't go by this way, it's too dangerous. I said how can you stop me, I'm just walking on the road. I have no money. They said we'll give you money. I just couldn't take money. I wanted to get away from the place. So you know the place where the electricity comes from. Is it Mandi? I said if you get me up to there, I can get a connection to Dharamsala or Punjab, but they said the pass we're going to travel through is very dangerous. But I kept following them, and they were very angry but they couldn't do anything about it.

Some distance ahead they stopped and opened their packets of food, and of course they had to give me some. They must have thought what a leech, what a chichar, but what could they do, I simply wouldn't leave them. I was quite weak, red eyes . . . no money. A little farther on we came to a small village and there they even got me milk and roti. In the morning again I was after them . . . but the grass was very slippery, and our feet kept getting caught, scratched, bruised . . . dying of cold, no warm clothes . . . Then we reached a point, a sort of main centre where buses left from. There was also a police post, a chowki. The two of them decided that they would leave me at the police chowki since I had attached myself to them. They took me to a sort of platform and said you sit here and we'll fetch you some water or something, and they slipped away . . . after all, they had to get rid of me somehow.

Then, as I was sitting there, the police came and I told them how I had got there, that I've come from Lahore and I'm related to so and so, and if you could get me to Dharamsala. They said what will you do there? I said I'll get in touch with the Deputy Commissioner who is on duty there . . . I told them I have no money, but please put me on a bus somehow. You see, there I was at the chowki. My legs were swollen, my body was stiff like this, I could hardly move. What they did, they put a wire, a chain, across the road to stop buses. A bus came, and they stopped it and said you have to take this passenger. They said our bus is booked and we have no room. They said you have to take this passenger. They said ours is a marriage party, we have no room at all. They said this poor unfortunate woman is a victim of circumstance, you have to take her, you must take her up to the place where the electricity comes from, the place whose name I can't remember at the moment. They said we have no seats. Then what they did, they opened the back door and in that little space they picked me up and put me, God help me always . . . I was so stiff I couldn't stand. The bus moved off and as it did my head began to spin and I began to throw up, I was half fainting . . . I didn't know what to do, I kept vomiting into my kurta, my kurta and dhoti, I kept filling my vomit into my clothes and I kept on being sick . . . I prayed to my god. I said, O god, you kept Draupadi's shame, look at what is happening to me now, O god, help me. As I was praying, the next stop came. I couldn't even look out of the window, I was crouched over my vomit-filled clothes. The door opened and a young man, tall and smart, wearing khadi, said mataji, behanji, you come and sit on my seat. I said no, no, leave me alone, I'm dirty, I'm filthy . . . I could hardly speak . . . and you know he said this after quite a distance, in fact it was soon after I prayed. He said my conscience does not agree, in this state you should not be sitting here. I have a front seat, you come and sit there, and I'll sit here. I said no, I'm dirty, I'll dirty the seat. He said, it doesn't matter . . . I kept crying, he simply picked me up and put me on the seat . . . I kept crying, I'm stiff, I'm fixed in this position, my limbs are locked. He didn't listen to anything, he put me on the seat, dusted all the dried vomit off my clothes, and put me there and went off to sit, I don't know where.

When we reached the place where the electricity comes from, the bus stops there, and from there I had to take another bus. I tried to sit up, and someone said to me, don't worry, when the bus comes we'll put you on it. I said but I have nothing, please help me to get to Dharamsala somehow, that's all I want. Then the young man stood up. He said, I live here, and work here. I have a house here, you come with me. I said no. He said, why? I said, no beta I can't. He said I cannot stand this, we can't leave you in this condition, you'll have to come. I said I can't climb the mountain. He said don't worry, I'll get another man and we'll take turns at carrying you up. His bungalow was quite high. Anyway in spite of my protests he took me up there, and put me down in the veranda of his bungalow. And then he called out, behanji, behanji, I have a mehman, a guest, for you behanji. Look we have a visitor. And, the door opened, and to my surprise, the woman who came out was my student!

My god, my god, behanji, what's happened to you, look at your condition! Kamla, it was Shakuntala, from Mahila Devi, the beautiful girl. She came and put her arms around me and cried and cried, saying look at your condition. I said are you Shakuntala? Yes . . . yes . . . Get away from me, I'm dirty, dirty . . . That very instant, she . . . she said this lady means more to me than my life. Every student loved her. And she got hot water, got me a set of clean and warm clothes, put on heaters, made up my bed, and gave me tea and put me into bed. I couldn't stop crying, and she kept saying behanji, why are you crying? You gave us the gift of knowledge . . . I said, Shakuntala, I don't know what to do, where to go, I don't understand anything. I said please send me to Dharamsala, I'll be eternally grateful to you . . . I have no money or anything. She said, don't make me ashamed . . . and in this condition I'm going to send you nowhere, you rest first, become able to walk and become strong, and then . . . this is your home, we're your children, this is my sister whose house it is. They kept me for ten or fifteen days and really looked after me, massages, doctors . . . I was happy but I also kept feeling I'm taking hospitality from someone I don't know well, I had a sort of complex. Later, they sent me to Dharamsala . . . there I went straight to the Deputy Commissioner. I explained to him how I had run away, I've come from such and such a place . . . I'm not asking anything of you except that you send me to Punjab somehow. I don't know where any of my relatives are except Dr Santokh Singh who is in Amritsar, so please send me there. He said, don't worry, we'll send you but first you come to my house. He called his driver and asked him to take me to his home. His wife was a patient of dama, asthma . . . she kept me for nearly a month and really looked after me. He said, I can't send you because the river is in full spate now and all the roads are closed. The moment things are better I will. At the moment the roads are very slippery and the jeep could easily skid.

* * *

KAMLA: One minute. Did no one in the family bother? Did they not get worried? What about Premi auntie?

DAMYANTI: Kamla, what did they know, or I know? For all they knew I could still have been in Kotra or dead or something . . . The time was such . . . no one knew about the other, nor did anyone have any interest, so what did they know about me? They must have thought she'll manage . . .

Part I HIDDEN HISTORIES

I cannot now pinpoint exactly when I became aware of the histories of women. I say 'became aware' because the process was a sort of cumulative one, where stories began to seep into my consciousness until one day when it became clear that there was something I should be actively seeking.

Even as I say this, it sounds strange to me. As a feminist I have been only too aware, sometimes painfully so, of the need to fold back several layers of history (or of what we see as fact) before one can begin to arrive at a different, more complex 'truth'. Why then, I have often asked myself, should the 'discovery' of women have come as such a surprise? But it did. Perhaps it was because the initial assumption I brought to my search was a simple one: the history of Partition, as I knew it, made no mention of women. As a woman, and a feminist, I would set out to 'find' women in Partition, and once I did, I would attempt to make them visible. That would, in a sense, 'complete' an incomplete picture.

There are, of course, no complete pictures. This I know now: everyone who makes one, draws it afresh. Each time, retrospectively, the picture changes: who you are, where you come from, who you're talking to, when you talk to them, where you talk to them, what you listen to, what they choose to tell you . . . all of these affect the picture you draw. Listening to Rana's story made me deeply aware of this.

I realized, for example, that if it had been so difficult for Ranamama to talk about his story, how much more difficult must it have been for *women* to do so. To whom would they have spoken? Who would have listened? I realized too that in my questioning, something I had not taken into account was that in order to be able to 'hear' women's voices, I had to begin to pose different questions, to talk in different situations, and to be prepared to do that most important of things, to listen: to their speech, their silences, the half-said things, the nuances. The men seldom spoke about women. Women almost never spoke about themselves, indeed they denied they had anything 'worthwhile' to say, a stance that was often corroborated by their men. Or, quite often, they simply weren't there to speak to. And what right did I, a stranger, an outsider, now have to go around digging into their lives, forcing them to look back to a time that was perhaps better forgotten? Especially when I knew that the histories I wanted to know about were histories of violence, rape, murder.

For a while, then, I held back from speaking to women: there were so many layers of silence encoded into these histories, I told myself, that perhaps I could make my exploration by looking elsewhere—surely I would still be uncovering some of the silences. I turned therefore to some of the very 'documents' that I had so often found wanting. Newspaper accounts, a memoir, and other sources helped me to piece together a story: a story of love and of hate, a story of four lives and two nations, a story that brought me back to the histories of women: the story of Zainab and Buta Singh.

Zainab was a young Muslim girl who was said to have been abducted while her family was on the move to Pakistan in a kafila. No one knows who her abductors were, or how many hands she passed through, but eventually Zainab was sold to a Jat from Amritsar district, Buta Singh. Like many men who either abducted women themselves or bought them, Buta Singh, who wasn't married at the time, performed the 'chaddar' ceremony and 'married' Zainab. The story goes that in time the two came to love each other. They had a family, two young girls. Several years after Partition, a search party on the lookout for abducted women traced Zainab to Amritsar, where she was living with Buta Singh. It was suspected that Buta Singh's brother—or his nephews—had informed the search party of Zainab's whereabouts. Their concern was that Buta Singh's children would deprive them of the family property, that their share would now be reduced. Like many women who were thus 'rescued', Zainab had no choice in the matter. She was forced to leave. Newspaper reports describe the scene as a poignant one: the entire village had assembled to see Zainab go. She came slowly out of her house, carrying her child, and clutching a small bundle of clothes. Her belongings were stowed in the jeep and as Zainab boarded it she turned to Buta Singh and, pointing to her elder daughter, is reported to have said: 'Take care of this girl, and don't worry. I'll be back soon.'

Not surprisingly, property figured in Zainab's recovery as well. Her own parents had been killed. But the family had received grants of land in Lyallpur as compensation for property they had left behind in Indian Punjab. Zainab and her sister had received their father's share, and an uncle had been allotted the adjoining piece. Rumour had it that it was the uncle who had been the moving spirit behind Zainab's rescue: he was keen that the land remain in his family, and he wanted Zainab, when found, to marry his son, which would then ensure the property would remain with them. The son had no interest in marrying Zainab, and as the story is told, part of his reluctance was because she had lived for many years with a Sikh. Discussion on this issue went on in the family for some time, and Buta Singh occasionally received snippets of news from neighbours and others who kept him informed.

Meanwhile, Buta Singh pleaded his case wherever possible—but to no avail. He tried to go to Pakistan, but this wasn't easy at the time. One day he received a letter from Pakistan—ostensibly from one of Zainab's neighbours, although no one quite knows—which asked him to go there as soon as possible. Zainab's family, it seemed, was pressing her to marry. Buta Singh sold off his land and put together some money, but he had not bargained for the difficulties of travel between the two countries. He needed a passport and a visa—for which he travelled to Delhi. There, he first took the step of converting to Islam, thinking perhaps that it would be easier to get to Pakistan as a Muslim. Buta Singh now became Jamil Ahmed.

And he applied for a passport, and a nationality: Pakistani. If that was what would get him to Zainab, that was what he would do. But acquiring a new country, especially in a situation of the kind that obtained at the time, was not easy. The High Commission of Pakistan accepted Buta Singh's application for Pakistani nationality, and fed it into the machinery. The question was not a simple one of changing nationality—if such questions can ever be simple. The two countries were virtually at war; deep-rooted suspicion of each other's motives was the order of the day; people could no longer move freely across borders—how then could the appeal of a man in love for nationality of the 'other' be accepted at face value? After many months, the application was rejected. (Interestingly, around the same time, according to newspaper accounts, a high-profile actress, Meena, wished to become a Pakistani citizen and applied for citizenship, which was immediately granted, and her 'defection' was made much of in the press.)

Buta Singh did not, however, give up that easily. He applied for a short-term visa, and because people in the Pakistan High Commission were familiar with him by now, he was granted this. Now Buta Singh, alias Jamil Ahmed, made his way to Pakistan. And he arrived to find that Zainab had already been married to her cousin. This could well have been the end of the world for him but by a strange quirk of circumstance, Buta Singh was given another chance to fight for Zainab. In his rush to find out about Zainab, he had forgotten to report his arrival to the police—to this day, Indians and Pakistanis are required to report their arrival in the other's country within twenty-four hours of actually reaching the place. For this oversight Buta Singh was asked to appear before a magistrate, and apparently he told the magistrate that he had been very distracted because of the history with Zainab, which is why he had omitted to report his arrival. The magistrate then ordered Zainab to be produced before the court, where she was asked to give a statement. It was at this point that all Buta Singh's hopes were dashed. Closely guarded by a ring of relatives, Zainab rejected him, saying: 'I am a married woman. Now I have nothing to do with this man. He can take his second child whom I have brought from his house . . .'

The next day Buta Singh put himself under a train and committed suicide. A suicide note in his pocket asked that he be buried in Zainab's village. This wish, however, was to remain unfulfilled. When Buta Singh's body was brought to Lahore for an autopsy, it is said that large crowds gathered outside; some people wept; a film maker announced he would make a film on the story. Later, a police party took his body to Zainab's village but was stopped from burying it there by people of her community. They did not want a permanent reminder of this incident, and Buta Singh or Jamil Ahmed was brought back to Lahore and buried there.[2]

[2] I have pieced together this account from newspaper reports, books and an unpublished manuscript: *Lahore: A Memoir* by Som Anand. There are many different versions to the Buta Singh-Zainab story now, particularly as it has acquired the status of a legend, so details vary in each. A film (*Shaheed-e-Mohabbat Buta Singh*) based on this story was recently released on Indian television.

* * *

In death Buta Singh became a hero. The subject of a legend, fittingly situated in the land of other star-crossed lovers: Heer and Ranjha, Sohni and Mahiwal. Zainab, meanwhile, continued to 'live', her silence surrounding her. She was unable to grieve and mourn her lover, and, in all likelihood, unable to talk. She was one among thousands of such women.

Zainab and Buta Singh's story stayed with me: it was a moving story, but more, I kept returning to it out of a nagging, persistent sense of dissatisfaction. As it was told, this was the story of a hero and a 'victim'. We learnt something about the hero: his impulsive nature, his honesty and steadfastness, his willingness to give up everything for the woman he loved, the strength of his love. But nothing about the victim. Try as I might, I could not recover *her* voice. What had Zainab felt? Had she really cared for Buta Singh or was she indifferent to both of the men in her life? How had the experience of abduction, almost certainly of rape, marked her? It was said that Zainab and Buta Singh were happy, that they were even in love. Yet, the man had actually bought her, purchased her like chattel: how then could she have loved him? I realized I had to go back to talking—if any women were still alive, this was perhaps the one way in which I could learn about their experiences, their feelings.

The decision wasn't an easy one. There is a point at which research becomes an end in itself. The human subject you are researching becomes simply a provider of information, the 'informant', devoid of feelings of her own, but important for your work. I did not want to be in this kind of violative—and exploitative—position. I decided, as I had done with Ranamama, that I would impose my own silences on this search. I knew by now that the history of Partition was a history of deep violation—physical and mental—for women. I would then talk only to those who wanted to talk about it. And I would continue to explore other sources to help me recover the histories of women. Providentially—or so it seemed at the time, for I realize now that once there is an involvement in something, you begin to take notice of things that relate to that—the next step offered itself.

* * *

In 1988, a women's journal, *Manushi*, published a review of a Gujarati book, *Mool Suta Ukhde* (Torn from the Roots). The book was a sort of memoir and documentary account by a woman called Kamlaben Patel, of her work with abducted and raped women at Partition. The story Kamlaben told was shattering. Nearly 75,000 women, she recounted, had been raped and abducted on both sides of the border at Partition. This figure would probably have been higher if Kashmir had been taken into account—perhaps close to 100,000. Apart from the rapes, other, more specific kinds of violence had been visited on women. Many were paraded naked in the streets, several had their breasts cut off, their bodies were tattooed with marks of the 'other' religion; in a bid to defile the so-called 'purity' of the race, women were forced to have sex with men of the other religion, many were impregnated. They bore children, often only to have them taken away forcibly. Sometimes families traded their women in exchange for freedom, at other times the women simply disappeared, abducted from camps, or as caravans of people marched across the border on foot. But that hundreds, indeed thousands, of women had been subjected to rape, and abduction, was now clear.

Kamlaben had worked with other women to recover and rescue many of the abducted women she talked about in her book. But it had taken her several decades to write about her work and how she had felt about it. Why, I wondered? Why had she chosen the path of silence? And what was it that finally decided her to make things public? I went in search of her—and found her, a small, upright woman, living alone but for a sort of companion-helper adopted daughter, in Bombay. 'You want to know why I didn't write about this?' she said, 'I'll tell you.'

> The reason I did not write my book earlier was because I could not accept what I saw during that time. I found it difficult to believe that human beings could be like this. It was as if the demons had come down on earth . . . it is when the demon gets into Shivji that he dances the tandav nritya, the dance of death and destruction . . . it was as if this spirit had got into everyone, men and women. Partition was like a tandav nritya . . . I have seen such abnormal things, I kept asking myself, what is there to write, why should I write it . . .

Kamlaben's silence was one thing. But what about the many families I had spoken to? Why had they made no mention of the rape and abduction of women? Were these deliberate erasures or could it be that I had asked the wrong questions? Or simply not listened to the nuance, the half-said things? I thought, perhaps I had missed something, perhaps people *had* talked about this. So I went back over my interviews. And, suddenly, there it was, in the odd silence, the ambiguous phrase. Two brothers whom I had spoken to in Delhi, survivors from the Rawalpindi riots, said of their family:

> At home we were my grandmother, grandfather, father, mother, three brothers, three sisters [one of the sisters lived in East Punjab]. Our aunt lived in Delhi, she was with us with her daughter, they were killed there. She had come to see us. In fact, all our family were killed. We two brothers were the only two who survived.
>
> . . . some were killed in the gurudwara and some elsewhere. Our grandmother and grandfather were killed in the house, they were killed by Pathans. The others . . . my mother, and younger brother were killed in the gurudwara. Our father managed to escape but was killed somewhere along the way . . . we were only a few left, and only some survived.

Among those who were killed, then, were several family members. But they'd made no direct mention of their sisters, two of them, who had 'disappeared' at the time. Everyone around them *knew* this story, they'd been part of the same community, the same village, and they spoke about it in whispers. 'Speak to them,' a neighbour told me, 'two of their sisters disappeared at the time.' The way he said it, it sounded as if this was something to be ashamed of. So I didn't ask. But it was when I went back over our conversation that it struck me that that awkward silence, that hesitant phrase was perhaps where the disappearance of the two sisters lay hidden: in a small crack, covered over by silence. I realized then that in this silence lay the many hidden histories of Partition, the histories that have always hovered at the edges of those that have been told, the histories that describe the dark side of freedom. As I began to search, slowly, inexorably, this history revealed itself.

Some months after I met Kamlaben, Sudesh and I came across a book

in a second-hand bookstore, a great big tome which proved to be a listing of thousands of women, Hindu and Sikh, who had been abducted
or were reported missing by their families after Partition. The book
made up 1414 pages in a large size. It carried a district-by-district listing of women and children who had been reported missing, some 21,809
names. Clearly an incomplete list, but a horrifying one nonetheless. The
two missing sisters were in there, as were countless others . . . young girls,
older women, children. Often, they were picked up by people from their
own village: one of the myths that historians of communal conflict have
held dear, and that victims of such conflict often help to perpetrate, is
that the aggressors are always 'outsiders'. This list, to me, was conclusive
proof of the opposite: so many women had been picked up by men of
the same village. So many *older* women had been abducted—women in
their fifties and sixties. According to social workers, this wasn't uncommon: because abductors often knew the circumstances of the women
they were picking up, they would take away older women, widows, or
those whose husbands had been killed, for their property. They would
then ask to become their 'sons'—a short-cut to quick acquisition of
property. A sample from this list is given in Table 1.

The book I found, which was published by A. J. Fletcher (Commissioner, Ambala and Jalandhar Divisions and High Powered Officer for
Recovery of Abducted Women and Children, India) and titled *List of Non
Muslim Abducted Women and Children in Pakistan and Pakistan Side of the Cease-Fire
Line in Jammu and Kashmir State*, was not released to the public 'out of deference' for the feelings of those whose relatives were listed there. In the
preface, Fletcher says:

> This volume is an up-to-date compilation, in alphabetical order, of the
> names and other particulars of Hindu and Sikh women and children ab-
> ducted in West Punjab (Pakistan) during the disturbances of 1947. This
> information was transmitted, from time to time, to the Government of
> Pakistan through Basic and Supplementary List[s]. The record of these
> Lists has now grown so bulky and scattered that references to particular
> entries are not only tedious and difficult but, at time[s], confusing. The
> names have now been grouped according to the districts in which they
> are reported to be living at present. For purposes of verification, it may

Table 1. Gujrat district

Serial No.	R. No.	Particulars of abducted person	Place and date of abduction	Particulars of abductors, custodians, etc.
851	GRT/S-2/ N-IIC	Piara Singh, 10 years, s/o Kaniya Lal, Vill. Kidar P.S. Khutalia Binka, P.O. and Teh. Phalia, Dist. Gujrat	Kidar, Distt. Grt. 28-8-47	Mian Sadar Din, s/o Nasar Din Kabsi, Vill. Gajan, P.O. and Teh. Phalia, Distt. Gujrat
852	GRT/B/ U-97W	Parmeshwari Bai, 28 years, w/o Haridayal, Vill. Gandhi Khel, P.S. Tajouri, Teh. Takimarwar, Distt. Banu	Gujrat 12-1-48	She is likely to be in or about Gujrat
853	GRT/B/ U-98W	Peeri Bai, 18 years, d/o Bhan Ram w/o Mool Chand, Vill. Hussokhail, P.S. Bannu, Tehsil Mirali, Distt. Bannu	Gujarat stn. 10-1-48	She is likely to be in or about Gujrat
854	GRT/B/ O-6C	Peshawari Lal, 9 years, s/o Pala Ram, Vill. Burk Bakhteda, P.S. Kadirabad, Teh. Phalia, Distt. Gujrat	Mandi Bahauddin 28-8-47	Lambardar Maulu, s/o Teja, Vill. Burj Bakhteda P.O. and P.S. Kidarabad, Teh. Phalia, Distt. Gujrat
855	GRT/B/ U-94W	Prakash Kaur, 22 years, w/o Pritam Singh, Vill. Dinga, Teh. Kharian, Distt. Gujrat	Dinga 18-4-47	She is likely to be found in or about Dinga, Distt. Gujrat
856	GRT/S-2/ UI6C	Pash, 6 years, d/o Sardari Lal, Vill. Chaukri Bhilowal, Teh. Kharian, Distt. Gujrat	. . .	She is likely to be found in or about Chakuri Bhilowal, Distt. Gujrat

Table 1. *Continued*

Serial No.	R. No.	Particulars of abducted person	Place and date of abduction	Particulars of abductors, custodians, etc.
857	GRT/S/1/ 0-8w	Pooro, 25 years, d/o Sardar Singh, Vill. and P.O. Bhagowal, Teh. and Distt. Gujrat	Bhagowal Aug. 47	Rahmat Khan and Ghulam Qadir, Bhagowal, Distt., Gujrat
858	GRT/S/1/ N-5C	Prakash, 10 years, s/o Mohan Lal, Vill. Khambi, Teh. Kharian, Distt. Gujrat	Latheri Aug. 47	Dalat Khan, P.O. and Vill. Khambi, Teh. Kharian, Distt. Gujarat
859	GRT/S-14/ 199W	Prem Devi, 40 years, d/o Jaman Ram, w/o Bhagat Ram, Vill. Batala, Teh. Bhimber, Distt. Mirpur	Batala	Bhola carpenter of the same village
860	GRT/S-14/ 2 01W	Prem Kaur, 34 years, w/o Ram Singh, Vill. Latheri, Teh. Kharian, Distt. Gujrat	Latheri Aug. 47	Subedar Anayat Khan of the same village

be necessary to make enquiries both at the original home of the abducted person and the place of alleged abduction.

2. The publication of this volume was not undertaken earlier out of deference to the feelings of the victims and their relations. The time has, however, come when the speedy recovery and restoration to relations of these unfortunate persons should be the paramount consideration and, whatever may be the feelings of abducted persons or their relations about the publication of the particulars contained in this volume, it is essential, for the early completion of this humanitarian work, that the necessary particulars of persons yet to be recovered should be readily available to the Governments of both countries. These particulars were reported by refu-

gees from West Punjab, to the authorities in India, at the points of entry into this country or, subsequently, at the places where they temporarily settled.

Families had reported their women missing. They had filed complaints with the police. Once the scale of the problem became clear, the State had to step in and take some action. The first thing to do was to prepare lists of missing women. These would then form the basis of their search. This, however, was not easy: often, three or four members from the same family, scattered in different places, would register the name of a woman. There was no system, at the time, of sharing and collating this information, so no list could be totally relied upon. The task of preparing such lists was assigned to Edwina Mountbatten's United Council for Relief and Welfare, who collated and sent names on to the local police in specific areas.

Nonetheless, the alarming growth in the size of the lists compelled both governments to act. As early as September 1947 the Prime Ministers of India and Pakistan met at Lahore and took a decision on the question of the recovery of abducted women. It was at this meeting that they issued a joint declaration that specified that: 'Both the Central Governments and the Governments of East and West Punjab wish to make it clear that forced conversions and marriages will not be recognised. Further, that women and girls who have been abducted must be restored to their families, and every effort must be made by the Governments and their officers concerned to trace and recover such women and girls.'[3] The assumption was that all those abducted would be forcibly converted to the other religion and, because they were forced, such conversions were not acceptable. Later, on December 6 in the same year, when the division of pens and pencils and tables and other assets had barely been concluded, and when several thorny issues still remained to be sorted out, this initial agreement was given executive strength through an Inter-Dominion Treaty. Interestingly, neither government denied that abductions had taken place—presumably they knew their men well—and both agreed to set up machinery to rescue abducted women from each other's territories. They agreed too that women living

[3] U. Bhaskar Rao, *The Story of Rehabilitation*, p. 30.

with men of the other religion had to be brought back, if necessary by force, to their 'own' homes—in other words, the place of their religion. It was a curious paradox—at least for the Indian State. India's reluctance (although recent history has questioned this) to accept Partition was based on its self-perception as a secular, rational nation, not one whose identity was defined by religion. Yet women, theoretically equal citizens of this nation, could only be defined in terms of their religious identity. Thus, the 'proper' home for Hindu and Sikh women who were presumed to have been abducted was India, home of the Hindu and Sikh religion, and for Muslim women it was Pakistan, home of the Muslim religion, not the home that these women might actually have chosen to be in. Theoretically, at Partition, every citizen had a choice in the nation he/she wished to belong to. If a woman had had the misfortune of being abducted, however, she did not have such a choice.

The machinery that was set up to recover women was to be made up of police officers, and women—social workers or those, usually from well-off families, who were willing to give their time to this work. Among such women were Mridula Sarabhai, Premvati Thapar, Kamlaben Patel and Damyanti Sahgal. In the long passage below Damyanti Sahgal describes how she came to be involved in such work.

*   *   *

Damyanti Sahgal:

My masi Premvati Thapar became a widow three months after her marriage. She had been taken out of school to be married, three months later her husband died and she went back into the school (the convent) as Miss Thapar. He was a mathematician, Devi Dayal. So there she did her FA, her BA, MA, double MA. Then she did her Tripos in Economics from Cambridge.

One day Mahatma Hans Raj, a well-known Arya Samaji of Lahore, came to meet my nana and said Thapar Sahib, we have come to ask you a major question. You know Arya Samajis never go anywhere without matlab and we have come to ask you for something. Whatever we ask for, you have to promise that you will give us. Then Thapar Sahib said at least give me some idea of what it is you're asking for. They said, no but you must promise us that you will give it, what we have come for we will take with us. You know Arya Samajis are very persistent people. My nana said well, think carefully and ask so that what you ask for is something that can be given. They said, well your daughter who has just returned, we would like you to give her life to us. There is a DAV college for girls here but there is no school and we want to put her in charge of a school, and she will have to work in an honorary capacity. My bhaiji said what are you talking about? I have spent so much on her education and she has had so many offers (suddenly there had been several job offers) and you're asking that I give her away, honorary you say. What will she live off? Where will she eat from? They laughed and said, Rai Sahib, don't speak like a child. You have three sons don't you? If you had had a fourth what would you have done, thrown him away? Think of her as your son, give her her share of the property and she will live off that. My nana . . . he wasn't willing, so much I have spent he thought and now, to just give her away . . . but Auntie Premi came out herself and said I have decided, I will do this, I will work for them. He kept saying Premi, don't, try to understand, but she was adamant. After that, masi, she used to work for a rupee a month . . . we all worked under her . . . a rupee a month . . .

You see she was such a fine person, such a personality, she had been doing social work all her life and so many people had worked under her in Lahore. So later, when she went to Mrs Nehru and asked if there was any work, Mrs Nehru said well, Jawaharlal is working on something. An agreement is being made between the two governments, you know all those women of ours who have been abducted, they are really miserable. We have to rescue them from the hands of those villains. And here the Sikhs have done the same thing, so we plan to open a recovery organization and I want to give you some work there. Masi said now I don't even have money, and I want very little . . . I need accommodation, a car and a chaprasi. Please get me this.

One day masi said to me, Danti, it's getting on to winter, and we have no money, no clothes, . . . you know, Auntie Premi loved clothes and things and she liked good clean living, she enjoyed life, and our almirahs in Lahore were full of our things and we even knew which families had taken our houses. Those days convoys used to go to Lahore and so we decided to go. Masi said Danti, let's go, we'll go to the DAV college camp in Lahore—from there we'll take government jeeps and go to our old homes and I'll collect some dhotis and a shawl. So we went. And we reached DAV college from where we got an escort jeep and went to masi's house. They welcomed us, the begums came out, we knew them, masi said I have come with a purpose, I left my almirahs locked here and I am freezing. I have come to collect some shawls and clothes. They said, what are you talking about? All that has gone in zait-ul-maniat, unclaimed property, and there's nothing left. Masi and I were shocked. They said, have tea, but we couldn't. They kept saying none of your things is here . . .

We came back to the camp and ate there. You see the camps would collect refugees and when there was a sizeable number, the convoys would leave and take them across the border. So we ate, dal and rotis, there used to be huge containers. And Mridula Sarabhai jumped on us. Masi used to know her, I didn't. I had heard stories about her. She said Miss Thapar, you are here. Masi said, yes, we came to get our clothes but were unable to get anything. She, Mridula Sarabhai, said but you know about this organization that is being started [the Central Recovery Organization to recover abducted women], they have decided that they're going to choose you as a director. And who is this, she asked, pointing to me. My niece, said my masi. Oh good, she'll come in handy for my work, she's just what I want. You see, Premi, when this organization starts, you will be the director there, and she will be the director here. I was sort of shy and of course the whole day I would do nothing but say my prayers and count my beads and roam about alone. I couldn't understand what was going on and I said, no, no, leave me out of this. But she said, no, I'll make her chief liaison officer and she said to my masi, don't take her back with you, she'll stay here and I'll soon get her an appointment letter. I asked what was going on and she said I'll make you director. I said director of what, she said recovery. I didn't know what recovery was or what director was. I couldn't put two and two together. She said no, no, it's done, it's done. I said I have no clothes . . . she said the jeep is going, it will bring your clothes. I didn't know what was happening . . . suddenly, masi had gone, I had no clothes . . . so then, you see I have this habit, when I have a problem I speak to my god, my thakur. I don't know anything, I'm just an instrument of his will. So I said to him what is this game you're playing? Here I have become a director and I have a letter in my hand, even my father and grandfather did not become directors, so now it's up to you to keep my pride.

Soon afterwards a message came that there was a young girl who had been abducted and she had been traced to somewhere close by, so what with one thing and another, we managed to rescue her. Refugees used to come there in huge numbers, they would collect there and once there was a large number the convoys would start off.

Part II HISTORY IS A WOMAN'S BODY

Seized by the problem of the large numbers of abducted women, the Indian and Pakistani governments arrived at an agreement, the Inter-Dominion Treaty of December 6, 1947, to recover as many abducted women as could be found. The operation came to be known as the Central Recovery Operation, and one woman in particular, Mridula Sarabhai, is said to have campaigned for it. Sarabhai wielded considerable influence with Gandhi and Nehru—she came from a powerful industrial family of Ahmedabad—and had been closely involved with Congress politics. She had submitted a fourteen-page note to Nehru outlining the necessity of recovering abducted women and used her influence to get the government to agree to mounting a recovery operation. At the 1947 Inter-Dominion conference where this was agreed, the Indian government returned the responsibility for the recovery of women to Sarabhai, appointing her chief social worker. She was to be assisted by a team, mainly made up of the police.

Within a short while, the initial agreement arrived at between the two governments was given legislative sanction: The Abducted Persons Recovery and Restoration Ordinance was transformed first into a Bill and later, in 1949, into an Act.[4] By the terms of this Act, the government of India set up an implementation machinery and, importantly, arrived at a working definition of what was meant by the term 'abducted person'.

This was essential because the affair was a complicated one: how to decide who had been abducted and who had not? What if a woman had gone of her own free will? These were things that took thought, that needed consideration. It was much simpler for an impersonal agency such as the State to set times, dates, figures to decide these thorny problems. So a date was fixed. The violence in Punjab had begun early in March 1947. Thus after March 1, 1947 any woman who was seen to be

[4] The Abducted Persons (Recovery and Restoration) Act, 1949 (Act No. LXV of 1949).

living with, in the company of, or in a relationship with a man of the other religion would be presumed to have been abducted, taken by force. After this date, all marriages or conversions that had taken place would be seen as forced, and would not be recognized by either of the two governments. No matter what the woman said, how much she protested, no matter that there was the odd 'real' relationship, the women had no choice in the matter. Many things were left unresolved by the fixing of this date: women who had children from mixed unions after the cut-off date — were they also to be considered abducted women? Or did the date relate only to those children who were conceived after March 1? The Act remained unclear on these issues.

In the work of rescue the chief social worker was to be assisted by a unit made up mostly of the police. The total unit comprised one Assistant Inspector General (ASI), two Deputy Sub-Inspectors of Police (DSPS), fifteen inspectors, ten sub-inspectors, and six Assistant Sub-Inspectors (ASIS). Together with women social workers, this force of police was empowered, in both countries, to travel into the other country in search of particular women, and then to carry out the 'rescue' or 'recovery' operation as best they saw fit. Social workers on both sides had to resort to all kinds of subterfuges to find abducted women. Often, the local police, meant to be accompanying and helping in the tracking down of women, would send ahead a warning and the women would be hidden away. Imaginative social workers countered this in a variety of ways — by adopting disguises, using false names, acting secretly and on their own, or just storming their way into homes where they suspected abducted women were being held. Here are two such accounts:

> In the mornings we used to go to find girls from the rural area. In the evenings we used to come to the head office, to the camp, and those women who had been rounded up from the area, they used to be brought to the camp where we would receive them. Then they used to be changed inter-dominion [i.e., between the two countries]. The only difference was that those workers were daring — they would go out and find women . . .
>
> We'd go selling eggs. We'd go into the villages, and we'd ask people for lassi, saying amma, amma, we have come from very far, please give us some lassi. So we'd sell eggs and ask for lassi. Then we'd tell stories, we'd say

we have come from Hindustan and you know, my younger brother, these bastard Sikhs have taken his young wife away, they've abducted her. He is bereft, and lonely. Do you know of any daughter of kaffirs in this area—if there is any such girl do tell us, maybe we can buy her and the poor man, at least he can set up home again. And the old women would know and they would often tell us there's a girl in such and such place . . . So there was all this about selling eggs and asking, amma, give us some lassi.

Or amma, I am hungry, give me something, and we would try to win their confidence and then we would ask them, or tell them we wanted to buy a girl . . . and we'd ask whether the people who had the girl would part with her, and then gently ask for the address . . . that was our way of getting information.[5]

*　*　*

Among the refugees who were leaving [from Delhi] there was a young man who had been married only a year and a half and whose young wife and two-month-old child had been lost. One day, someone told him that they had heard that she was in the custody of a Jat in Bhogal [an area in Delhi]. It was an old chamarin who gave the news. She had felt sorry for the girl and had promised that she would take her message across to her husband. The young man told me that his wife had even asked for his photo which he had sent her . . . the chamarin said she remembered him very much and Mithan, her abductor, made her work in the fields.

One day Sushila Nayyar had come to the camp. She said, come on, I'll come with you, where are these fields? Night was falling as we reached Okhla. But Sushila was fearless, and unhesitatingly she walked some twenty steps ahead of me, pushing her way through the bushes and fields. We met many other women but not the one we were seeking. Sushila walked into the house without a trace of fear, and I followed her. Ausaf, the husband, was calling out his wife's name, Jaan bi, Jaan bi, all the time. But there was no answer. And Sushila was giving the people a talking to: if the girl is with you, give her to us immediately. Tell me, where is she? At the moment, only I have come and I will take the girl away, no harm

[5] Damyanti Sahgal, personal interview.

will come to you. But if the police come you will be taken away to jail and punished. But there was no sign of the girl . . . and at nine at night we came back, dejected and unsuccessful.[6]

Later, it turned out that all the while Sushila Nayyar and Anis Kidwai were searching for Jaan bi, she was bound and gagged and locked up in the hay loft of the house she was in. Fearing that he would be found out, her abductor now took her with him and ran away to UP [Uttar Pradesh]. On the way, however, Jaan bi managed to escape: she ran to some Muslims reading the namaz, and told them her story. She was then restored to her husband, although she had lost her child. Not all tales ended so happily and there were thousands of women who were successfully spirited away, never to be found.

The fixing of dates and the enacting of legislation, however, did not do away with the many imponderables that had to be dealt with. Many women protested. They refused to go back. Impossible as it may seem, there were women who, like Zainab, had formed relationships with their abductors or with the men who had bought them for a price. At first, I found this difficult to believe, but there is a kind of twisted truth in it. One might almost say that for the majority of Indian women, marriage is like an abduction anyway, a violation, an assault, usually by an unknown man. Why then should this assault be any different? Simply because the man belonged to a different religion? 'Why should I return,' said an abducted woman, 'Why are you particular to take me to India? What is left in me now of religion or chastity?' And another said: 'I have lost my husband and have now gone in for another. You want me to go to India where I have got nobody and of course, you do not expect me to change husbands every day.'[7]

Mridula Sarabhai was instrumental in bringing many middle-class women into social work. Most of these women worked with Hindu and Sikh abducted women. In Delhi, at the two Muslim camps in Purana Qila and Humayun's tomb, there was another woman who took to social work on her own, and whose efforts related to Muslim women

---

[6] Anis Kidwai, *Azadi ki Chaon Mein* (Hindi), Delhi, National Book Trust, 1990, p. 131.
[7] Kirpal Singh, *The Partition of the Punjab*, p. 171.

abducted by Hindus and Sikhs. Anis Kidwai's husband, Shafi Ahmed Kidwai, was killed during the Partition riots in Mussoorie where he was working. Despite Kidwai's entreaties, he had refused to leave his office and his employees (he was a government servant) saying he could not abandon them, or his job. His death devastated Kidwai and she went to see Gandhi, in search of some sort of solace. Gandhi advised her to stop mourning and to involve herself in something, and Kidwai turned to social work with Muslim refugees. In the course of this work she had occasion to come across several cases of abducted Muslim women, and she writes movingly about their dilemmas. I quote from her at some length:

> In all of this sometimes a girl would be killed or she would be wounded. The 'good stuff' would be shared among the police and army, the 'second rate stuff' would go to everyone else. And then these girls would go from one hand to another and then another and after several would turn up in hotels to grace their decor, or they would be handed over to police officers, in some places to please them.
>
> And every single one of these girls, because she had been the victim of a trick, she would begin to look upon her 'rescuer' perforce as an angel of mercy who had, in this time of loot and killing, rescued her, fought for her, and brought her away. And when this man would cover her naked body—whose clothes had become the loot of another thief—with his own loincloth or banyan, when he would put these on her, at that moment she would forget her mother's slit throat, her father's bloody body, her husband's trembling corpse. She would forget all this and instead, thank the man who had saved her. And why should she not do this? Rescuing her from the horror, this good man has brought her to his home. He is giving her respect, he offers to marry her. How can she not become his slave for life?
>
> And it is only much later that the realization dawns that among the looters this man alone could not have been the innocent, among the police he alone could not have been the gentleman. But all were tarred with the same brush. Each one had played with life and death to save the honour of some young woman, and thousands of mothers and sisters must be cursing these supposedly 'brave men' who had abducted their daughters.

But by the time this realization came, it was too late. Now there was nowhere for her to go: by this time she is about to become a mother, or she has passed through several hands. After seeing so many men's faces, this daughter of Hindustan, how will she ever look at the faces of her parents, her husband?[8]

Kidwai's feelings for abducted women—'the reader will not understand how I, as a woman, felt on hearing these things,' she says—mirrored those of many of the other social workers who took on the task of recovering abducted women. Acting as dutiful servants of the State, they nonetheless responded to the women as women, and often helped to subvert the State's agenda, although much of the time they were also helpless and hampered by the fact that they had little choice but to carry out their assigned tasks. Kidwai describes her own feelings movingly:

... there were some women who had been born into poor homes and had not seen anything other than poverty. A half full stomach and rags on your body. And now they had fallen into the hands of men who bought them silken salvars and net dupattas, who taught them the pleasures of cold ice cream and hot coffee, who took them to the cinema. Why should they leave such men and go back to covering their bodies with rags and slaving in the hot sun in the fields? If she leaves this smart, uniformed man, she will probably end up with a peasant in rags, in the filth, with a danda on his shoulder. And so they are happy to forget the frightening past, or the equally uncertain and fearful future, and live only for the present.

They also had another fear. The people who wanted to take them away, whether they were friend or foe, how did they know that they would not sell them to others? After all, she has been sold many times, how many more times would it happen? The same police uniforms, it was these that had, time and again, taken her from here to there. What was there to reassure her that she could believe in the authority of the turban, that the person who wore it came from her relatives, and was not someone who had come yet again to buy and sell her. The stigma did not go away until she was dragged away and made to live with her relatives for a few days.

[8] Anis Kidwai, *Azadi ki Chaon Mein*, p. 142.

There remained religion, and what did these girls know about that after all? Men can at least read the namaz, they can go to the mosque to read the namaz at id, and listen to the mullah. But the mullah has never allowed women to even stand there. The moment they see young women the blood rises in their eyes. Be off with you, go away, what work do you have here? As if they were dogs to be pushed out of every place. The culprit is within them, but it is the women who are made to go away. If they come to the masjid everyone's namaz is ruined. If they come to listen to the sermon, everyone's attention is distracted. If they go to the dargah they will get pushed around by men, and if they participate in a qawwali mehfil the sufi's attention will be on worldly things rather than on God...

And friend, the God of this religion has never kept her very comfortably. But the new man with whom she is is like God. Let everyone talk, she will never leave this man who has filled her world with colour.[9]

Despite the women's reluctance (and not all women were thus reluctant, many were happy to be recovered and restored to their families) to leave, considerable pressure, sometimes even force, was brought to bear on them to 'convince' them to do so.

* * *

Damyanti Sahgal:

Two young men reported to me that their sister, Satya, whose marriage they had been preparing, had been abducted. They suspected Pathans had picked her up and they said somehow you must find her. I had heard that — I've forgotten which chak it was — that badmash Pathans had captured the daughter of deen dars and had taught her to ride a horse and that she now carried a rifle...

I learnt about Satya, that she was with dacoits and thieves and that she had become one better than them. They'd trained her and she even rode on horses. I told the SP [Superintendent of Police] that I want to go to this place and he said it's a very dangerous place. I said dangerous be damned, I want to go. You see what they used to do, they'd take information from us and send a message on ahead so that the person could be removed. No sooner would

[9] Anis Kidwai, *Azadi ki Chaon Mein*, pp. 142–43.

they hear the news than they would run away. And our own movements were so restricted—we had to be very careful about where we went and how we went. I used to move about a lot, other workers not so much. Anyway, on that day we had to go through farms and fields and the SP kept saying this was very dangerous and unsafe terrain. The poor woman who accompanied me! In the morning they sent a message on ahead that Satya should be spirited away. However, somehow or the other, after much running around we managed to get hold of the girl. When we had to bring her back to Gujrat, first we had to ask the SP to give us police protection for the girls. The Pathans followed us and appealed in court saying we're not ready to give up this woman, she's been a Muslim from the start. Even before Pakistan was formed she had actually taken on the Din religion and she was a Muslim. So the DC [District Collector] took the girl from me and let her go. Her brother kept shouting and protesting but he wasn't even allowed to meet her. I also said let her meet her brother at least, but no. He refused to listen. I was upset—I had risked my own life, gone through a lot of danger and hardship to get this girl and the DC then acquitted her! Then I—the first prime minister of Pakistan, what was his name? Yes, Liaqat Ali. He was in Karachi at the time. That was the time the Inter-Dominion Agreement had taken place about Indian women being returned to India and Muslim women being returned to Pakistan. I gave the reference of the treaty and sent a telegram to the Minister and said that with great difficulty I have caught this girl according to the Inter-Dominion Agreement but the DC has let her go. And I refuse to stay in Pakistan and continue to work there if there will be such frauds. He sent a wire that he was coming to Gujrat the next day and that Satya Devi should be brought to the railway platform to meet him. He said I'll see what I can do. So we were there waiting for the train. The Muslims got to know that our prime minister is coming and a *Hindu* woman has managed to call him. The news spread everywhere! And in this case . . . they had also heard that I had got the woman away from the Pathans and she was in handcuffs. Her brothers were with me, everyone was there. It was a very frightening case. Because dacoits and people take revenge and she had also become like that. And you will not believe it, there was not one person who was not there at the station! The SP, the DC . . . you name it, they were all there. They made me sit in a room. The military was also there. A captain. We were all waiting for the train. I thought how can I handle this? She's become a Muslim, the place is full of Muslims, I am alone. What will I say to him? What can I do?

Then I asked for paper and a pencil saying I wanted to write two lines and I wrote 'Janab-è-ali, you are a sensible man, you have the reins of Pakistan in your hands . . .' I praised him, I said the very fact that you are holding the topmost position in Pakistan, that you are the prime minister, shows you are an intelligent man. I am a silly woman, I have no idea of things. I want to say just this: I have got hold of just one ordinary, simple poor girl and the whole of Pakistan has come and collected here. I would like to ask you this—is this a way of helping in recovery? Is this what the Inter-Dominion Agreement was about? And the people here, have they sunk so low that for one woman thousands of men have come out? Is such a powerful fire raging in their hearts? In such circumstances how can you expect me to work? I wrote this letter—a small letter—and when the train came, I went straight to it. People began saying the train has arrived, the train has arrived. And what a train—all white, and done up with Pakistan flags all over, it was a sight to see! It stopped and the police took me there. What was his name? Liaqat Ali, he came out. He said, you are the person? I said, yes. You have a complaint? Yes. Please come into the train. I said I will come into the train Sahib, but you can judge the situation. So many people, for just one woman. What is this about? I can't understand what this is about. All I have done is to track one girl down and there's all this commotion and confusion. He got very angry. 'Where is the DC?' he shouted. 'Why are all these people here?' 'Sir, because of the girl.' 'Does it need so many people to protect one girl? Where is the girl? Have her brought here.' The police came with the girl, in handcuffs. I was standing here, he was there. The girl shouted: 'Who has come to take me? This bastard woman?' That was the saving grace. 'This woman has come to take me away? I will not go.' She had managed to get her shoe in her hand and was shaking it at me. Oh ho, he saw red. He said throw her in jail immediately and dismiss these policemen at once. These are orders. Transfer this SP immediately. Then he gave such a lecture there on the platform. He said I am proud of the Hindu workers. There is one girl representing India and your whole police force and officers felt the need to come out here. Look at this woman, how she's holding herself like a lion, and with no protection . . . He said [to the police] I am ashamed of you, what will become of you, how will you progress and reach anywhere? Instead of doing your job you are allowing her to raise her shoe at someone in front of me! Put her in chains and lock her in one compartment and the badmashes with her, lock them in the other compartment. He dismissed the policemen, transferred the SP, and also some others, then he patted me on the back, made me sit down next to him and said I am very very proud of you, not only of you but of India. He said this is amazing, you are facing this kind of thing, and what a frail person you are. Fifteen minutes we talked, then the train left, and I, all the people . . . they were surprised . . .[10]

Child, I had to stay. He gave them so many abuses, the SP, DC and others. I was so ashamed, I could hardly look up. He kept saying look at you, transfer this one, he's a shame. When I came back, one of them came to me and said I hope you are satisfied now, you are calm, your heart is calm, but all those poor men whom you have had transferred, have you thought of what will happen to their families, their children? What will they say to you? Think of you? Can you live with this? I thought this is a real problem, he's gone off and I'm stuck with this. And he said, 'In their houses today everything is silent and sorrowful, no food is being cooked there today, the children are hungry, and everyone is wondering who this woman from India is. Anyone who comes, she manages to prevail upon them, anyone who comes. For us she is like a monster.' I said, have they been dismissed? What else, he said, and what do you think will happen in those homes where no food has been cooked, there is no bread-earner any longer because his job has been taken away, you think they will bless you? Apart from curses what do they have to give you? I said but what have I done? He said you are the cause after all, you have made complaints and it is on those complaints that action has been taken. I then went to the SP. I said, why don't you do an enquiry . . . oh, what is it called now? Yes, I said please suspend them, you don't have to dismiss them. He said I can't undo the orders of the minister. Then I went to the DC and wept before him, and said please don't, but he was doing his duty and he said Mrs Sahgal, you saw how the minister was, what can I do? And I said yes I did see him, but how can this be, I don't even feel like eating anything my-self. Can you not somehow arrange for me to talk to him? He said, yes, that much I can do, I can get him on the telephone and if you speak to him, maybe something can be done, but you'll have to talk to him. Then he got him on the phone and I spoke to him and thanked him a great deal and then said there's only one thing I am sorry about and that is that—these dismissals,

[10] Damyanti's account of this incident is substantially correct, but she is mistaken in that the person she met was not the prime minister but Raja Ghaznafar Ali Khan, the Minister for Refugees.

they are a bit unfortunate. He said but they failed in their duty. I said, yes, Sahib, but you must think, the thing is that at this time everyone's mind is in a state of confusion, they thought it is their duty to protect Pakistan in this way, I thought it's my duty to get the girl, so I feel very bad. He said is this what you really want? I said yes, so he said all right. He then informed the SP that no action should be taken just yet. After that . . . I don't know where that girl went or what happened to her. But at the station I had said to her that her brothers were standing there, and she had cursed me and said you bastard woman what do I care and what business is this of yours?

At that time, the spectacle was amazing, you can imagine, if a young woman is brought along in handcuffs, and the police are on one side, and she is presented before authority . . . the brothers were on one side. But she was directing all her venom at me . . . this is the woman who caught me and brought me here, she is the one who has created all this.

No, I don't even know what happened to her, what the minister did about her future. But they took her away from me. Whether they sent her back to India or anything I don't know. In Gujrat I was told they had made camps. I was also told that there was a nawab in Gujrat who would sit on his throne and the abducted girls would be paraded before him and he would choose the pretty ones. The ones who were young, he used to feel them, the older ones he would give away. The girls could not do anything, no protest, nothing. He would say give such and such in category no. 1, or category no. 2, and the best ones, keep them in the zenana. Then I heard that two boys, whose parents had been killed, they had been kept also. I heard about this, and I went and asked them to return the boys. They said no we will not give these boys back. I said, why, you have a family of your own. The wife said yes, I have three boys of my own. Then why have you kept these? She said, there is a method behind this. We don't just simply pick up anybody, we don't just take the garbage. We choose who we take. Now these boys, they are studying alongside my boys, they have tuitions and both of them and my children they are all studying and then I will send them to England because I have money. These children are so intelligent that they will influence my boys, and when they marry, these two boys, their children will be very intelligent, and we have only one regret about the Hindus having gone away, that love has gone to the other side of the border, we want to bring that in here and multiply it. The children of these children . . . they are being brought up as good Muslims . . .

I didn't have any idea of what was happening, night and day I was caught up in this business of rescuing girls, and looking after them when they were handed over to me. I was busy and contented . . . But you know there is a place in Punj, there they had opened something where they had maulvis and they used to brainwash the girls that those girls who are leaving from here, Hindus and Sikhs will not accept them because they have lived with Muslims. Or, they used to tell them that your relatives will take you from here but they will kill you at the border. And they used to tell them things are so bad in India that you have to pay one rupee even to get a glass of water. Those who have gone are starving, and they used to do all kinds of dramas to scare them. Then they used to make them read the namaz to make them into proper converts. Then there was one who used to come and say that the father of such and such girl has come, and they would take the girl and show her some people standing down below from the roof, and would ask that she be released now that the relatives had come. So the girls would be set free, and then some ten days or so later the girl would come back, crying, weeping and saying that she had run away and come with great difficulty through the fields, etcetera saving herself from the Sikhs who were ready to kill her. And they would mix Musalmani girls with the Hindu girls, after all if there are two-hundred Hindu girls and a few Musalmanis are mixed with them, it is difficult to tell, and these girls would come and tell horror stories of how bad the Hindus and Sikhs had been—we had got them from all over the place, and we didn't really know them, so who knew what was what. They used to get them released and then she would come back, and tell these stories. Then the others would tremble. When they actually caught them, they would separate the men and the women and I don't know what they did with the men but they probably killed them. The girls they would take away, and oh yes, the old women, they'd keep them aside too. Women like me, what did they want with them? But they knew, you see, they would keep these old women, kill off their sons and make themselves their sons, they'd say amma take me as your son, and then they'd get their property. If they'd let these old women get away they or their families would get compensation in India and their property here would have to be confiscated, so they would keep them back. So it was a well thought out and well worked out thing . . . They had real courage and strength, they did. And the Hindus, you show them a piece of red cloth, or if there is blood on the road, out of fear they will leave the road and run away. They'll say we don't know who has been killed or who has killed. We are intelligent, brainy, and they are physically strong . . . Musalmaans are mutton headed, we are fish headed.

I don't know how many women I recovered, must be hundreds, maybe more. There was not one case I didn't catch myself. I don't think any worker can say that she got even one case. I caught them all myself and apart from this there were the ones who were brought to us, we had to accept them and give them receipts for these girls. They used to bring them and we used to have to give receipts. These were some fifteen or twenty cases and I used to move about so I knew about the cases.

*　*　*

'I have got nobody.' There was perhaps more truth in this phrase than many women realized: for several of those who did allow themselves to be 'rescued' or who were forcibly 'recovered', there was another trauma to face. Their families, who had earlier filed reports and urged the government to recover their women, were now no longer willing to take them back. In early 1948, at the sixteenth meeting of the Partition Council, it was decided that both dominions should take charge of refugees in their areas and that no refugees should be forced to return to their own areas until it was clear that complete security had been restored and the State was ready to resume responsibility for them. But for women they said:

> The Ministry of Relief and Rehabilitation has set up a Fact Finding Branch in consultation with the Red Cross, an enquiry and search committee with the special objective of tracing abducted women. Already, 23,000 names have been given to Pakistan. For the recovery of abducted women, the government depends at present on the active assistance of workers and prominent persons. On December 6, a conference of both Dominions was held at Lahore and it was decided that both Dominions should make special efforts to recover these women. More than 25,000 enquiries about abducted women who are in Pakistan have been received by the Women's Section of the Ministry of Relief and Rehabilitation . . . nearly 2500 have already been rescued . . . the main obstruction facing our rescue parties today is the fear harboured by the majority of abducted Hindu women that they may not be received again into the fold of their

society, and the Muslims being aware of this misgiving, have played upon the minds of these unfortunate women to such an extent that many of them are reluctant to come away from their captors back to India. *It has been mutually agreed between the two Dominions that in such cases they should be forcibly evacuated.*[11](my italics)

Forcible evacuation was one thing. The women's acceptance into their families was another. Such was the reluctance of families to take these women back, that Gandhi and Nehru had to issue repeated appeals to people assuring them that abducted women still remained 'pure'. 'I hear,' Gandhi said, 'women have this objection that the Hindus are not willing to accept back the recovered women because they say that they have become impure. I feel that this is a matter of great shame. These women are as pure as the girls who are sitting by my side. And if any one of those recovered women should come to me, then I will give them as much respect and honour as I accord to these young maidens.'[12] Later, in early 1948, Nehru made an appeal to the public. He said:

> I am told that there is an unwillingness on the part of their relatives to accept those girls and women back in their homes. This is a most objectionable and wrong attitude to take and any social custom that supports this attitude must be condemned. These girls and women require our tender and loving care and their relatives should be proud to take them back and give them every help.[13]

A number of pamphlets were published which used the story of Sita's abduction by Ravana, showing how she remained pure despite her time away from her husband. From all accounts, the 'purity' of the woman was of much more importance within India, to Hindus and Sikhs—perhaps because the Hindu religion places greater emphasis on purity and pollution. Apparently, abducted Muslim women were more easily

---

[11] Sixteenth Meeting of the Partition Council, 1948.

[12] Published as an appeal in *The Hindustan Times*, January 17, 1948. Quoted in *Selected Works of Jawaharlal Nehru*, Second Series, Vol. 5, Delhi, Jawaharlal Nehru Fund, 1987, p. 113.

[13] Quoted in G. D. Khosla, *Stern Reckoning: A Survey of the Events Leading up to and Following the Partition of India*, Delhi, Oxford University Press, 1949, rpt. 1989, p. 75.

accepted back into their families, and in Pakistan the All Pakistan Women's Association and other organizations worked hard at arranging marriages for many women who were recovered and returned. For Hindus, purity could, it seemed, more easily be accepted if the woman was alone, but if she had children, it became a different story altogether. The child born of a mixed union was a constant reminder of the violation of the woman, of the fact that she had had sex with a man of the other religion. So women were given a choice: keep your children with you, and stay—in all probability—in an ashram all your life, or give them up (such children were then kept in orphanages) and go back to your old family. There was also another problem: many women were pregnant. What was to be done with them? Social workers confirmed that pregnant women would either be sent away to appointed places to have their children (who were then often offered up for adoption) or they would be sent to be 'cleansed', in other words, to have mass abortions performed ('safaya', it was called). The State then financed mass abortions, out of a special budget set aside for the purpose, at a time when abortion was actually illegal. And apparently, a number of hospitals made their fortunes by doing this, as Damyanti Sahgal confirmed:

> In the Jalandhar camp, in Gandhi Vanita, there were a lot of marriages because most of the girls who came there were unattached. Young girls used to come there, and they were given training, and because people knew there were young girls there, we'd get a number of marriage proposals. We used to also find them jobs, get them to their relatives . . .
>
> Where there were girls who were carrying children from Musalmaan men, their families were very reluctant to take them back. For the woman, once the child is in her womb it is very difficult to leave it . . . but many women were forced to leave their children for the moment people knew this was a Musalmaan child, you know what society is like. That child would have had no future. Most of the women were recovered within a year or so, and families did take women back. But women who were pregnant, you know this Dr Kapur's clinic, they used to get abortions done there, and others would give birth and then hand their children over to the home in Allahabad. With children it was very difficult. And when the women left their children in Allahabad, they used to want to visit them,

to meet them. They were given a choice—they could keep their children with them—if, that is, their relatives would be willing to let them do so, if they would be willing to let the child live with dignity, if they would even look with respect on that child. Otherwise they had to give them up. It was a real problem. Each case was different. The mothers used to go to Allahabad . . . they would take time off from us and go there, what they did there we don't know, how they felt . . . we would give them a ticket and tell them go ahead and meet your children. What kind of future those children had . . . who knows?

Ashrams were set up in north Indian cities to house abducted women: in Jalandhar, Amritsar, Karnal, Delhi. Some of these were meant to hold women in transit until their families took them back. Often, families didn't: the women were now soiled. The family had made its adjustments to their absence, why should they now have to readjust, make new space, and take in a person who had become 'polluted'? So the ashrams became permanent homes for the women; there they lived out their lives, with their memories, some unspeakable, some of which they were able to share with a similar community of women. And there, many of them died, the only people who had suffered a double dislocation as a result of Partition. As late as 1997 some women still remained in the ashram in Karnal; until today there are women in the Gandhi Vanita Ashram in Jalandhar. There are many whose histories will forever remain hidden; others who don't even know their own histories. In Jalandhar there is a woman who is said to have been brought into the ashram when she was only a few months old. No one knows to which community she belongs; there is no idea of who her parents were. She is a child of history, without a history. The Gandhi Vanita Ashram at Jalandhar is today a home for destitute women and widows. 'When we set up the ashram,' one of the social workers told me, 'we looked all over for an appropriate space. And finally this spot was identified. It was actually a graveyard, a kabristan for Muslims, and on the bodies of the dead, we built the lives of women.' It was perhaps only because Partition was a time of dislocation and upheaval that it became possible for the Indian State to lay claim to a graveyard. And it was clearly because everyone was running for their lives that no one had the time to question this. But what sort of lives were actually built for the many women who lived on in ashrams, or were rejected by their families, is something we are not likely to ever know.

The recovery operation for abducted women continued for nine years after Partition, though recoveries began to drop off after the initial few years. In all, some 30,000 women were recovered, about 22,000 Muslim women from India, and about 8,000 Hindu and Sikh women from Pakistan. Many of these were, apparently, not listed in the reported cases with the governments. As time went on, the process of recovery became more and more difficult: apparently, the greatest hurdle in the way of forcible recovery was the women's reluctance to leave their children. Over time, differences developed between the key social workers in this programme. Rameshwari Nehru, for example, wanted the programme to be stopped, while Mridula Sarabhai was all for it to continue. In 1954, a special conference was held at which it was decided that some way should be found to ensure that abducted persons were not forced to go to the other country against their will. Special homes were then set up where unwilling persons could be housed and given time to make up their minds 'without fear or pressure'. How much of a free choice this actually gave women is another question.

*   *   *

Damyanti Sahgal:

After a year [in Jalandhar], I went to the Hoshiarpur camp. It was a big camp, some 1500 women, who had managed to get away or whom we had rescued, whose families had tried to kill them . . . we had some forty-five staff, and I got very caught up there. We had to rehabilitate these women, that was a rehabilitation camp, we had to do mental, physical and financial rehabilitation. This is what we were supposed to do, how many of us actually did it is another story.

The government had opened these camps, the women who had become orphans, or who were alone, they were put into camps. Hoshiarpur was a big camp and then there was Jalandhar. Then there was one in Karnal and many others. These were opened, and women like me were put in charge of camps, and how we did our work really depended on the individual. None of us was really qualified for this work, many of us were not educated. The government wanted to rehabilitate these women in every sense—our job was to make them forget their sorrow, to put new life into their veins, and to give them the means to be economically independent. This was a huge liability, and the mental adjustment used to take the longest; economically it was much easier. The government had given us industrial centres, like hosiery, tailoring, basket making, embroidery, weaving and spinning, we had all these things. For me, when I came back from Pakistan and before I went to Hoshiarpur camp, I had decided I had had enough. I don't want to do any more, I thought.

But Mrs Nehru was very taken with my work, and she insisted with Auntie Premi that I should be made to work. Earlier we had made recoveries, now the next step was rehabilitation, rehabilitation of the women who were recovered. She told me that they had opened a camp in Hoshiarpur, and the camp commandant was not very good there, and she had been getting bad reports—so she wanted me to be in charge there. I kept saying I don't want to do anything, but masi would not let me do this. Then one day Lady Mountbatten came and she had to be taken to the Hoshiarpur camp, so I thought I'd go—because I was getting a free ride. I went. They had made a lot of arrangements for the visitor. She first looked at the women who were spinning. To visitors they said these women earn quite a lot, some ten rupees a day, and then we went to the tailoring people and they said the same, the needlework girls said the same . . . and I began to wonder, spinning does not get so much money. If it is ten for spinning, it would mean three hundred for the month. I thought, I came back and told my aunt, and she said you are foolish, you should go there. She was a strong woman, full of life, strong, what a personality. She said, it's no use telling me. So they insisted that I go there, and Auntie Premi told me to come along with her, because she had to go there for an inspection. Once she was there, she said to me, why don't you stay and I'll come back tomorrow to get you. She just left me behind and said I'll come back in a few days and fetch you.

She told the people there, give her a bed and keep her here. So from that day I was appointed to that job. And then with me, it's like this that whatever work I get into, I put everything into it, and my god helps me to get success in it. After about a month, when the bills had to be made for all the income we had got, they brought the bills to me for the work jobs, and I said what is this? They said once you sign this, the individual workers will get paid, and it was when I saw these documents that I discovered that some women were earning five rupees, some ten for the whole month. At first I thought this was a daily document. Then I realized no one had earned more than forty for the whole month. I said is this every day's earning? They said no this is for the whole month. So I said but what about the time I came for the inspection? They said, that was for the visitors. Do you really think they can earn that much? I was shocked: I said to them but you lied so much. They said, no it wasn't really lies, what we meant was that if a person worked day and night, she could earn so much. Twenty-four hours. So it was all show.

The other thing I noticed was that if we were given a tailoring assignment from outside, it would be the technicians who would cut the clothes. They were the ones who were responsible. Independently the women could not do anything. If you bought a lot of fabric and placed it in front of the women, they would not be able to do anything! So I said, do you think the technicians will run around with these women wherever they go? Even in the hosiery department, it was the technicians who were responsible. The whole thing was heavy on show, wonderful show, but the reality was different. If there was a technician, there was a machine, and if the technicians were thrown out, the whole thing would come to a standstill. What kind of economic rehabilitation was this? As long as they were in the camp, they would get rations and they could earn a little, some ten rupees or so, but once they went out . . . they have no experience, they can't do hosiery, they have no machines, even if one of them buys a machine, then without the technician how will she work? If she puts a spinning wheel or a loom at home, what will she do? Here, the moment a thread snaps, the technician is there to help her but elsewhere . . . that means no future, nothing. The government wanted that after three years these women should learn to stand on their own feet. And what could we do with this kind of setup? I used to be very concerned about this. I couldn't sleep for many days, wondering what I could do. And because basically I am a religious person, I could not rid myself of the feeling that I was committing a sin, a sin. I thought, here I am, I've got an important post, I have become camp commandant, people are around to do salams to me, I have servants and helpers but . . . what am I doing about the real issue here? Then I prayed, and asked God what I should do. And it was at this time that I began to think of adult education.

From 1947 to 1948 I was in Pakistan, and then in '48 I took over in Hoshiarpur, and then I collected my staff, and we went in for adult education. I told the staff to make lists of all the widows who were below thirty-five, or thirty, I can't remember. I said leave the ones who are above this age. We got the lists, and there were some hundred and fifty or so who came within this age bracket. I then asked for a list of staff members, with their qualifications. Then I said, those who have failed matric, still, even if you have failed, there has to be one subject in which you are strong, so we had a column where they could put down the subject in which they were strong. And in this way I had a list in which I could see how many of my staff were strong in Hindi, how many in this subject and how many in that . . . so I then said, here we are working eight hours, but actually we aren't doing a lot. We do pray in the morning, but the country is in great difficulty, and yet we can't, for example, give any daan, any donation for we have nothing. But what we can give is our time, this we can do. We are not asking anyone for money, but I am asking you for a bit of time. For eight hours you give your time to the government, over and above that I'm asking that you give a bit of time to this work. So the list came, and on top was my name, and against it first of all I put a half hour, I was willing to give a half hour of my time . . . Then someone wrote half an hour, someone wrote a full hour and what with those forty or so staff members, we managed to get a lot of time donated. Then we looked at the list of women, and we divided up the staff, and we found that there were usually five women to a staff member. So that work could now begin. Then another problem came up: we needed pencils and notebooks. The government used to give an allowance of ten rupees a month to these women, how could they manage anything from this amount? They had to eat. So then I said, all right, whatever stationery you need you take from me. We couldn't take it from the women, they had no money. And we couldn't ask the government for they did not recognize our effort, so I said, never mind, just take it from me. And then I prayed, I asked the women to pray too, that our effort would be successful, that they would not have to wash dishes or do domestic labour and that they would be able to lead lives of dignity . . . then my director got to know. Later that evening, Miss Thapar got to know that I was planning to start adult education classes. She said, whatever such scheme there is, I know you will be the one to start it. The news spread, the staff and the women were there. A message came from Jalandhar. It said, I've heard you plan to start adult education classes. You do not realize that you are a government functionary, you cannot act of your own accord, you will have to have permission if you are to start anything like this. I thought to myself, what can they do? All they can do is to talk, they can't kill me after all, so I said to the women, tomorrow your classes will start. But then there was the problem: where would we hold these classes? And I decided they would be held under the mango trees . . . so that's what I told the women. Some of them had a little bit of Hindi and Punjabi while there were others, when they received their money they would put a thumb print, while others would be able to sign. I offered rewards to those staff members who would teach the women the fastest . . . this whole enterprise did so well, it was so successful, the government had set up so many industries, but everywhere there were these technicians who would earn a lot of money. The women could not go anywhere. But with a little education many of the women made a noise about the technicians. Then the technicians got worried about losing their jobs. If they didn't show any work, they'd be out. And again I got shouted at for doing something that might put them out of work. Anyway . . . the first set of women, some eighty women, the first year, some of them were old enough to be grandmothers! Some had studied up to one point, some to another, many were ready for the 'middle', some had studied in the vernacular. And then another question came up: that of their ages. Most jobs had an age limit . . . so we had to get together new affidavits. They had to fill in their educational qualifications, but we needed an age certificate first. I told the staff that there is a government rule that anyone over the age of twenty-eight can't get a job. I don't know what the logic was, but that was the rule. So we did some rough calculations—we took off some time for the educational opportunties some of the women had lost, and then a year for something else, and a few months for job searching, and then tried to see how many women fit the bill. But my workers said, behanji, these lists have now become very small. I said how—how will we find them jobs? Make the lists bigger. They said, but how? I said just do it, orders are orders. They all looked at me, thinking behanji has gone mad. Then we had to get the affidavits done. I went to the magistrate, to the Assistant Deputy Commissioner, what was he called—I forget now. Oh yes, Mr Puri. I telephoned him and said I need to come and see you and he said, yes please do come, what is it you need. I told him I needed to get some affidavits signed. He said, what sort of affidavits. So I told him that these women had to take the exam for the eighth standard, and this was their first entry so we needed an age certificate. He said, these women's age? Where are they? Bring them here. The women were outside. I said, why do you need to see the women? He said, if I am signing the affidavit, I need to see them. I tried to dissuade him. He said don't be funny, I have to see the women. I said, for what? He said, am I being funny or are you? I said you want to see the women? You have to sign the affidavit, that's all. He said, Miss Sahgal, you are a strange person, at least bring the women in. I said all right, if you insist. So we brought the women in. [laughing] Poor man, we had written down their ages as twelve, eighteen, fourteen . . . he looked at them and said, these are the women? They are *these* ages? I said you sign the paper, why are you wasting your time and mine, what does it matter? He said Miss Sahgal, look at that woman, her hair is white. I said, congratulations, well done. Don't you know that people's hair goes white even at a young age? Today, even twelve-year-olds have grey hair — haven't you seen any? I can show you lots! Today, one can't rely on hair at all, you never know when hair might go grey! Even at age twelve. Look at that one, he said, she has no teeth. Oh ho, I said, you have such sharp eyes, for a man. I said to her, bibi, you fell down from the roof did you not, the other day? She said, yes, yes behanji. Yes I did and my teeth broke, what could I do? He said, Miss Sahgal, you are trying to make a fool of me. I said, Puri sahib, the girls are in front of you, you can see the truth for yourself, why should I fool you. He said, they have wrinkles on their faces. I said to him, how observant you are, you notice so many things. I said, Look Puri sahib, tell me what you ate at home this morning. He said, so now you are trying to turn the tables on me. I said, no, I genuinely want to know what you had for breakfast this morning. You must have had milk, fruit, toast, butter on it, egg — all this at least your wife must have given you. This much I can tell you, more I don't know. And me too, I have had plenty. But look at these poor women, they get nothing. The government gives them ten rupees. What can they eat with this? They have to starve, that's why their faces are so wrinkled. Once they get enough to eat they will be all right. He said, you are a real Jatti. Look at these women, one has no teeth, another has grey hair, a third is wrinkled . . . I said, oh ho, Puri sahib, what is it you want? He said, tell me the correct age of these women. I said, okay, you write what you want, and I'll accept what you write. How, he said. Why not, I said. Use your pen, and take an oath and write when they were born and I'll believe you. He said, how do I know? So I said, if you don't know, how do I? You will also put down an estimate, and so will I. I said have you seen their faces? They come from the village. Do you think even one of them will know her birth date? What do they know, these women? They will tell you lies, I am also lying, you have to give a false signature, since we are all liars together, none of us will speak. Do you think these women can say when they were born? Neither can I, I was not there, nor can you. So what can we do? For forty-five minutes we argued and argued. He said what should I do? I said I know nothing, I am doing this in God's name, and why don't you do the same? I told him if you can swear when they were born, which hour, which day, I'll take your word for it and countersign it, but you don't know, neither do I. If you can't, I can't.

Anyway, he signed! And with these women then we got an excellent result.

5
'HONOUR'

Part I OUR WOMEN, YOUR WOMEN

Almost from the beginning the recovery operation was fraught with difficulty and tension. In the early stages Pakistan protested the involvement of the Military Evacuation Organization (MEO) and suggested its duties should be confined only to guarding transit camps (these had been set up to house abducted women who had been recovered and were awaiting being sent to their 'home country'). The actual work of rescue, they suggested, should be given to the police. The Indian government was reluctant to do this because they claimed that in many instances the police themselves were the abductors of women—and if social workers are to be believed, there was truth in this claim. Abduction by people in positions of authority happened on both sides. In Montgomery, a tahsildar of Dipalpur, while participating enthusiastically in broadcasting appeals for information about abducted women, is said to have kept an abducted woman with him for eight months. In another instance, two assistant sub-inspectors of police went to recover an abducted woman, and themselves raped her.[1]

For several years after the initial treaty was signed, the fate of abducted women was of considerable concern to the two governments. Legislative Assembly records for the years following 1947, as well as newspapers and periodicals of the time, show an ongoing concern and debate about various issues: the unequal pace of recovery in the two countries, the number of women who had been recovered, where the largest number of recoveries had taken place, why the Indian government was allowing Pakistani social workers free access to the agreed-upon areas when Pakistan had arbitrarily decided to close off certain areas, why it was that fewer Hindu and Sikh women had been recovered from Pakistan and more Muslim women from India, why the Indian government did not slow down the pace of recoveries of Muslim women until more Hindu and Sikh women were found, and so on.

The Ordinance which enabled the Indian government to recover ab-

[1] Kirpal Singh, *The Partition of the Punjab*, p. 171.

ducted Muslim women from India was due to end on December 30, 1949. Fifteen days before this date the government's representative, Gopalaswamy Ayyangar, introduced a Bill in the Assembly—the Abducted Persons Recovery and Restoration Act. The Act remained in force till 1957, after which it was not renewed. By this time, the pace of recovery had slowed down considerably—many women were untraceable and others had 'settled' into their new homes—although the occasional search was still carried out.

Inside the Constituent Assembly where the provisions of the Bill were being debated, many speakers were in agreement that the recovery effort was one that should have been mounted, that it was 'humanitarian' in its objectives. And indeed, it is true that the State could hardly have remained indifferent to the fate of its citizens: neither to the women who had been raped and abducted nor to the pleas of another group of citizens, their families and relatives. However, the debate in the Constituent Assembly also provided Indian political leaders with the opportunity to use the question of the recovery of abducted women to pronounce on something quite different: the character of Pakistan. At the bottom of this lay the profound sense of betrayal that the creation of Pakistan had meant for many Indian political leaders who saw themselves, and India, as secular, and tolerant. Speaker after speaker in the Assembly emphasized what they saw as Pakistan's recalcitrance in keeping to the terms of the joint agreement. Such behaviour, they said, was not what one would expect from a civilized government. It was, rather, a reflection of two things: the typical uncivilized character of Pakistan (made up, as it was, of Muslim men who had fought for a communal State and who were therefore communal by nature) and the much more humane—and civilized—approach of the Indian State. At the same time, the fact that the Indian State was unable to press Pakistan to return as many women as India was recovering was seen as a sign of weakness on its part, an inability to draw the other country in line. Professor Shibban Lal Saxena (UP General) said he was deeply dissatisfied at the 'failure of our government to be able to infuse a proper spirit in the other Dominion to restore our sisters to us.' He suggested India retaliate and do something commensurate with the gravity of the situation, not only because that was the right thing to do 'by our sisters' but also because India had a 'tradition'. 'Even now,' he said, 'the Ramayana and Mahabharata are revered. For the sake of one woman who was taken away by Ravana the whole nation took up arms and went to war. And here there are thousands and the way they have been treated . . . Our sisters from Kashmir were actually sold in the bazars and whatnot was done to them.'[2] There were other criticisms, and a suggestion that the restoration of Hindu and Sikh women abducted in Pakistan should have formed part of the Ceasefire Agreement.

While one member even suggested 'open war if need be' another said:

> If there is any sore point or distressful fact to which we cannot be reconciled under any circumstances it is the question of the abduction and non-restoration of Hindu women. We all know our history of what happened in the time of Shri Rama when Sita was abducted. Here, when thousands of girls are concerned, we cannot forget this. We can forget all the properties, we can forget every other thing, but this cannot be forgotten . . .
> *As descendants of Ram, we have to bring back every Sita that is alive.* (my italics)

The feeling that Pakistan needed to be brought in line was echoed by others who felt, to use the words of Pandit Hriday Nath Kunzru, that the restoration of Muslim women to 'their rightful home' (i.e., Pakistan) was a 'great moral duty'. 'We cannot refuse to fulfil our obligations because others decline to fulfil theirs.' He was of the view that Pakistan ought to be made to feel that it was not an act of merit but of degradation to keep unwilling persons within its own territory and to 'compel them to give up their own religion and to embrace Islam'.

Suggestions for retaliatory action were, however, turned down by the government's representative. In response to Pandit Thakur Das Bhargava's statement that he saw no reason why 'a country is not justified in keeping these [Muslim] girls as hostages for some time', Gopalaswamy Ayyangar, speaking for the Indian government, held that such behaviour did not behove a 'civilized' government. Rather it was India's responsibility, given its modern, secular, rational outlook, to persuade the other country to behave in a manner that would be 'consistent with its claim to

---

[2] *India: Constituent Assembly of India (Legislative) Debates, 1949.* Unless otherwise stated, all further references to the debates in this section are taken from the debates of this year.

be a civilized government'. He reminded his colleagues that abductions had taken place on both sides: 'We are not the monopolists of virtue and the people in the other dominion are not the monopolists of vice — we are as guilty as they have been.'

Like its men, the Muslims who had abducted Hindu and Sikh women, Pakistan too became tarred with the same brush. It was not civilized, it had not displayed moral standards. Renuka Ray, from West Bengal, was clear that: 'India is not going to succumb to the ideas of Pakistan. India has her own objectives and standards and whether Pakistan comes up to them or not, it does not mean that India is to go down to the level and the lack of moral standards displayed by Pakistan.' Pandit Thakur Das Bhargava said: '. . . so far as we are concerned, we know how to honour our moral obligations.' The clear implication was, of course, that Pakistan did not. Among this clamour about who was moral and who not, there was the occasional voice that tried to bring the discussion round to the key actors involved in it: the women. Shrimati Ammu Swaminadhan from Madras said: 'I am very sorry that some of the members said that there should be retaliation. I think that is a most inhuman thing to do because after all, if two Governments are not agreeing with each other, that is not the fault of these innocent girls who have been victims of cruel circumstances. We should not think in terms of retaliation at all . . .'

A second thorny problem was what to do with women who resisted being recovered. These women presented a problem for the State: the law did not allow them to exercise the choice that, as individuals and citizens of two free countries, should have been their right. Both countries had agreed that after a certain date, neither forced conversions or marriages would be recognized. What was to be done if a woman claimed that the relationship she was in was voluntary? Who would sit in judgment on this? The tribunals that had been set up to decide disputed cases were made up of police officers from the two countries. Were they, people asked, competent to decide on the truth or otherwise of a woman's claim? Faced with this difficult question, Gopalaswamy Ayyangar was not willing to admit the possibility that any such claim could be genuine. 'Women or abducted persons are rescued from surroundings which,' he said, 'prima facie, do not give them the liberty to make a free choice as regards their own lives. The object of this legislation is to put them in an environment which will make them feel free to make this choice.' But how could placing the women in a different environment—usually a camp—make them feel free to make a choice? They had little freedom to move in the new environment; they were surrounded by police and social workers; they were pressured—often very subtly—to return to their families. For those who now had children by their abductors or the men they were living with, the choice was no longer merely an individual one.

The minister's views found support among other members, but there was also opposition. Renuka Ray (West Bengal) said that even if there was one case among a hundred in which there was a woman who did not wish to go back, the government needed to pay attention to it. 'After all,' she said, 'in some cases legalized marriages do take place and we have to be very cautious to see that such women who do not wish to cancel such a marriage after so much time has elapsed are not due to our over-zealousness also sent back.' Earlier, another woman, Purnima Banerji, had cautioned the government in this respect. She pointed out that considerable time had passed since many women had been taken away. During this time they

> have lived in association with one another and have developed mutual attachment . . . Such girls should not be made to go back to countries to which they originally belonged merely because they happen to be Muslims or Hindus and merely because the circumstances and conditions under which they have been removed from their original homes could be described as abduction.

Adding his voice to the concern for the double trauma women would have to face, Shri Mahavir Tyagi said that these girls had already been the victims of violence: 'would it not be another act of violence if they were again uprooted and taken away to the proposed camps against their wishes?'

The minister, however, was firm. He did not wish to change this clause that denied women a choice and give them the freedom to decide. He claimed that there had been 'hardly any case where, after these women were put in touch with their original fathers, mothers, brothers or husbands, any one of them has said she wanted to go back to her abductor—a very natural state of feeling in the mind of a person who was, by exercise of coercion, abducted in the first place and put into a wrong environment.' He insisted that he had not come across a single case 'of an adult abducted woman who had been recovered and who was pushed into Pakistan against her will,' although he did admit that when the woman was 'first taken into custody her wishes are not taken into account. The idea is that in the environment that she is in at that moment, she is not a free agent, she has not got the liberty of mind to say whether she wants to leave that environment and go back to her original environment or whether she should stay here.'

If the resistance of women to being recovered was a problem to deal with, so was the much more difficult question of what to do with their children. Curiously, many members who had held that abduction was a shameful and immoral act were quite willing to have women leave their children behind with their abductors. 'You must realise,' said Pandit Thakur Das Bhargava, 'that all those children born in India are citizens of India. Supposing a Hindu man and a Muslim woman have married. Who should be the guardian of the offspring?' When a Muslim woman is restored, he said, she would go to Pakistan. Once there, she might change the religion of the child. But the child would continue to be treated as illegitimate and would be 'maltreated and perhaps killed'. Between father and mother, he asked, who is entitled to guardianship? The question of children was perhaps the most vexed one in this discussion—deeply emotional, it was sought to be decided 'objectively', 'practically' and 'unemotionally'—but while Assembly members may have been able to be unemotional, the mothers clearly could not. Kamlaben Patel pointed to the difficulty of this problem: in Hindu society, she said, a child born of a Muslim father and a Hindu mother would not be acceptable, and if the relatives of the recovered women did not accept their children, the government would then be faced with the problem of large numbers of destitute, unwanted children. This was perhaps the rationale behind the suggestion that children be left with their 'natural fathers'. I shall come back to the question of children later.

* * *

The Assembly was not the only place where the fate of women was discussed. A similar, and different, discussion on the fate of abducted women took place in the pages of newspapers and journals at the time. The *Organiser*, the mouthpiece of the Rashtriya Swayamsevak Sangh (RSS), took on the issue with gusto. On December 29, 1949 the front page of the *Organiser* carried a story entitled 'Pakistan the Sinner: 25,000 Abducted, Thousands Sold.' The story ran as follows: 'For the honour of Sita, Sri Rama warred against and destroyed Ravana, when filthy Khilji beseiged Chitoor its thousands of women headed by Rani Padmini all clad in gerua [saffron] saris, mounted the funeral pyre smiling, ere the mleccha [impure] could pollute a drop of the noble Hindu blood. Today, when tens of hundreds of Hindu women are spending sorrowful days and unthinkable nights in Pakistan, the first free government of the Union of Indian Sovereign Democratic Republic has nothing but a whimper for them.'

This article and its subsequent accusation that Pakistan actually deserved the epithet 'Napakistan' (impure) was typical of the kind of thing the *Organiser* voiced regularly in the years following Partition. The rape and abduction of Hindu and Sikh women by Muslim men formed the backdrop against which accusations were levelled at Pakistan for being barbaric, uncivilized, lustful. The very formation of the nation of Pakistan out of the territory of Bharat (or, the body of Bharatmata) became a metaphor for the violation of the body of the pure Hindu woman. The Indian State was regularly assailed for its failure to protect its women and to respond to Pakistan, the aggressor State, in the language that it deserved. More than ever, the need of the hour for Hindus was to build up 'a strong and virile state backed by a powerful army', because, as one Chaman Lal, author of a book entitled *Hindu America* put it, 'we have become such extreme pacifists that despite receiving kicks . . . we continue to appeal to the invaders in the name of truth and justice.' If the invader was to be responded to in kind, what was required for the removal of this grave 'national' weakness was the 'Kshatriyaisation'[3] of the Hindu race.

For many writers in the *Organiser* the rape and abduction of women was a shameful, but predictable, event, for what else could be expected

[3] *Organiser*, July 10, 1947.

of Pakistan, a nation 'built on the predatory desire for Hindu property and Hindu women [which] took practically no steps to checkmate the lust and avarice of its champions.'[4] There was, however, another reality. Muslim women had also been abducted by Hindu and Sikh men. How could this be explained? In the debates in the Constituent Assembly this was seen as an 'aberration', these men had clearly fallen victim to 'evil passions'. The *Organiser* wasn't quite prepared to admit that Hindu and Sikh men had been guilty of abductions. Rather, they had 'sheltered' Muslim women. In an article entitled 'During the War of 1947' the writer claimed:

> During the Hindu Moslem War in the Punjab in the summer of 1947, passions ran high. Lakhs of people were slaughtered on both sides. But the war—the worse than war, abduction—on women, *a notorious and age old practice of Muslims* (my italics) made the Nation writhe in pain and anguish. Thousands of Muslim women, widowed and abandoned, were left in Hindu majority areas also. But as soon as recovery work started, most of them, till then sheltered by the Hindus, were handed over to the authorities. Hardly any Muslim women remain in Bharat against their wishes. *It is significant to note that some of them were abducted by Muslims themselves.* (my italics)[5]

Hindu men thus, while occasionally falling victim to evil passions, were seen by and large as being harmless, even weak, and certainly not lustful. 'The Hindu mind,' readers were told, 'is broad enough to do justice to others but not bold enough to demand justice.'[6] This is because India has a great tradition, a magnanimous culture that has ensured that:

> throughout the ages and even at the pinnacle of her armed might, when she could easily have swept the continent she never assumed the tyrant's role. While other people take pride in savage campaigns launched by their ancestors for enslavement, exploitation and forcible proselytization of their brother human beings, India, pregnant with the wisdom of her illustrious seers, and true to her hoary culture, remembers only the key days

[4] *Organiser*, December 14, 1949.

[5] *Organiser*, December 14, 1949.

[6] *Organiser*, December 14, 1949.

146

of her glory when the impact of her glorious civilization was felt far and wide.[7]

This ancient tradition then was what made the Hindu male tolerant and civilized, such that, even having (mistakenly?) abducted Muslim women, he was willing and ready to hand them over to the State or the authorities, the moment the call was given. It was also this tolerance — hitherto important — which in the moment of crisis, rendered the Hindu male incapable of protecting his women. This then, is the reason for the call to arms, to fight and retaliate in the language of the Muslim State.

In a similar vein we are told by one writer that

Tens of thousands of our pious mothers and sisters who would faint at the sight of blood were kidnapped and sold for so many rupees, annas, pies. I have seen some of them recovered from that holy land. Their foreheads bore tatoo marks declaring them 'Mohammad ki joru' [Mohammed's wife], 'Mian Ahmed ki joru' [Mian Ahmed's wife], 'Haji Hussain ki joru' [Haji Hussain's wife], etc., etc. . . .

Their [that of refugees in general] early and effective absorption in the economy and society of the regions of their adoption is the *primary duty of every national of Hindustan.* The task is not easy. It bristles with difficulties. That is obvious. But no less obvious is the fact that the problem is *a challenge to our manhood, no less than to our nationalism.*[8] (my italics)

This easy equation of manhood and nationalism was not unusual — it needed men to protect the honour of the motherland. For many writers of the *Organiser,* then, during this period it became important to establish the purity of Mother India, the motherland which gave birth to the Hindu race and which was home to the Hindu religion. The country, whether referred to as Bharat, or Hindustan, was imaged in feminine terms, as the mother, and Partition was seen as a violation of its body. One issue of the *Organiser* (August 14, 1947) had a front page illustration of Mother India, the map of the country, with a woman lying on it, one

[7] *Organiser,* November 30, 1949.
[8] *Organiser,* July 10, 1947.

THE OTHER SIDE OF SILENCE

limb cut off with Nehru holding the bloody knife responsible for doing the severing. Of Bharat Mata it is said elsewhere that 'it is this steadfast faith in her religion that has saved Hindustan from extinction through countless centuries . . . she has run the gauntlet of conquest and bond-age, she has been wrought upon by fear, persuasion and temptation to sign away her old faith and choose another, but she refused to part with her religion which is her soul.'[9]

In this homily there was a lesson too for those abducted women who had so easily fallen prey to, or chosen to accept the religion of the 'other'. If to be a good Hindu woman was equal to being a 'good' mother, the very real fact of their cohabitation—enforced, perhaps even voluntary —with Muslim men represented a real threat to this ideal and there-fore had to be dealt with. The responsibility fell on their husbands and brothers, to fight for them, to go to war, even 'to burn themselves to ashes' if need be, and to bring them back into the fold despite their 'pol-lution'. As 'Kamal' (a pseudonym for a regular writer) put it, 'Not only is Bharatvarsh our mother and we its children, she was the Deity and we her devotees. She was sacred. To go out was to go to foreign, impure, barbaric lands and so a purification on return was necessary.'[10] Another article quotes Ram as saying to his brother: 'O Lakshman, this golden Lanka doth not please my heart. The Mother, the country of our birth, is sweeter than the joys of heaven itself.'[11]

In sharp contrast to the image of the Hindu mother was that of the Muslim woman. Although she appeared only infrequently in the pages of the *Organiser*, readers were nonetheless warned of the dangers she carried. In an article entitled 'Life in Sind', Hoondraj Kripalani be-wailed the fact that Hindus were being abused and insulted at every step. 'Even in your own house you are not safe. Muslim women would enter your house on the pretext of enquiring whether you have anything to sell. And after a few minutes they will tell you that they have come to stay. You cannot drive them out, for you dare neither touch them nor get them removed by anyone else . . .' He goes on to add an ingenious

[9] *Organiser*, November 13, 1948.
[10] *Organiser*, September 25, 1947.
[11] *Organiser*, August 19, 1948.

warning to his Hindu brothers: 'You may persist for two or three days in living with them, but then, of course, there is the real danger of these Muslim women crying aloud at night. And then where do you stand?'[12] Clearly, then, there was no way in which Hindu men could be anything but helpless in the presence of aggressive Muslim women who insisted on inserting themselves into their lives.

* * *

Mass-scale migration, death, destruction, loss—no matter how inevitable Partition seemed, no one could have foreseen the scale and ferocity of bloodshed and enmity it unleashed. 'We had thought,' said Faryad, a carpenter from Delhi, 'that once independence came, the streets of Delhi would be paved with gold, awash with milk. Instead, all we saw was rivers of blood.' Still less could anyone have foreseen that *women* would become so significant, so central, and indeed so problematic. However inadequate they may be, there are some steps that the State can take to help people rendered homeless, or to compensate those who have lost properties. But how do you respond when there has been mass rape of women and abductions on such a major scale, especially when the problem is further compounded by the fact that many of the abducted women say they actually wish to remain with their abductors?

Independent India in 1947 was a fledgling State—embattled, deeply contested, even fragile—thrown immediately into dealing with problems of enormous complexity. No matter how much people found to approve or disapprove of in the actions of the State, there was almost nothing at the policy level that could be acceptable to everyone. Most dissatisfactions, however, had to do with material things: how much compensation, the recovery of property, etc. Where women were concerned, the debate entered another realm altogether—that of the honour of the nation, and of its men.

Partition itself—the loss of a part of itself to another—was just such a loss. Although Partition had also brought independence, there was a deep sense of shame, almost of inadequacy, that India had allowed a part of itself, a part of its body, to be lost to the other nation. Through-

---

[12] *Organiser,* August 19, 1948.

out the nationalist movement one of the most powerful symbols for mobilizing both women and men had been the image of India as the mother, Bharatmata. Now, Partition represented an actual violation of this mother, a violation of her (female) body. The picture carried by the *Organiser*, with the woman's body mapping the territory of India, and Nehru cutting off one arm which represented Pakistan, is a powerful and graphic reminder of this.

If the severing of the body of the country recalled the violation of the body of the nation-as-mother, the abduction and rape of its women, their forcible removal from the fold of their families, communities and country, represented a violation of their bodies as real—not metaphorical—mothers. Each woman who had been taken away was actually, or potentially, a mother. Within the givens of motherhood, her sexuality could be contained, accepted and legitimized. But as a raped or abducted mother, and further as an abducted mother who actually expressed a desire to stay on with her abductor, this sexuality was no longer comprehensible, or acceptable. How could motherhood be thus defiled? The fact that this had actually happened could be put down to the chaos of the time. But allowing it to continue: how could families, the community, the nation—indeed, how could *men* allow this state of affairs to continue? The women had to be brought back, they had to be 'purified' (and this meant that they had to be separated from their children, the 'illegitimate' products of their 'illegitimate' unions), and they had to be relocated inside the family and the community. Only then would moral order be restored and the nation made whole again, and only then, as the *Organiser* points out again and again, would the emasculated, weakened *manhood* of the Hindu male be vindicated. If Partition was a loss of itself to the 'other', a metaphorical violation and rape of the body of the motherland, the recovery of women was its opposite, the regaining of the 'pure' (and this purity had to be constantly re-emphasized) body of the woman, essential, indeed crucial for the State's—and the community's—self-legitimation.

Extensive as it was, then, the detailed discussion in the Assembly on the Abducted Persons Recovery and Restoration Act had very little to do with the *women* who were its subject. This of course is nothing new, for even today discussions that are said to be about women often have little or nothing to do with them, but provide an opportunity to re-hearse other agendas. Similarly, the debate in the Assembly was an exercise in restoring or reaffirming the self-image of India.

Perhaps the most stark question that faces us is why did it become so important for the Indian State to go to such inordinate lengths to recover abducted women? Why, equally, did the Act that empowered the government to do so need to be quite so sweeping in its powers? In the early days, the State could hardly have acted differently, given the considerable pressure families brought to bear on it. But as time went on, and the conditions of recovery became more and more difficult—it was clear, for example, that many women did not want to leave because they had children—why did the State continue the recovery operation?

And if the question of women's recovery became so important for the State, we might well pose an additional question: why then did it become equally important for the kind of discourse we have seen in the *Organiser*? In both instances, the woman as a *person* did not count, her wishes were of little consequence, she had no right to resist, defy nor even to appeal, for the Act denied even that basic freedom. Not only was she to be forcibly recovered, but if she disputed her recovery, she was (after 1954) allowed to put her case before a tribunal, but beyond that—if the tribunal's findings were seen as unjust—she had no recourse. There is no escaping the question, then, that if *women* were so inconsequential in something that was so centrally of concern to them, what was it that lay at the heart of the recovery operation?

National honour: the honour that was staked on the body of Mother India, and therefore, by extension, on the bodies of all Hindu and Sikh women, mothers and would-be mothers. The loss of these women, to men of the 'other' religion, was also a loss to their 'original' families. These, and not the new families which the women may now be in, were the legitimate families, and it was to these that the women needed to be restored. If this meant disrupting the relationships that they may now be in, that they had 'accepted' for whatever reason, this had to be done. The assumption was that even if asked for their opinion, women would not be able to voice an independent one because they were in situations of oppression. And there was some truth in this. But the obverse was also true: that even in their 'own' families women are seldom in situations where they can freely voice their opinions or make a choice. Nonetheless, these were the families which were held up as legitimate; women therefore had to be removed from those 'other' non-acceptable families and relocated into the 'real' ones. This, for the State, was the honourable thing to do.

If colonialism provided Indian men the rationale for constructing and reconstructing the identity of the Hindu woman as a 'bhadramahila', the good, middle-class Hindu wife and mother, supporter of her men, Independence, and its dark 'other', Partition, provided the rationale for making women into symbols of the nation's honour.

This was not surprising. If independence in 1947 represented 'the triumph of anti-colonial nationalism', then Partitition, equally, represented the 'triumph of communalism',[13] something which has had far-reaching consequences for the India of today. Communalism came to be associated mainly with Pakistan, India could take upon itself the mantle of its opposite: thus Pakistan came to be represented as the communal, abductor country, refusing to return Hindu and Sikh women, while India was the reasonable, and civilized non-communal country, fulfilling its moral obligations.

[13] Aijaz Ahmed, 'Some Reflections on Urdu', in *Seminar* 359, July 1989, 25.

Part II A TRADITION OF MARTYRDOM

The violence that women faced in the aftermath of Partition is shrouded in many layers of silence. If we hear little about the rape and abduction of women in historical accounts, what we do know about violence in general relates only to men of the 'other' community. There is seldom, if ever, any acknowledgment (except perhaps in fiction) that Hindu and Sikh women could have become the targets of Hindu and Sikh men. Yet in the upheaval and the disruption of everyday life, Hindu men could hardly have become miraculously innocent. One of the myths that survivors increasingly—and tenaciously—hold on to is how communities and families held together in this time of crisis: how then can they admit such disruption from the inside, and by their own members?

It was in 1986 that I first came across stories of family and community violence. At the time, I had no idea of its scale and it was only gradually that I learnt exactly how widespread it had been. Mangal Singh was one of the first people I spoke to when I began to collect stories about Partition. In Amritsar bazar where he lived, Mangal Singh was considered something of a legend. The last surviving brother of three, he had made his way over to Amritsar in August 1947 with nothing but the 'three clothes on my back'. Once over the border, Mangal Singh occupied a piece of vacant land, left behind by Muslims who had moved to Pakistan. 'My heart was heavy,' he said, 'and this space was open, large, empty. I thought let me stay here, this emptiness is good for me, this emptiness and clear space.' Here, he set up home and began the painful process of scratching together a living and starting life again. With small amounts of money borrowed from relatives and friends ('if you needed a few hundred or even thousands of rupees for anything, you were able to get them because people helped out'), he started a shop that sold fans and electrical spare parts. In time, he married and started a family. When I met him, Mangal Singh was in his seventies, a grandfather, surrounded by his large, extended family. His sons ran the business while he spent most of his time with his grandchildren.

Many people had urged me to talk to Mangal Singh, and I was curious about him. His legendary status in his neighbourhood came from the fact that, at Partition, he and his two brothers were said to have killed the women and children of their family, seventeen of them, before setting off across the border. I found this story difficult to believe: how could you kill your own children, your own family? And why? At first Mangal Singh was reluctant to speak to me: 'What is the use of raking all this up again?' he asked. But then, after talking to his family, he changed his mind—they had, apparently, urged him to speak. They felt he had carried this particular burden for too long. I asked him about the family that was gone. He described them thus: 'We were people of substance. In those days people had a lot of children—so we had many women and they had many children . . . there were children, there were girls . . . nephews and others. What a wonderful family it was, whole and happy.'

Why, then, had he and his brothers thought fit to kill them? Mangal Singh refused to accept that the seventeen women and children had been killed. Instead, he used the word 'martyred':

After leaving home we had to cross the surrounding boundary of water. And we were many family members, several women and children who would not have been able to cross the water, to survive the flight. So we killed—they became martyrs—seventeen of our family members, seventeen lives . . . our hearts were heavy with grief for them, grief and sorrow, their grief, our own grief. So we travelled, laden with sorrow, not a paisa to call our own, not a bite of food to eat . . . but we had to leave. Had we not done so, we would have been killed, the times were such . . .

But why kill the women and children, I asked him. Did they not deserve a chance to live? Could they not have got away? He insisted that the women and children had 'offered' themselves up for death because death was preferable to what would almost certainly have happened: conversion and rape. But could they really have offered themselves? Did they not feel any fear, I asked him. He said, angrily:

Fear? Let me tell you one thing. You know this race of Sikhs? There's no fear in them, no fear in the face of adversity. Those people [the ones who had been killed] had no fear. They came down the stairs into the big courtyard of our house that day and they all sat down and they said, you can make martyrs of us — we are willing to become martyrs, and they did. Small children too . . . what was there to fear? *The real fear was one of dishonour. If they had been caught by the Muslims, our honour, their honour would have been sacrificed, lost. It's a question of one's honour . . . if you have pride you do not fear.* (my italics)

But who had the pride, and who the fear? This is a question Mangal Singh was unwilling to address. If accounts such as his were to be believed, the greatest danger that families, and indeed entire communities, perceived was the loss of honour through conversion to the other religion. Violence could be countered, but conversion was somehow seen as different. In many ways their concern was not unfounded: mass and forcible conversions had taken place on both sides. Among the Sikhs particularly, the men felt they could protect themselves but they were convinced that the women would be unable to do so. Their logic was that men could fight, die if necessary, escape by using their wits and their strength, but the women had no such strength to hand. They were therefore particularly vulnerable to conversion. More, women could be raped, impregnated with the seed of the other religion, and in this way not only would they be rendered impure individually but through them the entire community could be polluted, for they would give birth to 'impure' children. While the men could thus save themselves, it was imperative that the women — and through them, the entire race — be 'saved' by them.

A few years after I had spoken to Mangal Singh I began to look at newspaper reports on Partition, searching for similar accounts of family violence. On April 15, 1947 *The Statesman*, an English daily newspaper, had carried the following story:

The story of 90 women of the little village of Thoa Khalsa, Rawalpindi district . . . who drowned themselves by jumping into a well during the recent disturbances has stirred the imagination of the people of the Punjab. They revived the Rajput tradition of self-immolation when their menfolk were no longer able to defend them. They also followed Mr Gandhi's advice to Indian women that in certain circumstances, even suicide was morally preferable to submission.

About a month ago, a communal army armed with sticks, tommy guns and hand grenades, surrounded the village. The villagers defended themselves as best they could . . . but in the end they had to raise the white flag. Negotiations followed. A sum of Rs 10,000 was demanded . . . it was promptly paid. The intruders gave solemn assurances that they would not come back.

The promise was broken the next day. They returned to demand more money and in the process hacked to death 40 of the defenders. Heavily outnumbered, they were unable to resist the onslaught. Their women held a hurried meeting and concluded that all was lost but their honour. Ninety women jumped into the small well. Only three were saved: there was not enough water in the well to drown them all.

The story referred to incidents of communal violence in Punjab which had actually begun some months before Partition, in March 1947. Early in this month, a number of Sikh villages in Rawalpindi district were attacked, over a period of eight days (March 6–13, although in some places sporadic attacks continued up to 15 March). The attacks themselves were said to be in retaliation for Hindu attacks on Muslims in Bihar; also the Sikh political leader, Tara Singh, is said to have made provocative statements in Lahore to which Muslim political leaders had reacted. It is futile to speculate whose was the primary responsibility: the reality is that once it became clear that Partition would take place, both communities, Muslim and Hindu, started to attack members of the other. In Rawalpindi district, in the villages of Thamali, Thoa Khalsa, Mator, Nara and many others, the attacks ended on the 13th of March, when the army moved in and rescued what survivors were left. In many villages the entire population was wiped out; in others, there were a few survivors.

A small community of survivors from these villages lives in Jangpura and Bhogal, two middle-class areas in Delhi. It was from them that I learnt a little more about the 'mass suicide' in Thoa Khalsa described above. Because they could lay claim to this history, survivors from Thoa Khalsa, even today, seemed to have a higher standing among the Rawalpindi community, than the others. People spoke of them, as they had done of Mangal Singh — in tones of awe and respect. Conversely, the two brothers from a neighbouring village who had lost their sisters to abductors were spoken of as if they were the ones who were somehow at fault. Clearly the women's 'sacrifice' had elevated their families, and their communities, to a higher plane. The first person from whom we heard the story of Thoa Khalsa was Basant Kaur, a tall, upright woman in her seventies. According to her, she was one of the women who had jumped into the well, but because it was too full she did not drown. I reproduce below a long excerpt from her interview.

* * *

Basant Kaur:
'I keep telling them these stories . . .'

My name is Basant Kaur. My husband's name was Sant Raja Singh. We came away from our houses on March 12, and on the 13th we stayed out, in the village. At first, we tried to show our strength, and then we realized that this would not work, so we joined the morcha to go away. We left our home in Thoa Khalsa on the 12th. For three or four days we were trapped inside our houses, we couldn't get out, though we used to move across the roofs of houses and that way we could get out a bit. One of our people had a gun, we used that, and two or three of their people died. I lost a brother-in-law. He died from a bullet they fired. It hit him and he died. So we kept the gun handy. Then there were fires all around, raging fires, and we were no match for them. I had a jeth, my older brother-in-law, he had a son, he kept asking give me afim (opium), mix it in water and I will take it. My jeth killed his mother, his sister, his wife, his daughter, and his uncle. My daughter was also killed. We went into the morcha inside the village, we all left our houses and collected together in the centre of the village, inside the sardaran di haveli, where there was also a well. It was Lajjawanti's house. The sardar, her husband, had died some time ago but his wife and other women of the house were there. Some children also. They all came out. Then we all talked and said we don't want to become Musalmaan, we would rather die. So everyone was given a bit of afim, they were told, you keep this with you . . . I went upstairs, and when I came down there was my husband, my jeth's son, my jethani, her daughters, my jeth, my grandsons, three granddaughters. They were all killed so that they would not fall into the hands of Musalmaans. One girl from our village, she had gone off with the Musalmaans. She was quite beautiful, and everyone got worried that if one has gone, they will take all our girls away . . . so it was then that they decided to kill the girls. My jeth, his name is Harbans Singh, he killed his wife, his daughter, his son . . . he was small, only eight days old. Then my sister-in-law was killed, her son and her daughter, and then on the 14th of March we came to Jhelum. The vehicles came and took us, and we stayed there for about a month and then we came to Delhi.

In Delhi there were four of my brothers, they read about this — the camp — in the papers and they came and found us. Then, gradually, over a period of time the children grew up and became older and things sorted themselves out. My parents were from Thamali. Hardly anyone survived from there. You know that family of Gurmeet's, they had two sisters, the Musalmaans took them away. It's not clear whether they died or were taken away, but their bodies were never found . . . Someone died this way, someone that, someone died here and someone there, and no one got to know. My parents were burnt alive.

That whole area was like jungle, it was village area. One of my brothers survived and came away, one sister. They too were helped by a Musalmaan, there were some good ones, and they helped them — he hid them away in his house — and then put them into the vehicles that came, the military ones. The vehicles went to Mator and other places. In Mator, Shah Nawaz made sure no harm came to them. People from Nara managed to get away, but on the way they were all killed. Then my brothers read the papers and got to know. My husband, he killed his daughter, his niece, his sister, and a grandson. He killed them with a kirpan. My jeth's son killed his mother, his wife, his daughter, and a grandson and granddaughter, all with a pistol. And then, my jeth, he doused himself with kerosene and jumped into a fire.

Many girls were killed. Then Mata Lajjawanti, she had a well near her house, in a sort of garden. Then all of us jumped into that, some hundred . . . eighty-four . . . girls and boys. All of us. Even boys, not only children, but grown-up boys. I also went in, I took my two children, and then we jumped in — I had some jewellery on me, things in my ears, on my wrists, and I had fourteen rupees on me. I took all that and threw it into the well, and then I jumped in, but . . . it's like when you put rotis into a tandoor, and if it is too full, the ones near the top, they don't cook, they have to be taken out. So the well filled up, and we could not drown . . . the children survived. Later, Nehru went to see the well, and the English then closed it up, the well that was full of bodies. The pathans took out those people who were at the top of the well — those who died, died, and those who were alive, they pulled out.

Then they went away—and what was left of our village was saved, except for that one girl who went away.

I was frightened. Of course, I was . . . we were also frightened that we would be taken away by the Musalmaans. In our village, already, in the well that was inside the village, girls had jumped in. In the middle of the night they had jumped in. This happened where the morcha was. The hundred . . . eighty-four women who jumped in they were just outside, some two-hundred yards away from Lajjawanti's house. In the morcha, the crowd had collected in Lajjawanti's house. She was some seventy, seventy-five years old. A tall, strapping woman. She did a lot of seva of all the women, she her-self jumped into the well. Many people were killed in the morcha, and the Musalmaans climbed on top to kill others, and then many came and tried to kill people with guns, one of them put a gun to my jeth's chest and . . . and we began to jump in. The others had died earlier, and we were in the morcha, the well was some distance away from Lajjawanti's house, in a garden. There were two wells, one inside and one outside, in the garden. My nanan and her daughter, they were both lying there . . . close by there was a ladle, I mixed afim in it, and gave it to them, and she put it in her mouth . . . she died, and I think the village dogs must have eaten her. We had no time to perform any last rites. An hour or so later, the trucks came . . . just an hour.

She did path, and said don't throw me away, let me have this afim, she took god's name and then she died. We had afim because my jeth's son used to eat it, and he had it with him and he got more and gave it to everyone. My jeth's son, his daugher-in-law and his daughter, they died in Jhelum later, when we were going to the Dinia camp, on March 15 or so. The camp was close to the Jhelum. Four days we fought, and we remained strong, then around the 12th we got into the morcha, on the 13th our people were killed, and then the trucks came in the evening and took us to Rawat, a village.

They brought us there [to the well]. From there . . . you know there was no place . . . nothing to eat, some people were eating close by but where could I give the children anything from . . . I had barely a few paise . . . my elder son had a duvanni (two annas) with him, we thought we could use that . . . my brother's children were also hungry . . . but then they said the duvanni was khoti, damaged, unusable . . . [weeping] such difficulties . . . nothing to eat . . . we had to fill their stomachs . . . today they would have been ranis . . . so many of them, jethanis, children . . . I was the youngest . . . now I sit at home and my children are out working and I keep telling them these stories . . .

they are stories after all . . . and you tell them and tell them until you lose consciousness . . .

* * *

They have told them, don't listen to her stories . . . We mark the day, 13th March in Bhogal, martyrs day . . . what did Gurmeet tell you? Did he tell you about Thamali? Thamali was my parent's home. They took young girls away from there—did he not tell you? In our village there was one temple and one gurudwara, but no masjid. The Muslims came from outside. In Thamali there were a few Musalmaans, those who ground wheat, grain, channas . . . They used to participate in some customs, it was a sort of ritual. They did nothing, they used to eat our salt.

My husband? My nephew killed him, my nephew. Because they had killed the girls, his daughter, sister, grandchildren, with their kirpans, and then my jeth's son had a pistol and he killed his mother, his uncle . . . then my nephew killed my husband with a pistol. He had a small daughter, one-and-a-half years old, she also ate pistol shots. Yes, my husband was killed by my nephew as I told you, he killed him because my husband said he did not want to become a Musalmaan. Imagine . . . fifteen, twenty thousand people, and we had four guns. Those also they took away. The same thing happened in Thamali, they had collected all the weapons, but then they had to part with them. Then they killed them. My nephew was young and strong. My jeth's son . . . he had shops. It was not this boy's father who died from burning, but my other, older jeth. I had eight jeths. This boy, he also killed himself after this. I have a son who killed his wife, his daughter, a small son . . . one jeth came to Rangabad, where his son was, one died from burning, another one—the eldest—kept watching all that was going on, he did not say anything, people thought why kill this man, he has no children, no daughter, no son, nothing. Two of my jeths had no children . . . All this had happened before, and then we jumped into the well. All this had happened earlier, some things happened on the 12th, some on the 13th and then, as night fell, the military trucks came to take us away. Four women were pulled out of the well, they held them by the arms and pulled them out, the Musalmaans. Four women, one was really beautiful, she had eight children, she was saved. She threw her children in and then jumped in after them, but she was saved . . . You see, you work it out, many died, but when the water could not rise any more, those near the top were saved. Wives, grandchildren, daughters-in-law, Bahmanis, we had some higher castes in our village, their women, with their children . . . later, Nehru came to our village, he wept. Then they closed down this well, and later, they went with the military to open it. Some months later, at the time I was coming to Delhi. From Dinia camp, my brothers brought me. My brothers were here, they used to run trucks.

In our village there were a few Musalmaan families, but we never had any problem. We lived together, there were marriages, we would attend them, we lived fairly close to each other. Close by there were other villages where you would find Musalmaans, Tihai, Saintha, Sadiok, Sadda, small villages. I was born in Peshawar. I was about nineteen or twenty when I came to Thamali, though I was married in Thoa Khalsa. My father was ninety years old when he was killed. He was in Thamali when he retired, he kept taking a pension for a long time. Around forty or forty-five rupees. Just before 1947 his pension went up to ninety rupees. My father said, child, all the other sisters have gone, you are the only one left, it's time for you to go. I said no need, I'll go when I need to—after all we lived well so . . . I also take a pension now, but it's in my husband's name, not mine. Why should I lie? We brought four boris of sugar into the morcha, two of chuaras, boris of moongphalis, and a few other things, you see you used to buy wholesale, so we had mountains of stuff with us, gur, rice, etc. The Jhelum river was some twelve miles from us.

There were Hindu houses in our village, maybe thirty, forty or fifty. And the rest of the village was with the sardars. There were twenty or twenty-five houses of Bahmans, Thoa was like a town, it was quite big. The Hindus did their own work, the same sort of things, shops, cloth shops, hundreds of things. The same give and take. The Sikhs were all kattar Sikhs, they all had pattas from Maharaja Ranjit Singh's time.

There was a wave of violence, it began in Rawalpindi and Lahore. Then it was as if they had decided on a day, let's finish them off on this day. Things happened in Rawalpindi, but no one got killed, all the deaths took place in the villages around. At first, I think it was in Rawat, the place where there used to be a committee [a market] of donkeys, of horses—you don't understand what a committee is do you? Child, it was a mela, people would come from far away to Rawat to sell their horses and donkeys, there was a thana there also. The violence was then in Choa, Thamali, Thoa, Nara, Bewal—they did not leave anyone here, they took all the weapons . . . We had four guns, they took them away. There were two more, with two men, a servant and another who had come on leave from the military, they too had weapons. From Rawat, things spread to Pindi, and then it came to our villages.

*   *   *

The abduction and rape of women, the physical mutilation of their bodies, the tattooing of their sexual organs with symbols of the other religion—these acts had been universally condemned. But no mention was made of family violence by anyone—neither the families, nor the State, nor indeed by historians. And yet, its scale was not small. Virtually every village had similar stories. Gurmeet Singh, a survivor from village Thamali, also in the same district, described their flight:

> On the night of the 12th of March we left at 4 A.M., in the early hours of the morning. Our own family, all the people, we collected them in the gurudwara and got some men to guard them. We gave them orders to kill all the young girls, and as for the gurudwara, to pour oil on it and set it on fire.
>
> We decided this among ourselves. We felt totally helpless—so many people had collected, we were completely surrounded. If you looked around, all you could see was a sea of people in all four directions . . . wherever the eye could reach, there were men. After all, you get frightened . . . people collected together to comfort each other. But then we found we were helpless . . . we had no weapons, whatever little we had they had taken. Then they took a decision in the gurudwara that all the young girls and women . . . two or three persons were assigned the task of finishing them off. Those in the gurudwara were asked to set it on fire with those inside . . . first, we killed all the young girls with our own hands; kerosene was poured over them inside the gurudwara and the place was set on fire . . . women and children, where could they go?

Over the years, as I spoke to more and more people, both men and women, I was to come across this response again. The tone adopted by *The Statesman* report above was similar to that adopted by families when they spoke of the hundreds of women they had 'martyred' in order to 'save' the purity of the religion. Some time after we met Basant Kaur,

I came across Bir Bahadur Singh, her son. He gave us a more detailed account of incidents of community violence in Thoa Khalsa.

In Gulab Singh's haveli twenty-six girls had been put aside. First of all my father, Sant Raja Singh, when he brought his daughter, he brought her into the courtyard to kill her, first of all he prayed, he did ardaas, saying sachche badshah, we have not allowed your Sikhi to get stained, and in order to save it we are going to sacrifice our daughters, make them martyrs. Please forgive us.

Then there was one man who used to do coolie work in our village. He moved forward and . . . caught my father's feet and he said, bhapaji, first you kill me because my knees are swollen and I won't be able to run away and the Musalmaans will catch hold of me and make me into a Musalmaan. So my father immediately hit him with his kirpan and took his head off. Then Nand Singh Dheer, he said to my father, Raja Singa, please martyr me first because my sons live in Lahore . . . do you think I will allow the Musalmaans to cut this beard of mine and make me go to Lahore as a sheikh? For this reason, kill me. My father then killed him. He killed two, and the third was my sister, Maan Kaur . . . my sister came and sat in front of my father, and I stood there, right next to him, clutching onto his kurta as children do. I was clinging to him . . . but when my father swung the kirpan (vaar kita) perhaps some doubt or fear came into his mind, or perhaps the kirpan got stuck in her dupatta . . . no one can say. It was such a frightening, such a fearful scene. Then my sister, with her own hand she removed her plait and pulled it forward . . . and my father with his own hands moved her dupatta aside and then he swung the kirpan and her head and neck rolled off and fell . . . there . . . far away. I crept downstairs, weeping, sobbing and all the while I could hear the regular swing and hit of the kirpans . . . twenty-five girls were killed, they were cut. One girl, my taya's daughter-in-law, who was pregnant . . . somehow she didn't get killed and later my taya's son shot her with a pistol . . . but she was saved. She told us, kill me, I will not survive. I have a child in my womb. She was wounded in the stomach, there was a large hole from which blood was flowing. Then my mother and my uncle sat together and Harnam Kaur—her name was Harnam Kaur—she said, give me some afim (opium). We arranged for afim, people used to eat it those days . . . in a ladle we mixed afim with saliva . . . she said the *japji sahib path* . . . just as the *japji sahib bhog* took place so did her bhog. Completely as if she was pre-pared for death . . . few people can do that . . . she had death in her control and it was only when she wanted it that death took her. For nearly half an hour she did the *path* . . . half an hour and then as she spoke her last shlok she also ended. She knew she would die . . . so much control . . . over death.

Later, Bir Bahadur Singh also witnessed the incident in which women jumped into a well to take their own lives, rather than let their 'hon-our' be put to test. This incident has today acquired almost an iconic significance by being fixed in a television film, *Tamas,* where numbers of tall, upright Punjabi women stride determinedly and proudly towards the well which is to receive their sacrifice for the sake of their religion. The reality must have been rather different. Descriptions from survivors (most of whom are male), however, tend to re-emphasize the 'heroic' and 'valorous' aspects of these tragic deaths. In Bir Bahadur's words:

> . . . at the well Sardarni Gulab Kaur . . . in my presence she said sachche badshah, let us be able to save our girls . . . this incident of the twenty-five girls of our household had already taken place . . . so she knew that Sant Raja Singh had killed his daughters and other women of his house-hold . . . those who are left we should not risk their lives and allow them to be taken away. So, at the well, after having talked among themselves and decided, they said, we are thirsty, we need water, so the Musalmaans took them to the well . . . I was sitting with my mother, this incident of the twenty-five women had taken place . . . so sitting at the well, Mata Lajjawanti, who was also called Sardarni Gulab Kaur, she said two words, she jumped into the well and some eighty women followed her . . . they also jumped in. The well filled up completely; one woman whose name is Basant Kaur, six children born of her womb died in that well, but she sur-vived. She jumped in four times, but the well had filled up . . . she would jump in, then come out, then jump in again . . . she would look at her children, at herself . . . till today, she is alive.

Some negotiations had clearly taken place between the attackers and the victims in most of the villages. Kulwant Singh, another survivor, this time from Thamali, remembers a meeting at which an understanding was reached (between the two communities) that 'we would be let off'. According to Kulwant Singh, the amount negotiated was between sixteen and thirty thousand rupees and the laying down of all weapons. Having done this, 'at night they started fires and some of our sisters, daughters and others, in order to save their honour, their relatives, our veers, they martyred them and in this way at that time some of our women and children were killed. In the gurudwara there were piles of bodies.' There is no record of the numbers of women and children who were killed by the men of their own families, their own communities. Unlike in the case of abducted women, here families did not report the deaths of their women, for they themselves were responsible for them. But while abducted women then entered the realm of silence, women who were killed by families, or who took their own lives, entered the realm of martyrdom.

Stories of this kind of mass suicide, or of women being killed by their own families, are legion. Today, half a century later, these and other stories still survive, and are held up, not only as examples of the bravery and manliness of the Sikh race (although it is the women who died, nonetheless, the decision to sacrifice their lives—attributed, in this instance, to the men—is seen as the defining act of bravery, for it also 'saves' them from a fate worse than death), but also as examples of the heroism of the Sikh women who 'gave up' their lives 'willingly' for the sake of their religion. In the remembrance rituals that take place in gurudwaras these incidents are recounted again and again each year to an audience of men, women and children and the women are exhorted to remember the sacrifice and bravery of their sisters and to cast themselves in the same mould. Should the quam, the race or the dharam, the religion, ever be in danger, they are told, your duty is clear. The 'sacrifice' of the many women who died such deaths during Partition is compared, as in the *Statesman* article, to the extreme 'sacrifice' of Rajput women who undertook mass immolation when they lost their husbands in war. It is not unusual to draw a direct and almost linear link between that sacrifice and this. Talk of the martyrdom of women is almost always accompanied by talk of those women whose lives were saved, at the cost of those which were lost, and although there may not be any direct condemnation, it is clear that those who got away are in some ways seen as being inferior to those who 'offered' themselves up to death to save their religion. In response to a question about whether there were any women left in Thoa Khalsa after the mass 'suicide' of ninety women, Bir Bahadur Singh said:

> Yes, many women were still left in our village. Mostly our family women died, and then the ones who jumped into the well. But the others were saved. Because the Musalmaans saw that they were killing themselves. The ones who sacrificed . . . if the women of our family had not been killed, and those who jumped into the well had not taken their own lives, the ones who were left alive would not have been alive today.

'The ones who were left alive would not have been alive today.' Clearly, for Bir Bahadur Singh, as for many men, the words 'being alive' (inasmuch as they related to women) had little to do with their literal meaning. What would have happened to women if the others had not 'given up' their lives? In all likelihood, they would have been raped, perhaps abducted and further violated, almost certainly converted. All of these were tantamount to death. But the sacrifice of some women saved the lives of the others—women and men. The implication all along is that the power of such a supreme sacrifice worked to frighten away the aggressors, that once they saw how strong the women were, how determined to preserve the honour of the community, they backed off in the face of such power. And through such a supreme sacrifice the women merely lost their lives—or exchanged them for an eternal life of martyrdom—while the community managed to retain its honour. Implied in these accounts was the assumption that the honour of the community lay in not allowing its women to be violated. In normal times, men can be the guardians of such honour through their responsibility of guarding the woman's sexuality. But at abnormal times men need to fight to retaliate in attacks and the best way of guarding their honour is to not allow the women to be violated.

As Bir Bahadur said: 'My father took the first step, and then the rest of the work was done by Sardarni Lajjawanti . . . Mata Lajjawanti . . .

saved all the other Sikhs by sacrificing her life . . . this made around one hundred girls.'

And yet, things were not always so clear cut, for when it came to saving themselves, all sorts of other arguments were brought in. In each case, however, the common factor was the dispensability of women. In many villages where negotiations had taken place, often women were traded in for freedom. In Thoa Khalsa too, as survivors tell it, there was one particular woman who was said to be involved with a Muslim. Before the attacks actually began, the attackers asked that she be given to them as the price of freedom for the entire village. As Bir Bahadur said:

> It was like this, when all the fighting started, then there were also attempts at settlements. After all, a fight means a settlement. So the Musalmaans came to make a settlement. They said they would allow us to stay on in our homes if we gave them that girl. There was one Musalmaan, he was quite strong. He was a kind of loafer, he used to work the land, but he wanted this girl. He had some kind of relationship with her. They kept asking for this girl, saying if you give her to us, we'll send the Musalmaans away. *And people were discussing this, saying she is a bad girl anyway, she has a relationship with him, what's the use of keeping her? You see, when it comes to saving your life, nothing counts.* (my italics) So a sort of decision was taken to give her away . . . At the time, there was no question of what she wanted. It was a question of the honour of the village.

In the end, the woman was not given away, and the negotiations failed. Later, the Muslims came and took her away from a transit camp where the survivors of Thoa Khalsa were housed. From all accounts, she went willingly, and was married into a Muslim family. Throughout his account Bir Bahadur continued to reiterate the sacrifice made by the men and women of his particular family. He, his family, other surivors of Thoa Khalsa, all feel they owe their lives to those who died:

> All around us there were fires. What can a person do? I think really all honour to those people who killed their own children, who jumped into wells. And they saved us . . . you take any household of martyrs and you will find it will take root and grow. Blood is such a thing, that as you water a plant, a tree, so also the tree grows, so does the martyr's household.

Recalling the time he said: 'Even today when I remember it . . . I cry, it helps to lighten my heart. A father who kills his daughter, how much of a victim, how helpless he must be . . .'

* * *

It is not my contention that the women who died thus in family and community violence were all victims, forced into taking their own lives, or murdered by their kinsmen. Or that they were mere victims of a 'patriarchal consensus' arrived at by their men and the elders of the community. But how can we ever arrive at the 'truth' of these incidents? As with abducted women, there is no way in which we can easily recover the voices of women themselves. With the exception of Basant Kaur, all the accounts I have quoted from above are by men, and clearly, we cannot unproblematically take their voices to reflect what the women felt. I think the lines between choice and coercion must have been more blurred than these accounts reflect. For example, when Bir Bahadur Singh spoke of a few women who jumped into the well several times and who survived, he made no mention that one of them was actually his mother, Basant Kaur. So that, when she described the incident with herself as the protagonist, we did not, at first, believe her. Later, when it was confirmed that she was indeed the same woman, I could only conclude that Bir Bahadur had not mentioned that she was his mother because in having escaped death, she could not be classed with the women who had, in fact, died. Much easier, then, to speak of the sister who died an 'honourable' death, than the mother who survived.

In Thoa Khalsa, and its surrounding areas, the attacks had continued for some eight days, and it was on the last day that the mass drowning took place. For these few days virtually everyone in the village was aware of the many discussions that went on. As the survivors tell it, although the men led the discussions, some women were involved in them. Key among these, in Thoa, was Sardarni Gulab Kaur, otherwise known as Mata Lajjawanti, a fairly important figure in the village, as her husband, Gulab Singh, had been. As survivors tell it, not only did she take the decision, but she also 'fearlessly' led the women to the well, upholding the tradition of the strong, upright, courageous Punjabi woman. If the women were aware of the discussions, perhaps even involved in them, can we then surmise that in taking their own lives they were acting upon a perceived (or rather, misperceived) notion of the good of their community? Did their deaths corroborate the ideology—and were they a part of this ideology?—that the honour of the community lay in 'protecting' its women from the patriarchal violence of an alien community? The natural protectors by this reckoning are the men, who at this particular moment are unable to offer such protection. Because the women knew this, can one then suggest that they could well have consented to their own deaths, in order to preserve the honour of the community? Were they then consenting victims/agents of the patriarchal consensus I have spoken of above? Where in their 'decision' did 'choice' begin and 'coercion' end? What, in other words, does their silence hide?

Is there any satisfactory way of arriving at the truth of these things? Choice, after all, is not simple to reconstruct, and it might well be said that my reading of its conflicted existence back into this incident is dictated more by my involvement in the contemporary discourse of feminism, than by the incident itself. Yet, for me, this incident, and the many others like it, are important for they shed light on much more than the question of choice or coercion, of whether the women were victims or agents of their fate. I am struck by the fact that nowhere in the different discourses on Partition do such incidents count as violent incidents, that somehow when we speak of the violence of Partition, we do not touch upon the violence within ourselves, within families, within communities. Instead, such acts are represented, in so much of what we say and do, as valorous acts, shorn of the violence, and indeed coercion, that must have sent so many women to their deaths. Nor do we ever consider the ramifications, in terms of the further violence they can and do lead to, of such acts; or indeed the symbolic significance they come to acquire over the years, and the use they are put to to instigate further violence.

One of the myths about violence of the sort we have seen in Partition is that it is largely male: that women, in times of sectarian strife, are the victims of violence, not its perpetrators, not its agents. Much of this is, however, predicated on how we understand violence: I believe that our notions of violence are so patriarchal that we find it difficult to think in terms of women, those custodians of the domestic sphere, as violent beings. Yet, whether the women who died in Thoa Khalsa actually offered themselves up for death or not, the manner in which they 'chose' to die was no less violent, though certainly different, from what one might cynically term the routine, and visible, violence of Partition. And further, as long as violence can be located somewhere outside, a distance away from the boundaries of the family and the community, it can be contained. It is for this reason, I feel, that during Partition, and in so much of the recall of Partition, violence is seen as relating only to the 'other'. This obscures the very important fact that many women of Hindu and Sikh communities must have seen the men of their own communities as being perpetrators of violence against them—for just as there were 'voluntary' suicides, there were also mass murders.

Women faced violence both from their own families and their own communities. I would like to end this account of family and community violence with a story of a woman, Prakashvanti, whom I met in the Gandhi Vanita Ashram at Jalandhar. One of the three remaining Partition survivors in the ashram, Prakashvanti's story goes as follows: she and her husband and small child lived in Sheikupura. In 1947, she was some twenty years old. When Partition began to seem like a reality, Hindus from her village gathered together in the local rice mill for safety. Shortly afterwards, the mill came under attack, and the attackers began to loot the place. Prakashvanti's husband came to her and suggested he kill her, else, he told her, 'they will dishonour you'. She remembers little after that, except that she was hit by her husband, and she lost consciousness. The attackers clearly left her for dead and, later, when she recovered, she and two girls hid behind some sacks, waiting for the attackers to leave. Later, Prakashvanti found the body of her husband, and her child lying with many others. Did she not feel anger at him, I asked her. She said: 'what could he do? He was alone.' She did not defend her husband, but she did attempt to explain what she saw as the 'logic' of his action. I have often wondered whether that was what the women whose deaths I have spoken of above told themselves. But for those who recount these stories today as stories of heroism and valour, of sacrifice and honour, there is another, more realistic agenda.

As we can see in the remembrance rituals for the Thoa Khalsa incident, for men, the potential for violence on the part of their own women, or their agency in this respect, had to be contained and circumscribed. The women could not, therefore, be *named* as violent beings. This is why their actions are narrated and sanctified by the tones of heroic, even otherworldly, valour. Such narratives are meant to keep women within their aukat, their ordained boundary, which is one that defines them as non-violent. Their actions are thus re-located into the comfortably symbolic realm of sacrifice — their role within the home anyway — for the community, victimhood and even non-violence. To actively remember these women as symbols of the honour of the family, community and nation is then also to divest them of both violence and agency.

Part III BIR BAHADUR SINGH

'You take any household of martyrs and you will find it will take root and grow . . .'

The reader will by now be familiar with Bir Bahadur, whose words I
have quoted extensively above. I have, nonetheless, chosen to include the
full text of his interview here, because there are many other things Bir
Bahadur spoke about, and which struck me as important and significant, which I have not referred to above. This interview was carried out
in 1990 in Delhi. At the time, Bir Bahadur was in his sixties. As with
many people, I met Bir Bahadur quite by accident. For some months,
Sudesh and I had been talking to people, survivors of the Rawalpindi
riots that had taken place in March of 1947 — in Bhogal and Jangpura.
As often happens when you are talking to people of a community, one
person leads you to another, and that contact to another and so on. At
first someone directed us to Bir Bahadur's mother, Basant Kaur. She lived
in a newish house in Bhogal. And it was during one of our interviews
with Basant Kaur that we met Bir Bahadur. A tall, striking man with a
flowing white beard, Bir Bahadur ran a small, but successful general mer-
chant shop in Delhi. Of all the people we spoke to, Bir Bahadur was the
one most directly involved in politics. Apart from being a member of
the Shiromani Gurudwara Prabandhak Committee (SGPC), he had been
active in helping Sikh families in the aftermath of Indira Gandhi's assassination in Delhi. As well, he seemed to be in regular contact with a
number of Sikh politicians and to be closely connected with them. Because of the suspicion that came to attach to many Sikhs after 1984, Bir
Bahadur was arrested and jailed on grounds of being a terrorist. He describes the incident in detail in this interview, and brings out, starkly and
poignantly, the sense of betrayal that he and many other Sikhs felt after
1984. Bir Bahadur and his family suffered considerable material losses in
1984 and, in this interview, his sense of betrayal comes from two things:
the fact that none of the guilty had, till the time of writing, been punished, and the fact that the government chose to ignore and do nothing
for 'those people whose blood was spilled to make this country independent.' By this he means the Sikhs who came across at Partition, and who

both fought the 'other' as well as sacrificed their own families. Sikhs like his father, who is mentioned in the interview as a victim, someone burdened with the knowledge of having killed his own kin for the honour of the community and country. And equally, Sikhs like his sister Maan Kaur, who 'became a martyr' in the cause of the Sikh religion at the hands of his father.

When I first listened to Bir Bahadur's story, and every time I have gone back to it since, I have been struck by the combination of pride, grief and sense of real loss with which he describes the incidents relating to the deaths of women. His sister, Maan Kaur, killed by his father is, for him, not only a woman who gave up her life to save the honour of the community, but also one of the people whose sacrifice should occupy a place in the struggle for independence of this country. In the remembrance ritual that takes place in the local gurudwara every year it is often Bir Bahadur who comes and recounts the stories of women who 'killed' themselves, and of those who were killed. These valorous acts of martyrdom are what, for Bir Bahadur, set Thoa Khalsa apart from other Sikh villages in the area. He seems to imply that the men of Thoa did not allow their women to be abducted, that they did not show this sign of weakness. Instead, they avoided this by making the women into martyrs.

On one of the occasions that we met Bir Bahadur we were carrying with us the book that I have referred to earlier, which has a district-by-district listing of all the Hindu and Sikh women who were abducted in Pakistan. We wanted to ask him about this book, whether he recognized any of the names in it. But before we could do so, Bir Bahadur asserted that there were no names from Thoa in our book, since the men of Thoa had protected their women. This is not correct of course. Thoa Khalsa does figure in the book, as do many other villages, but we realized that it was essential for Bir Bahadur to deny rape and abduction in Thoa in order to justify the 'martyrdom' of the women: if the specific purpose of the 'martyrdom' had been to prevent rape and abduction, and if those had taken place anyway, it would have been pointless. So many deaths would have gone to waste.

In Bir Bahadur's statements there is no sense of censure, no questioning of the logic that makes men kill people of their own families. One of the stories often told about Partition is how families tried to barter their daughters for freedom. Bir Bahadur describes one such story when the villagers decided to give a girl away in order to secure their freedom. 'When it comes to saving your life,' he said, 'nothing else counts.' They were stopped from doing so by Bir Bahadur's father, who then took the decision to 'martyr' the girls and women. I was struck by the fact that in all of this Bir Bahadur saw his father as a victim, as someone who was helpless (majboor), an instrument of God's will. When he tried to kill his own daughter, the father did not succeed the first time round. He tried again, this time successfully: in Bir Bahadur's eyes both the father and the daughter knew what they were doing. Although no words were exchanged between them, 'just the language of the kirpan was enough'.

Bir Bahadur also speaks movingly of the ways in which Hindus and Muslims related to each other. He places the responsibility for Partition at the door of the Hindus who, according to him (and he includes Sikhs in this), did not even give the Muslims the consideration due to a dog. Nonetheless, at a later stage in his life, Bir Bahadur turned more centrally to politics: I have not met him for many years but I believe that he is now a member of the BJP (the Bharatiya Janata Party, a right-wing majoritarian party). This would explain why, despite his initial openness about Hindu-Muslim relations, he comes back to asserting the age-old BJP arguments about the rapid increases in population among the Muslims. Throughout his interview, I am fascinated by the co-existence of seemingly paradoxical situations: first, his identification with Hindus and his recognition of how they treated Muslims; then his growing sense of a Sikh identity and a simultaneous sense of alienation from what he sees as a Hindu State; then his empathy, at Partition, with Muslims and his fear that now they will take over the Indian State; and underneath this, somewhere, his political loyalties and his religious identity. To me, this interview became important for all of these reasons.

* * *

Bir Bahadur Singh:

My name is Bir Bahadur Singh. My father's name is Sant Raja Singh. My village is Thoa Khalsa, zilla Rawalpindi, tahsil Kahuta. Our village was in district Rawalpindi, it used to be seen as a model village because in the whole area, if you left out Gujjar Khan, Thoa Khalsa was the largest tahsil.

There were wholesale shops and approximately fifty to sixty large traders. And the smaller villages that surrounded ours . . . they had no shops, these were Musalmaan villages, that was why everyone would come to Thoa Khalsa to purchase things and jathas and jathas would come for this. For example, a woman from one of the Musalmaan villages, if she was going to buy something, she would not go every day to make her purchases, instead she would buy provisions for a whole month, because otherwise the markets were quite far for them. And some twenty, twenty-five men and women would get together and come to get their provisions, and there would be a good crowd, like in a kasbah. In Thoa Khalsa . . . the main thing about this place was that Sant Attar Singh ji, who is from Mustawana Sahib, he made Gurudwara Dukh Bhajni Sahib here. This gurudwara was very well known and respected and people would come to it from far away. Twice a year there used to be a mela there and thousands of people, both Hindu and Sikh, would collect for this. Even Musalmaans would be there in large numbers, Musalmaans also paid homage to this saint. The place where I belong, Thoa Khalsa, close to that there is one Saintha village, in this village the population is some thirty or forty families. Along with that there are some smaller villages. In Saintha my father had a shop, and my early upbringing was in that village. My teachers were Musalmaans and our house was the only Sikh house there, the rest of the village was Musalmaan.

. . . In our area the people who used to live in towns, in the kasbahs, there were small villages where they would go to set up shop, and they used to live there with their families. And I remember that from the time I was admitted into school, in the first class, till class five, I studied there . . . There was a Musalmaan woman, dadi dadi we used to call her. Her name was ma Hussaini, and I would go and sit on one side in her lap, and her granddaughter would sit on the other side. I used to pull her plait and push her away and she would catch hold of my jura, my hair, and push me away. I would say she is my dadi and she would say she is my dadi. Look at this: that girl was small when we used to play together, I was in the fifth class, she was younger than me, and now her son has become a young man, he was in Dubai and from there he wrote to me, calling me mamuji. The girl wasn't even married then, and her son is forty now, he saw my letter in his grandparents' home and asked who is this. He was told by his mama that this is also your mama, your uncle. Such good relations we had that if there was any function that we had, then we used to call Musalmaans to our homes, they would eat in our houses, but we would not eat in theirs, and this is a bad thing, which I realize now. If they would come to our houses, we would have two utensils in one corner of our house, and we would tell them, pick these up and eat in them and they would then wash them and keep them aside and this was such a terrible thing. This was the reason Pakistan was created. If we went to their houses and took part in their weddings and ceremonies, they used to really respect and honour us. They would give us uncooked food, ghee, atta, dal, whatever sabzis they had, chicken and even mutton, all raw. And our dealings with them were so low that I am even ashamed to say it. A guest comes to our house, and we say to him bring those utensils and wash them, and if my mother or sister have to give him food, they will more or less throw the roti from such a distance, fearing that they may touch the dish and become polluted . . . the Musalmaans dealt with us so well and our dealings with them were so low. We, if a Musalmaan was coming along the road, and we shook hands with him, and we had, say, a box of food or something in our hand, that would then become soiled and we would not eat it: if we are holding a dog in one hand and food in the other, there's nothing wrong with that food. But if a Musalmaan would come and shake hands our dadis and mothers would say son, don't eat this food, it has become polluted. Such were the dealings: how can it be that there are two people living in the same village, and one treats the other with such respect and the other doesn't even give him the consideration due to a dog? How can this be? They would call our mothers and sisters didi, they would refer to us as brothers, sisters, fathers, and when we needed them they were always there to help, yet when they came to our houses, we treated them so badly. This is really terrible. And this was the reason Pakistan was made. They thought, what is this, what has happened? How can this be?

Two people living in the same village and one loves the other so much while the other hates him so much that he will not eat food cooked by his hand and will not even touch him . . . if a Musalmaan shook hands with you and you had something in your hand, you could take it that the thing was finished, destroyed . . .

We don't have such dealings with our lower castes as Hindus and Sikhs did with the Musalmaans. I'm really saying that today I feel ashamed of this. I went to a Musalmaan's house and he asked what will you eat. I said what will I not eat, you tell me. I'll eat everything. What is there in eating and drinking? If you go to someone's house and they hate you so much that you

have to pick up your own plate and go and have yourself served in this way . . .
am I a human being that I will eat in your house like this?

Brahmanism was there in Sikhi also, it was there and we were all caught
in this dharam kanta, this dilemma that was why the hatred kept growing.
Otherwise there was so much love, so much love that you . . . if you look at
these stories I tell you of my younger days, till today I get letters . . . even our
own first cousins, real relations, were not so close to us as our Musalmaan
friends. It was only when we came here after Pakistan was created that we
realized that the woman we used to call our dadi was not our real dadi, she
was a Musalmani. She used to have a garden of fig trees, and she had kept one
tree for me and she would not even give the fruit of that tree to the masjid,
she had reserved it for me. Her grandson also died saving me. I was small,
and you know the ploughs that kisans have . . . to dig up the ground . . . the
man stands on his legs, like this, and there is a bull in front. I was standing
once between his legs, his name was Arif . . . and a snake went past and sort of
leapt towards me, as I was standing between his legs. Arif was without anything on his feet . . . you know kisans don't have shoes or anything, and he did
like this and the snake bit him. Only one grandson she had and he too died.
But she never once said a word, never a word of blame . . . in fact she used
to say that my grandson's sprit is alive in this young boy . . . so God-fearing
a woman was she. Till today in my life I have never seen a woman like this.
She used to use the plough herself . . . yes, herself. Her husband had died
while she was still young. And Musalmaans often marry a second time, but
she is the only woman I have seen in my whole life who did not do that, who
could and would do everything with her hands, she is the only woman I have
seen who would and could work a plough . . . otherwise women generally do
not touch the plough. Yes, in Punjab you see them on tractors. Now they
even drive them. So in this way we had very close links and relationships with
Musalmaans. This is only brahmanvad, and politics which have brought ruin
on us. Brahmins have cast such spells, bound people in such devious webs
that perhaps for the next hundred generations to come we will have to suffer
this punishment they have made for us. I feel that our elders were so guilty
towards the Musalmaans, that they sinned so much against them that for the
next hundred years we deserve to suffer whatever punishments there are for
us. We deserve them, we have sinned so much.

The Musalmaans believed in us, trusted us so much . . . that for example
those who were workers . . . those who used to serve . . . if a money order

came for someone no one would go to their homes to deliver it. There was one post office . . . as in our village there was one post office and there were many small villages around. They used to have to come themselves to collect the post and money orders.

[The post office] was in Thoa Khalsa, and the postman would not reach people's mail to them or get money orders to them. That was why when Musalmaans went to work away from their homes, they would give our address as the place to receive their money orders . . . and money would come for them there. My father used to make entries in his register scrupulously . . . this belongs to so and so, this belongs to so and so . . . and then people used to come and buy their provisions out of this. In a sense this was like getting advance money. If there were a hundred money orders for a hundred rupees each, that would be ten thousand rupees, so you could use those ten thousand rupees to buy rations, or you could use five and keep the rest to run the shops . . . those people trusted us so much. But we did not even think we should treat human beings as human beings . . . I am not saying that you should change your religion and become a Musalmaan, after all, religion has its own place, but what I am saying is that humanity also has a place and we simply removed that, pushed it aside as if it did not exist. The same people who used to look up to us, when they were asked about Partition and asked how the Sikhs dealt with them . . . if I am telling you how badly we treated them, then when a Musalmaan will speak to a Musalmaan obviously he will exaggerate a bit and tell him about this in more detail. And of course there is no doubt in this that all the Musalmaans said that we dealt with them very badly and that they could not continue to live with us. No doubt. Why should they stay with us? Why? By separating they did a good thing. We were not capable of living with them. And all the punishment we have had at their hands, the beatings they have given us, that is the result of all this. Otherwise real brothers and sisters don't kill and beat each other up. After all, we also had some sin in us . . . to hate someone so much, to have so much hate inside you for someone . . . how can humanity forgive this?

*　　*　　*

In Thoa Khalsa when the fighting and trouble began, then for three days they kept fighting, our jawans kept fighting for three days and chasing the Musalmaans out. . . . When the Musalmaans came in thousands we kept fighting, but in the end it was decided to come to an agreement. Some Musalmaans came forward to discuss this. In the agreement they made one condition . . . there's one girl, she's still in Pakistan . . . actually everyone knew about her, even I knew and I was a child, so the whole village must have known . . . something that a child knows the elders also have to know . . . she had a relationship with one of them. So the Musalmaans said, give us this girl. But my father said, look, we're not the type of people who work like this, you want money, you take it, you want anything else you have that, but . . . even in Kabul Kandhar when Ghazni took our girls away, we brought those girls back, and today you are asking us to give you this girl, absolutely not. And they, they were seven brothers, my father and his brothers, and two sisters, and the children of all the brothers and sisters, even these added up to some twenty-five or twenty-six girls, leaving aside the boys . . . so those young people . . . the young people, the newly married girls and the unmarried girl . . . my father and my uncle, Avtar Singh, they collected them in one place, they collected them and said to them, whatever may happen we are not going to agree to this condition, we would rather kill you all. There was no protest at this, no noise, all of them, all the women said kill us . . .

There were some 1000–1200 people in the village. There was one Sardar Gulab Singh—we had all collected inside his haveli, it was a large house, all of us had collected there . . . in Gulab Singh's haveli twenty-six girls had been put aside. First of all my father, Sant Raja Singh, when he brought his daughter, he brought her into the courtyard to kill her, first of all he prayed, he did ardaas, he said sachche padshah, we have not allowed your Sikhi to get stained, and in order to save your Sikhi we are going to sacrifice our daughters, make them martyrs, please forgive us. Then . . . there was one man who used to do coolie work in our village, he moved forward and . . . he stepped forward and caught my father's feet . . . Ram Singh caught his feet and he said, Bhapaji, first you kill me because my knees are swollen and I can't run away . . . you will all run away and I will not be able to and the Musalmaans will catch hold of me and make me into a Musalmaan. So my father immediately hit him with his kirpan and took his head off. After that, Justice Harnam Singh, who was Chief Justice of Punjab, Justice Harnam Singh, his behnoi, meaning his father-in-law's sala, he, Sardar Nand Singh Dheer, he said to my father, Raja Singha, please martyr me first because my sons live in Lahore . . . do you think I will allow Musalmaans to cut this beard of mine and make me go to Lahore as a sheikh? For this reason kill me. My father then killed him. He killed two, and the third was my sister Maan Kaur . . . my sister came, and sat in front of my father, and I stood there right next to him, clutching on to his kurta as children do. I was clinging to him . . . but when my father swung the kirpan (vaar kita) . . . perhaps some doubt or fear came in his mind, or perhaps the kirpan got stuck in her dupatta . . . no one can say . . . it was such a frightening, such a fearful scene. Then my sister, with her own hand she removed her plait and pulled it forward . . . and my father with his own hands moved her dupatta aside and then he swung the kirpan and her head and neck rolled off and fell . . . there . . . far away. I crept downstairs, weeping, sobbing and all the while I could hear the regular swing and hit of the kirpans . . . twenty-five girls were killed, they were cut. One girl, my taya's daughter-in-law, who was pregnant . . . somehow she didn't get killed and later my taya's son shot her with a pistol. Then he killed himself, he and his father both, they became shaheeds, martyrs . . .

She was saved. That girl, she said to us, kill me because I will not survive. I have a child in my womb, how can I survive? She was bleeding. Then my mother and my uncle, they sat by her, her name was Harnam Kaur, and they got some afim (opium)—those days people used to have afim in villages—then they mixed the afim with their spit and heated it up. She began the *japji sahib path*, and said *vahe guru*, let me become a martyr, and just as the path came to an end, so did her end come. It was really as if . . . you know it is rare that a human being prepares for death in such a way, as she did. She really had death in her control, and when she wanted death to take her away, it did. Nearly half an hour she did the path herself, and as the last sloka came to an end, so did she. She knew, she was dying. The last sloka . . . *Pan guru pani pita, mata tat mahat* . . . I can't remember it well. But her life became complete at the time. The same night, there were two young girls, and it was decided to throw them into a well in the haveli. In the morning we thought they would be dead. It was a very deep well, in Rawalpindi district the wells were very deep and if you looked into them, you could not see into the depths. In the morning we heard voices chanting the path coming out of the well. So we asked the Musalmaans, we told them that two of our girls had gone to fetch water and they have fallen into the well, can you help us to get them out. So they brought ropes, and then we got the girls out, and they were still alive, even the bangles on their wrists were not broken! There was one Hari Singh, he signalled to me to go away. He was trying to speak but could not. He indicated to me through sign language that the Musalmaans had cut his tongue off because he had refused to become a Musalmaan. He had said he did not want to have his head cut off, but he'd be willing to have his tongue cut off. Not even one person agreed to become a Musalmaan. We all left and went to the edge of the river.

*   *   *

In 1945 we had come to Thoa Khalsa from Saintha. After six months we went there and when we came back we got two camel loads of gifts: kaddu, pethas, mangoes, dal, ghee and nearly sixteen maunds of things as gifts from the Musalmaans there, rations, sixteen maunds of stuff. Just as they gift things to pirs, to saints they gave things to us. From every house, atta, ghee, dal and so many things, they left these things in our house.

The Musalmaans used to farm, or do service. Sometimes one person in the family would be in the military. They would send money back—that too used to come in our name. They were good people. They would not steal, nor frighten us, or threaten us. Even when they knew that Pakistan was going to be formed, they were keen that we should leave so that we would not come to any harm. We came away from there honourably. And when the trouble started, the people came from there. You know that Ma Hasina whom I mentioned to you, her son, Sajawal Khan, he came to us and said we could stay in his house if we wanted to. He came with his children. But we were doubtful, and today I feel that what he was saying, the expression on his face, his bearing—there was nothing there but sincerity and compassion, and we, we misunderstood him. We had all been through so much trouble, and they came to give us support, to help us, and we refused.

In Rawalpindi, those who were shopkeepers, they had their own lands, and they also kept property of the Musalmaans as guarantee. Say, they would lend money against the land, so they did this too. And there were Sikhs who used to do zamindari as well. They had cows and buffaloes at home, and they needed fodder etc., for them, so they used to use this land which they had kept on guarantee. Apart from that they were mostly shopkeepers, small margins, clean work. They had low overheads. I remember, I was in the fifth class and my father said to me, beta you do a lot of fazool kharchi, unnecessary expenditure. Don't you know that we need money for our day-to-day expenditure in the house? You must be careful about spending money. People earned enough to keep them, and they were happy. I would open our shop in the morning. My father would come back from the gurudwara around nine and sit in the shop. He'd wake at four, bathe, do his path, go to the gurudwara and then come and sit in the shop. Whatever I know today I have learnt from him, clean, honest business. If a small girl came, he'd call her daughter. If it was an older one, he'd call her sister. He'd treat everyone with respect.

We used to buy material from Gujjar Khan. The stuff used to come on camels, and the shopkeepers would go and collect it. There were no trucks in those days. There were buses, from Thoa Khalsa to Rawalpindi, and back. About twenty kilometres. The Musalmaans, the Hindus and Sikhs, there was so much to-ing and fro-ing between the communities that no one bothered about small things. The Musalmaans were more large hearted, production was with them, grain, fruit, everything. And they were generous. Whenever anyone went to their homes, say if a Sikh went, they would give us presents, sukhi ras it was called, uncooked things. In fact if a Musalmaan did not give this to a Sikh, he was not thought well of by Musalmaans from the other villages. They would say, Shahji came and you did not give anything. No one would ask, but on their own two, three people would bring things. And they used to say very calmly, you don't eat things cooked by us, but sometimes the utensil they would bring . . . you see we used to drink milk from their houses, but the milk had to be in an unused utensil, a new one. But we never asked what difference it would have made if we had actually drunk out of the same cup. Just wash it and drink. What would have happened? If we had been willing to drink from the same cups, we would have remained united, we would not have had these differences, thousands of lives would not have been lost, and there would have been no Partition. Are Musalmaans not staying in Hindustan, or Hindus in Pakistan? This is not even so much because of politics as it is because of Brahmanvaad. And these days I fear, I wonder if the Harijans will not do the same thing with us that the Musalmaans did. A time will come when Harijans, whom we call sudras, even today we do not give them our girls, we do not take their boys, we don't give them any respect. I tell you this is very dangerous, they can rebel. Look at what Kanshi Ram is saying in his meetings—he says he does not need Brahmanvad. You see, the anger is beginning. Our relations, our attitude should be the same towards Harijans, Sikhs, Musalmaans, anyone, we should not treat people differently. A person who has four friends, he should be proud that he has one Musalmaan friend, one Hindu friend, one Sikh friend and so on. I try very hard to make sure that I have friends in every class.

* * *

When the trouble began [in 1984] many of my friends—I have one friend, Guptaji, Manohar Gupta, he came and stood in front of my shop when the attackers came. He said to them this is my shop. They said but it says Bir Bahadur Singh. He said, yes, that is my name. Three days he kept us with him in his home. He gave us a divan, and he made us rehearse what we would do if there was trouble. He said, in case there is danger, if they break down the doors, he gave me some sindoor powder, and he said if this happens, we will all sit downstairs and we will say that it is our guruji who is visiting. He told me you will have to open your hair, and you sit and we will all sit round you and start praying and we will say our guruji has come. I tell you when a person is willing to pray to you, to make you his guru, to save your life, what greater thing is there? This is true nobility. My Musalmaan friends phoned, Hindu friends, and of course there were the Sikh friends . . . what happened with the Sikhs in 1984, we are so sad about this. My whole family was finished in Pakistan, and my two brothers and my mother, we came here. We did not get any land, nor a house, we got no help from the government, and we scraped every penny together, we worked ourselves really hard and made a small farm for ourselves, and then our homes, everything was looted and destroyed. I had bought four thousand ducks from the Government of India—I had taken permission to buy them. I had this dream that I would put them in all the ponds in UP [Uttar Pradesh] in villages where Harijans live. I wanted to make so much production in UP of duck eggs, because they are full of vitamins, because they are better than hen eggs, and it costs less also because ducks live off the stuff in ponds. They were destroyed, my tube-well was uprooted and destroyed. This was in district Ghaziabad. And the people who did this were identified, but there was no action. What the government should have done is that those people whose blood was spilled to make this country indpendent—if we had not had any love for our country, then it would have been a different thing—if we had become Musalmaans, we could have stayed on. But we said no, our links are with Hindustan. At the time Master Tara Singh had said that Hindus and Sikhs are one. And we are, I believe that we are. My village Thoa Khalsa, behind our shop there there is a temple, and that temple must be some thousand years old. And the gurudwara is some two or three hundred years old. The Sikh religion isn't older than that. This means that my great-grandfather, or my other ancestors, they must have gone to the temple to pray. After all, they could not have gone to the mosque. They must have gone to the temple. So then, how could we be separate? In the Guru Granth Sahib also there is a reference that we are one. And the Hindu is our root. If the root dies, where will the tree be? For Hindus, the Sikhs are warriors. If you kill the warriors, who will save your home? It's a separate thing that if everyone rounds on the one warrior in the home, then of course he will retaliate. I don't approve of what happened in 1984, till today there has been no punishment and I feel really sorry that other people have been implicated with FIRS [First Information Reports] being filed against them. And once a person is hanged, I believe the whole thing is over. But this kind of persecution . . . it's not only a question of Simranjit Singh Mann, but every Sikh has begun to think, to wonder what will happen to us. Even after one person has been hanged, to carry on punishing people. Last year I was caught . . . shall I speak this into your tape recorder? I want to. On October 24 Prabodh Chander, a Congress minister in Punjab, died. He was a friend of mine. Another friend of mine, Virinder Singh, and I had gone to his home and on our way back on Prithvi Raj road there was a car, and some people were lying wounded on the road, and a couple even seemed dead. One of them I recognized, he was Buta Singh's son and he was crying out, asking people to stop. No one was willing to stop. I stopped, I took Buta Singh's son, his gun man, his friend, and I took them to hospital, the American hospital and admitted them there. My car was covered in blood, but I did this because of insaniyat, humanity, I couldn't not. One person was dead, but the wounded one — he was a Hindu — we took him to hospital and admitted him there. Then, it had hardly been fifteen days (and I thought foolishly that I would get some kudos for this — I remember telling Buta Singh about the incident and he even thanked me) when I was lying ill at home they came and caught hold of me. You must have read about this in the papers. The news they carried was that five major terrorists have been caught in Delhi near Gurudwara Bangla Sahib. That they were meeting there at two A.M. at night, and we caught them, they have very strong links with Punjab terrorists and they had planned to blow up Parliament House and to kill Rajiv! Had we been terrorists, Buta Singh's son was with us, what more did we need? We could have taken him away, got money from Buta Singh and from the terrorists, but we acted like human beings, yet Buta Singh kept us in jail for five months, labelling us terrorists. For twenty-four hours we were in a room eight by six feet, there was no light. We wrote letters to the governor, and asked for light. I used to keep doing path, I did four bhogs there. It was like being in the hangman's cell and the whole time the jailers used to keep telling us Billa was hanged here, so and so was hanged here, and before being hanged they are brought here, into this room. Then we hang them. I also used to think sometimes, those who had died, I used to think I saw them sometimes in the night, it was as if an image of theirs had appeared before me, a sort of sketch. Maqbool Bhat, Billa, Ranga . . . whoever is hanged, they would say, we bring them here. All bail applications, even up to the High Court, were rejected. And finally they had to give it in writing that we had arrested Bir Bahadur Singh but he had no direct involvement. This was in 1987 October, and in December the High Court released me, and in 1988 May or June the government gave it in writing in the sessions court that there was no involvement. I am not a terrorist. I am a member of the Shiromani Gurudwara Prabandhak Committee that's all.

In jail we were alone, yes alone. All five of us were kept separately, alone. The hanging room has two portions, one where the person to be hanged is kept and the other which is empty. We were kept in those, there was a small bathroom, three by something, full of water and mosquitoes, and that's what we had. The latrine was also there and our food was also handed to us there. We used to think that we were the children of patriots, we used to see the prisons they spent time in. But I — this experience could have turned me into a terrorist if I had been that way inclined.

I have a lot of anger, but I don't have the strength to fight. I have a family, I have daughters, how can I take this on? Had I been twenty-two years old, certainly something would have happened. There must be hundreds of cases like this, like mine, where young people have turned terrorist. After all, this is the State, and they need to see — a seventy-year-old man, they've turned him into a terrorist. Look at my record. I've been chairman of the Municipal Corporation, a member of the SGPC, I have no cases against me, I lead an honest life. Look at my family background, my father . . .

My father was a nationalist, he was in the forefront of the fight for independence. He spent time in jail, that's why my mother gets a pension. On the one hand they give you a pension, and on the other they label you a terrorist. And this is the sort of stigma that sticks so much that even your own brothers and sisters don't want to have anything to do with you. I used to see my wife and my children, often I could not even see their faces properly, and we would only talk in gestures. Between them and me there would be police . . . what can you say? Where is the justice in this? Is this a democracy? To catch hold of someone like this, and turn him into a terrorist, someone who is a member of the SGPC, this is a major sin, it's something I shall never forget all my life. How they dealt with us. Even so, India is our land, all Sikhs think like this, no one wants Khalistan. The slogan, *raj karega khalsa* [truth will prevail], this is something that has been around from the start.

* * *

The thing is, the maximum attack came on the Sikhs because Sikhs are visible. Between Hindus and Musalmaans there isn't so much visible difference. So I suppose there must have been a fear that in thinking someone to be Hindu they might actually have been attacking a Muslim. The Sikhs are easily recognizable. And they pulled out their kirpans. You know that after killing my sister my father killed seven Musalmaans. Seven. He had no enmity with them. In fact there was a great deal of love. But when it came to the crunch, and this happens with the Sikhs, then the kirpans come out. Guru Gobind Singh has filled the Sikhs with this kind of spirit, it can't be done away with. Even the English realized this. It's only this government . . . yet despite what has been happening to us these last forty years or so, you can see that Sikhs have been creating history afresh the whole time. In 1984, I called the governor, and I said I am really sad to see what is happening. I'm a member of the SGPC but I can't even go out to ask people how they are. He said, what do you want? I said, I want to go to the riot-stricken areas. He gave us a car and people, and I think I must have been the first Sikh to go all over the city. I went to Shakarpur, I went everywhere. They sent people with me. I am grateful for this. In Shakarpur, we were helping the wounded, and taking them to a santa da dera, there was a girl lying on the road, and her infant was looking for her breast to drink milk. So we stopped the car, and I said to her, bibi, but she was dead. So we picked up the child, and sent it to the camp. This is the condition in which we found women. The young people who saw this, how can they build up trust in anything? After all, trust begets trust, and distrust creates distrust. I told you we doubted Sajawal Khan at the time, we should have trusted him. Trust is a big thing. Even the enemy deserves trust . . . he will not lie and cheat if you show you trust him. Even the dishonest ones will not do so.

The two girls in the well, their father had been wounded by the Musalmaans. His leg had a bullet in it. He was our leader at the time, Pratap Singh Dheer. One of the girls was called Mahinder Kaur. We used to pick up his charpai, his cot, and whatever he said we would do. If he had said we should become Musalmaans, we would have done so. But he said, we would rather let ourselves be cut up into small pieces, but we will not convert . . . We will not change our religion, to save our lives. He said, I am half dead anyway. You can cut me up into small pieces, and with each piece you can ask me again, but I will not convert. And as he said this, Lajjawanti and the other women jumped into the well. So then the Muslims said, here they are killing themselves. And they decided to go on to Thamali, which was four kilometres from Thoa. Our village was a bit closer, and was surrounded by small hills. It was very beautiful. And many people had come to loot. People who went to the village afterwards said not even bricks were left to take away. From our village the mob went to Thamali where there had been fighting for some days. There was one very brave lady, a relative of mine, Dewan Kaur, she wore a pagri and went to fight. Her body was found some distance away from the village. People kept telling her not to go alone and she said what nonsense, I am Guru Gobind Singh's daughter, and she fell upon them like a fury.

Yes, many women were still left in our village. Mostly our family women died, and then the ones who jumped into the well. But the others were saved. Because the Musalmaans saw that they were killing themselves. The ones who sacrificed . . . if the women of our family had not been killed, and those who jumped into the well had not taken their own lives, the ones who were left alive, would not have been alive today. The Musalmaans had come for this. You'll forgive me for saying this, but the Musalmaans from our village, they were not so good. Our children for example, they were clean, they dressed well. The Musalmaans would not bathe for eight days together. And soap was an unheard of thing. Then they would look awful. And our women were beautiful, which is why they had planned to take them away. But my father was determined not to let this happen. History does not change every day, and we are not born every day. How much longer do we have to live, he said. Maybe ten years, maybe twenty. And then what? We still have to die after that. We'll die with honour. And the rest of the work . . . my father took the first step, and the rest of the work was done by Sardarni Lajjawanti. There were only two advocates in our area: one was justice Harnam Singh and one was Sant Gulab Singh.

Justice Harnam Singh reached the High Court, and Gulab Singh became a sant, he went in this direction, he was a man of a higher order, a literary man. Mata Lajjawanti was his wife, and she saved all the other Sikhs by sacrificing her life. So twenty-six and . . . this made around a hundred girls. Then, the Musalmaans in our village . . . there was one Hari Singh. There was another, a granthi whom they caught hold of and took away. First they cut his hand, then his arm, but he kept refusing to become a Musalmaan. He said you can kill me if you like. They killed him. Then one of our relatives, Gurbaksh Singh Dheer—he's dead now. They kept a gun on his chest. Tell us where your father is. Tell us where your father is. The father had escaped at night, he travelled some twenty kilometres to Rawalpindi, where he approached the District Collector, and managed to get the military from there. The real sacrifice was made by Mata Lajjawanti, and the girls who jumped into the well. Look at the weapon she found, how suited to the time it was. She took inspiration from Sant Raja Singh. She saw that he had cut his own girls. Then, these girls and those, what was the difference? If they took even one of these away, it would bring dishonour. The girl that they were talking about, we brought her with us. She was alive . . . we brought her with us into the camp, from there she ran away and went to Montgomery, and she married a Musalmaan. She still lives in our village.

It was like this, when all the fighting started, then there were also attempts at settlements. After all, a fight means a settlement. So the Musalmaans came to make a settlement. They said they would allow us to stay on in our homes if we gave them that girl. There was one Musalmaan, he was quite strong. He was a kind of loafer, he used to work the land, but he wanted this girl. He had some kind of relationship with her. They kept asking for this girl, saying if you give us this girl, we'll send all the Musalmaans away.

And people were discussing this, saying she is a bad girl anyway, she has a relationship with him, what's the use of keeping her? You see, when it comes to saving your life, nothing counts. So a sort of decision was taken to give her away.

At the time there was no question of what she wanted. It was a question of the honour of the village. My father said, how can this be. Our history says that in Kabul and Kandhar Ghazni took girls away, and those girls we brought back into people's homes, and now we should just say take our girls away, just to save our lives? How can we do this? This girl is my daughter. He said, all of you stand aside, I'll show you how we give this girl away. So he put his girls aside, and then he went out into the maidan, and he fought and made the Musalmaans run away. Then we picked up the charpai on which Pratap Singh was—he said, let's give the girl. Then when the military came, the girl came with us in trucks. First we went to Jhelum . . . no, to Gujjar Khan. Then at night, we went to Rawat, then to Wah camp, we stayed there, and the girl was also there. Then there were some relatives of hers in Montgomery. There had not been much trouble elsewhere yet . . . when trouble began in our Rawalpindi, people were still comfortable in their homes elsewhere. The trouble started for us in March. In Jhelum there was one Sardar Harnam Singh, he helped people a lot. He would collect things from all over and distribute them. We were in such a bad state that we had nothing at all, not a penny. Once I stuck my hand in my pocket and came up with a two-anna piece and I gave this to my nephew and said go and bring some cholas. On the way to Rawat. We were fiercely hungry. In a way the entire hunger and thirst had been killed . . . when you are holding your mother by one hand, another child by another and carrying a younger brother at the same time, where do you have the capacity to feel hungry?

But after all, a human being is a human being. And people do feel hungry. So my nephew, I remember that he told me that the coin was khota, damaged. And I cried. Then I put my hand in my other pocket and I found a letter of my father's, a letter that he had written to his sister-in-law. It must have just been in that pocket by chance. And I had one chaddar—a shawl—of my father's, sometimes I would read the letter, sometimes I would touch and kiss the shawl. I kept that letter for many years. Now I don't know where it is. Whenever I was full of grief at something, I would weep,

I would take comfort from it. But tears are also a good sign. All that overflowing is good. How much I cried that day when I learnt that coin was damaged.

In Rawat camp there was a room in which a durrie was spread. Just as we were about to settle down we were told this was not for us, and that there was another room. So we picked up our sheet and sacking, whatever little stuff we had, and in that we found a small potli, a handkerchief made into a bundle, in which were tied fifty rupees. When I opened it and found the fifty rupees, I said, there are fifty rupees here, do they belong to anyone? And of course they must have belonged to someone. But everyone was in such a state at the time, each one had left behind thousands, so no one was going to stand up and claim fifty. Perhaps they'd been there from before, or they came with the durrie. But no one claimed them. So we kept it, and with those fifty rupees, keeping track of every little bit, we managed to get through the next two months. Then some relatives of ours in Peshawar, they sent us a money order for fifty rupees, and with those some relatives of ours who were in Delhi brought us here. We had nothing. We were young, though, sixteen or so years old, and you know this condensed milk, and sardine fish — the sardine fish is flat. So the fish tins would serve as katoris, and condensed milk cans would serve as tumblers. We used to take off the edges with stones, and use the cans. Even the best of people would say, please pick up one for us too. You know the military people, they would eat and throw the tins away, and we'd pick these up, hammer them into shape and turn them to use. Then we'd give them away, tayaji, you take one, chachaji, you take one. To everyone we gave these. My first form of aid that I gave was this. We had collected some for ourselves, but to all relatives and others, I used to pick these things up, clean them up very carefully and then give them away. And when the time would come to eat, we would pull out these tins as our utensils. Gradually the camp people did give us utensils, and we managed to have bowls and tumblers. But at first it was only this. And then, gradually, we came here.

Yes, that girl. When we came, we were close to Montgomery, from there they took her away. It was done with a lot of pomp and celebration. Then in the village we learnt that she was living close to the bus stand, she had married that man and she was heavy with child. He took her away. She was quite beautiful. She was married. Her son must be grown up now, with children. They had a hotel. Her husband died only some two years ago. She was extra beautiful. There are some things like that . . . she was the reason for many deaths. This was all a well-thought-out scheme. All the villages were surrounded in one night. The situation was like this there that if there was one village of Sikhs, there were some thirty or forty villages of Musalmaans. So where will the Sikhs go? They have to drink water, eat, get rations. You see, the Musalmaans have done some dreadful things—they have never fought a battle in the battleground. Out in the open. They will come and stab you in the back. A Musalmaan can't fight a Sikh face to face. They'll set fire to things, your home, your village. So when they surrounded the village, they kept on setting fire to houses, and fire is such a scary thing, and the moment a person sees smoke, he gets frightened. We were fully surrounded. All around us there were fires. What can a person do? I think really all honour to those people who killed their own children, who jumped into wells. And they saved us . . . you take any household of martyrs, and you will find it will take root and grow. Blood is such a thing, that as you water a plant, a tree, so also the tree grows, so does the martyr's household. In our house, my son died—this was after Pakistan was formed. After our marriage, on a farm. Here where I am at the moment, there has been no death. So after all, there is some barkat, some good. Somehow even fate understands that if virtually all their household has been destroyed, at least for some time what is left must be preserved. Bravery is never laid waste is it? We have grown and developed according to the dictates laid down by fate—I have five sons. My mother would weep all day when she remembered those incidents. She would cry, almost sing the dukhan about her family. All day long she would cry. But Vahe Guru must have heard her. Now we are three brothers, we all have children, I have five boys, grandchildren, we have a good, large family and now my mother complains that she isn't even able to sleep because there is no peace in the family! So you should be happy that fate has turned this miracle for you.

* * *

I had two sisters. One was in Calcutta at the time. The other was the first one to become a martyr, and she did it with such courage. I did not see anyone else with my own eyes. She sat just like this, on her haunches, and behind her stood my father, while I stood next to him. Father and daughter could not see each other. He was behind her. He sat. He did ardas with his kirpan out. And then, when he tried to kill her, something came in the way perhaps, or perhaps a father's attachment came in the way. Then my sister . . . no word was exchanged. Just the language of the kirpan was enough for the father and daughter to understand each other. They both were sad that this vaar, this hit went waste. Then my sister caught hold of her plait and moved it aside, and my father hit like this, and her head fell . . .

Some people were upstairs and some were down. The whole village was there . . . there were a few rooms downstairs, and some upstairs. There wasn't any long scheme, but suddenly they realized that their whole household would be destroyed, all the girls were young. The only difference was that my father was the youngest of the seven brothers. Avtar Singh, whom I spoke to you about, the girl who had a child in her womb, this was her first child . . . what was I saying? The chacha and nephew were young. The elder brother's son and the chacha were roughly the same age. They were all young men. There were so many men in the household. After all, if there were twenty-six girls, you can imagine how many men there must have been. Fifteen or twenty young people. They all thought, we will be destroyed and the chacha said this is right, you must do it. So they all stood behind him. If the Musalmaans take these girls they thought . . . who knows how long we will live. Suppose today that they had not done this, would my sister's name not be among the abducted women listed in this book that you have with you today? [The reference is to a book containing a list of abducted women that we had with us.] These are the same people who saved lives. They said we will kill our girls instead of leaving them to rot. Look through this whole book and you will not find the name of our village there. The names that you find here, from Thamali and other places, these poor girls had no choice. Say if some ten people come, and take away our girls, what can I do? There were so many people, there seemed to be no end to them. It seemed as if the world had broken its borders and people had poured forth.

Yes, there were people who took their girls away. Only our household was left, the others went down. Upstairs, we were alone. Those who were left upstairs were finished. They did not kill men. I was upstairs, they didn't kill me. They just put me aside. I have never seen such a frightening scene. Even today when I remember it . . . I cry, it helps to lighten my heart. A father who kills his daughter, how much of a victim, how helpless he must be. It's as if his insides are being ripped open when he thinks that someone will take my daughter away. And all my life, I will have to . . . they wanted to take them away for religion.

It was exactly the same thing [as 1984]. People were forced to shave their hair, forced to convert. It was exactly the same thing. People have fought, they died. There was a woman whose husband worked in Delhi and he was transferred to Ambala, and her brother worked in Patiala, he was transferred to Delhi. So he thought, my sister has such a big house, we'll stay there. So the husband lived in Ambala and the brother and sister were in Delhi. The woman had children. They lived near Palam in Palam colony, and there they were surrounded, the sister begged and pleaded with them not to kill her brother. They told her, you get away, we do not kill women and we won't kill you. But in front of her, and she told me this, they started hitting him with spikes and they killed him and left him. She was left alone with her brother's body. She kept wondering what she could do. Sometimes she would break a bit of wood from the window. Another time, she took out some ghee. Then she found a book, a chair . . . whatever she could lay her hands on, she put together, and built a cremation pyre for her brother. Still, she could not burn him fully. All this because of an attitude . . . If Pakistan was made it was made because of our attitude. And it is the Sikhs who have helped to create Hindustan. *We* have held its flag aloft. Before Musalmaans, what does history say? If there was an attack, the Sikhs would come forward. The Sikhs were after all Hindus who became Sikhs. And now Hindus think they are separate. Or Sikhs think they are separate. We are the sentries, the gatekeepers if you like, the soldiers of the entire Hindu society. You can call us any of these things. Sardar, elders, youngers . . . but if we are alienated . . .

You see how the population of Musalmaans is increasing. I think there were seven crores when Pakistan was made. I don't think I am wrong in this. Now there are some sixteen. In forty years if this has happened, in the next forty will it not multiply more? I had a Musalmaan friend, I used to fight the corporation election from Bhogal. He, Iqbal, came to me and said it's my child's birthday. You must come. I said certainly I'll come. Then I asked him, Iqbal Sahib, how many children do you have? He said, forget it yaar, I'll tell you that later. So I said again, tell me, or should I tell you how many I have? I have five sons and two daughters. He said forget it friend, I'll tell you another time. In case you think there are too many. I said tell me, how many are there? He said, eighteen. Eighteen children . . . if you multiply these eighteen, what will happen to our votes. This should not happen. In the name of Khalistan you put down the Sikhs, and then you try to make the others happy. This is not desh bhakti, love of your country. This is kursi bhakti, lust for power. Desh bhakti is if you think of the whole of Hindustan as azad. Hindustan became azad because of the gurudwara movement. And the hundred and seven people who were hanged because of the freedom struggle, ninety-two of these were Sikhs. Ninety-two out of a hundred and seven are Sikhs. You can work out the ratio yourself. These people, are they a martial race? They are strong people, we should keep them on our side. Our wise women say that if a cow is wise, and she gives milk, what does it matter if she even kicks you once in a while. It's the same thing with us. But the one who does not give milk, who should care for her?

6
CHILDREN

No history of Partition that I have seen so far has had anything to say about children. This is not surprising: as subjects of history children are difficult to deal with. The historian may well ask: how do you recover the experiences of children, as children? As a tool of history, memory is seen to be unreliable at the best of times, with little to offer by way of 'facts'. Childhood memories filtered through the prism of adult experience — these may be acceptable as autobiography, but not necessarily as history. How, then, do we make sense of the experiences of children?

Where Partition history is concerned, this is particularly important. So much of this history is woven around children that their invisibility now, in it, is tragic. India and Pakistan did not fight over children as they did over women, or indeed over Harijans. But it was the bodies and beings of abducted children that posed the greatest challenge of all: for while an abducted and raped woman could be brought back into the fold of religion, and could, in a manner of speaking, be 'repurified', a child, in whom the blood of two religions was mixed in equal quantities, was not so easily re-integrated. If numbers mean anything, they would force our attention towards children. Nearly 75,000–100,000 women are said to have been abducted at Partition. It took a decade of searching to locate a fraction of that number. Even if we imagine that half the number of abducted women had children, that gives us a figure of nearly 50,000. And apart from these there were the numbers of children who were abandoned, or who simply got left behind — of these we have no record. Can we afford to ignore these histories?

But while most records were lacking in information about children, virtually everyone I spoke to mentioned the hundreds of abandoned, destitute, lost children: some that families had left behind, others who had been abducted, some who were in hospitals and never knew what happened to their families, some who lost all relatives. Savitri Makhijani, a record collector with the United Council of Relief and Welfare, the parent organization set up under the leadership of Edwina Mountbatten to coordinate relief and rehabilitation work among non-government organizations, described a time when a large camp was closed down in Lahore. At the time, a few months after Partition, she was with the School of Social Work in Delhi. Shortly after the camp closed down they received information that there were some dozen children who had been left behind, who seemed to belong to no one. What was to be done with them? The children were sent to Delhi, and housed in a home by Mridula Sarabhai. Social workers from the School of Social Work then put out advertisements on All India Radio, asking for offers of adoption. A large number of postcards began to pour in — but here too, as in everyday life, everyone first wanted a boy. And yet, most of the children who had been left behind — again as in everyday life — were girls. What was to be done? Finally, most were adopted. And then, one man returned the little girl he had taken, she was too 'naughty' he said. Most people, according to many social workers, were looking for domestic help, rather than looking to adopt a child. 'Naughtiness' was clearly not what was wanted. Savitri was unable to remember what had happened to that little girl. But, like other social workers, she did confirm that while young boys were preferred for 'legitimate' adoption, young girls were much in demand for 'other services'. I quote from her:

> When we came to Delhi I was doing social work. We had just reached Delhi. We learnt that Hindus had migrated, and some of the Indian doctors had been sent to Pakistan to render medical aid to the Hindus in the camps. Pakistan did not have too many doctors, and even if they did . . . so the Indian government had sent Indian doctors. And when they were winding up camp, a stage came when there were eight or ten abandoned children left in the camp. So these Indian doctors brought those children back to India because they could not possibly leave them there. Even if it was a Muslim child — though they knew these were Hindu children . . . At the time Rameshwari Nehru and Raksha Saran were running a kind of home . . . so they put them there. And from the school one of our teachers, who was guiding our social work, she went on All India Radio to make an announcement that we have these eight or ten children — would somebody volunteer to adopt them. It was a small number . . . eight or ten children is not that many. I was still in the School of Social Work and we started receiving postcards. And everybody first wanted a boy, then

they wanted a good-looking and healthy boy. Nobody wanted girls. Anyway, one man came along, he took a girl and within two or three days he brought her back, saying she was too naughty. Now what do you expect a child to be if not naughty? After that . . . I don't know what finally happened to those children, but this is an incident where the Hindu parents abandoned their children. You know people's mental makeup changed, the important thing was to save themselves, so they left the children behind.

* * *

Four decades after Partition, I met Trilok Singh. Trilok Singh was nine years old when his father and two uncles decided that they would have to kill the women and children of their family in order to escape to India. Their village, it had been confirmed, would go to Pakistan. The Sikhs were already under attack, and with every passing day the violence was drawing closer. Mangal Singh (Trilok's uncle) and his two brothers knew that while they could manage to escape — or die in the attempt to do so — the women and children of their family had little chance. They took a decision to do what had by now become common in Hindu and Sikh families: kill those who were seen to be vulnerable — women, children, the old and infirm. It wasn't only that these people would make escape difficult and cumbersome, it was also that they — women particularly — could be raped and, being 'weak', could be forced to convert: both things which would be an insult to their religion (and their manhood). Children too could be converted, or simply taken away — this happened among both communities, so it wasn't an imaginary fear.

Trilok heard the male elders of his family discussing the impending family deaths. They called it martyrdom. But somehow, at nine, he knew he did not wish to die. So he pleaded with his uncles and his father. He said he was willing to take the risk of escaping and being killed en route. But he wanted them to give him the chance to at least try. They did. Others in the family did not have this choice. Seventeen of them died at the hands of their men, while young Trilok escaped.

When I met him Trilok lived in a village a bare thirty kilometres from Amritsar where he ran a cloth shop. Despite himself, he remembered the time. 'I don't want to,' he said, 'I want to put it behind me, but it

keeps coming back.' After the death of his father and one of his surviving uncles, he and Mangal Singh were the only two who remained of
their 'original' family. Now both of them had 'new' families and, under-
standably, neither of these families had any interest in the traumas that
assailed these two men. In a curious kind of sharing, Trilok and his uncle
kept in touch, but they seldom, if at all, talked about 'that time'. It was as
if both understood the 'betrayal' that underlay their relationship—but
for his pleading Trilok would also have been killed with the other members of his family. He knew, when he faced Mangal Singh, that he could
have met death at the hands of this man. But, by the same token, both
were tied to each other in a sort of 'conspiracy' of silence: the deaths
hung around them like a constant presence. But they were never referred
to. Occasionally, when Mangal Singh went to the Golden Temple for
his annual remembrance ritual, a forty-eight-hour prayer in the name of
all those who had died, Trilok would accompany him. They would pray,
and silently remember those who had died, and return to their homes.
No other family member accompanied them on this private pilgrimage.

*　*　*

Trilok's story was not unusual. Many of the people whose stories I heard,
in their fifties now, had been children then. They told these stories as
adults, describing an experience they had had as children. Unlike older
people, as children they often did not even have the language to describe
the experience, to make sense of it for themselves, to tell it to others.
It took Trilok several years to be able to speak about what he had been
through. Many children grew up in orphanages or homes for the destitute; others made their way through life on the streets, and some had
the privilege of being adopted into homes. In most of their lives, there
probably was no one to whom they could recount these experiences, nor
perhaps would they have been able to. Adults going through experiences
of trauma and pain have, to hand, a history of different experiences, their
own or those of others, to draw upon, to refer back to. But children have
little of this: the vocabulary of rupture, of the enormous tearing apart
of their lives—where will they find this? Many children, Partition survivors, developed severe psychological problems, and found they could
not live in families. Kulwant Singh was one such child.

When I met him Kulwant Singh was close to sixty, a gentle, tall and thin man with a flowing white beard, and one arm cut off at the elbow — a legacy of Partition. 'I work in a hospital as a technician,' he told us, 'and spend the rest of the day in prayer and social service.' As part of his daily routine — by way of giving thanks to Guru Nanak for saving his life and making it possible to survive — Kulwant Singh gave two or three hours of his time to social service in the Sisganj gurudwara in Delhi. He would go there every day, clean and swab the floors, man the counter where people left their shoes, and do anything else that was required of him. Partition had been for him, as for many others, a traumatic experience. He lost virtually all his family. He remembers lying by the side of his dead father, with the heat of the flames rising up all around him. In an attempt to ward off the attackers, people from his village had laid a sort of barrier of thorns. This proved no obstacle at all and Kulwant has a vivid sense of thorns on one side and flames on the other.

> I was small; my mother, when she saw my father being killed — they cut him up into a hundred pieces, the first blow they struck on his neck, and then they cut him into a hundred pieces — at that time I was trembling, at my feet there were many bodies, there were fires all around, I was dying of thirst, they heard my voice — my mother lifted my head and my chachi took my feet . . . the six-month-old daughter, first of all they did ardas and threw her into the fire, and then they said, bibis, our izzat is in danger, will we save our honour or our children. And then turn by turn they threw their children into the fire . . . my mother, she took me and put me down by my father's body, where there was fire all around and I felt so thirsty and because of the heat, my legs got burnt.
>
> [Later] I got up, my hands were cut, blood was flowing from my body, my body was burnt, I fell down, then they picked me up and where they brought me, I was walking on thorns, huge thorns, but at that time I could not feel them.

Kulwant spent more than a year — till March 1948, well into Partition — in Rawalpindi, in hospital. When he was well, he came to his relatives in Delhi. But he found it difficult to settle down in the family. His relatives then applied to an ashram and Kulwant Singh was admitted there.

Then after that, I came and stayed with some of my relatives for two or three years, but things were not too good, and my chacha's son Tarlok Singh applied saying that I should be admitted into a hostel as I was full of grief, unhappy. At that time I was admitted to a hostel here in Ashram where earlier there was a subzi mandi and then Kasturba Niketan came here. I lived in the hostel nearly sixteen years, I did my matric. And then I got my claim, Rs 5,000 or so. After that I got a quarter, a place to live and then, thanks to the maharaj, I got a job in Jayprakash Navain (JP) hospital, Maulana Azad Medical College. Then till now I am doing service. This is my life.

Once he managed to make his way to Delhi, Kulwant became one of the many subjects of the State's rehabilitation plan. He was placed in an orphanage, where he stayed till he was old enough to go out looking for a job. In this too, he was helped by the State: displaced persons and refugees were given a kind of priority in job placement, and Kulwant was one of the lucky ones. His permanent government job allows him to live a reasonably comfortable life.

If Kulwant was lucky enough to be at the receiving end of State welfare policies, there were others who were not, and for whom the experience of 'that time' is marked by a sense of bewilderment and incomprehension. I remembered hearing the story of Murad, who did not know how old he was when Partition took place, though he knew he was a child. At the time that Satti Khanna and Peter Chappell interviewed Murad, he was in his forties, a tonga driver in Lahore.

He cared for me. A schoolmaster accepted me and I started living with him. He was more sympathetic to me than my own relatives and looked after my needs. I would take his cattle to the grazing ground. Then the controversy over Pakistan and Hindustan came up . . . nobody was ready to keep me. Unwillingly, an older uncle took me in.

I would always be out playing. A few Sikhs lived around our village on the main road. People said he plays outside all the time. There are bullets flying around, he will get killed. But I was always out playing. My maternal uncles took me to their homes. They thought I would be killed while I was playing out on the streets. One day we were inside the house, my uncles came in and sat down. Sikhs came! Daughter fuckers!

First they knocked my uncle down . . . I thought I would also be killed and I tried to get out. Sugarcane chaff was piled at the back. I jumped into it and wrapped myself with the stuff . . .

Murad was found lying in the chaff by another of his 'uncles'. Together, they made their way to a nearby camp—the only place where they could be relatively safe. 'It was miserable,' he said, 'if they saw a Muslim, they would kill him . . . Near the camp was a sugarcane field, but there was no food to be had: we just lay on the ground and passed the time.'

Murad's story mirrored that of hundreds and thousands of children whose lives were torn apart as a result of Partition. Once in the camp, he boarded a lorry bound for Pakistan. Over the border, he remembers being put down by the driver and told to find his way. 'Nowhere to go, I thought. I did not know the way.' He followed someone who seemed to know where they were going. A child, he was still careful enough to know that money was important: 'I would not spend the few coins I had. They would be needed if things got worse.' Stumbling and making his way through the widespread death and destruction he saw around him, Murad remembers coming across an old woman at Attari, near the border. He said to her: 'Mother, I want to stay here.' 'Where have you come from?' she asked him. 'From a well to an abyss,' said Murad. She gave him food, offered him a roof over his head, but Murad moved on: 'I have no family,' he said, and left.

For many years Murad lived the life of a destitute, with the occasional bit of work, sometimes in the vegetable mandi, other times helping with odd jobs. At some point, he made his way to Lahore, where he began to help cart and tonga drivers by looking after their horses. He earned two annas per horse. 'The time passed,' he said. One day he asked the chaudhry of the tonga drivers if he could be allowed to drive a tonga. He was told he did not know the roads. But luck was with him: a cart driver had left his job, there was no one to take his place, and Murad was told he could have a go. He did, hesitantly finding his way around the city by asking passengers and people on the street. And gradually, he had a job, a bit of money, and a sort of life.

'There is not much to think about Partition,' Murad said. His key memory of that time is his fear that he had nothing to fall back upon—

no money, no family. Where can you go, he said, if you have nowhere to go? He would spend disturbed nights, especially at festival times. He remembers the discussions about Partition and the talk of having to leave. 'Where,' he says, 'Where the hell can we go? . . . They would say, to your Pakistan. Where will Pakistan be? I would ask. "Somewhere near Lahore". But I haven't seen Lahore. People would ask, is Lahore a city? I didn't know. I had never been there. No, they would insist you too will go to Lahore. But how? Where I have been born is Lahore for me, but anyhow we were dragged to Lahore.'

* * *

Partition children. Listening to these stories, or simply reading about them, I had to constantly remind myself that it was *children* we were talking about—these stories, told by adults, were stories about what had happened to them as children. Six, eight, nine, eleven, ten . . . these were the sorts of ages they had been then. I have often wondered at the role memory plays in such cases. How far back can people be said to remember, and how much of this recall is 'accurate'? Did any of these people even wish to remember that time? Indeed, did they actually have a choice in the matter? If they were children, how reliable were their memories? Ought they to be discounted as mere childhood fabrications? These are difficult questions to answer. When Kulwant Singh spoke to me about the women of his family killing first the children and then themselves, I could not help feeling that these were the words, and indeed the interpretation, of an adult. Could he have noticed all that he had spoken about as a child? How else would memory have reconstructed the details? Or was it that his adult mind was now building on stories he had heard of that time?

Yet his wife told us that he still had nightmares, that he woke in the middle of the night feeling an intense heat rising up around him, the flames which surrounded him as he lay by his father's body in 1947. Another Sikh living in Bhogal in Delhi, who had actually been part of a killing spree as a child, would often wake in the night screaming. His wife said he could not forget the screams of the Muslims he had helped to kill. Could Trilok Singh actually have remembered the details of his pleading with his uncles and father and then his escape as clearly as he did? At age nine? Or were these reconstructed from the accounts of others around him? If so, ought they to have been taken seriously or not? All I have is questions, and more questions.

* * *

In November of 1948 Anis Kidwai visited Irwin Hospital in Delhi — she was looking for abandoned, deserted children — Partition children. A group of people from Jamia, including Kidwai's friend Jamila Begum, had got together to provide shelter for these children. Kidwai found a number of children of all ages in the hospital — someone had a head wound, another a broken leg, a third a broken arm. One little girl — she couldn't have been more than five years old, according to Kidwai — sat around happily, singing and playing. 'You seem to be fine,' Kidwai said to her. 'Yes, I came here with my aunt [actually her ayah],' replied the girl, 'but she's dead now.' And with that, she began to introduce the children. 'This is Rashid,' she said, 'everyone in his family is dead, and that is Zainab, her family is also dead, and over there is Nabu — they slit his mother's throat . . .' and she continued to laugh as she said this.

Kidwai's attempt to find a home for these children was probably part of a private enterprise — social work taken on by concerned citizens. There were many such initiatives, but, since people kept virtually no records, it is difficult to know if the government had any role in them (although the government had also set up a number of homes and orphanages). Someone donated a house, others gave their time, and Kidwai went round to hospitals locating children. One little boy said his home was in Lucknow, although he knew no more than that. Firoze Gandhi offered to take him there and help locate his family. On the way, the child got off at a station to drink water and came rushing back. Gandhi asked if he would go again to fetch water for him, but the child refused saying there were too many Sikhs at the station and he was frightened of Sikhs as they would kill him. Another young girl had a different story to tell: asked what her name was, she said, Sita-Hasina. What is your father's name? Again, a Muslim name and a Hindu one. To whom did this child belong? A Hindu family or a Muslim one? Or one that was 'mixed'? Now that the lines had been drawn between Hindus and Muslims, where was the child to go? If she was Muslim, her home was in Pakistan, if Hindu, in India. Sita-Hasina defeated all attempts at being slotted, to allow boundaries to be fixed for her. But eventually, on Gandhi's advice, was sent off into the care of the Kasturba Trust in Delhi.

But all cases were not so simply solved. Often, the children were not that easy to locate. When Kidwai set off to look for them in Delhi's hospitals, she was struck by how few there were. Everywhere there was talk of hospitals being full of children, indeed every hospital was said to have a children's ward for abandoned children but when Kidwai got there, there were no children to be found. 'What happened to these children, I have still not been able to figure out. Where did they disappear to? Perhaps they got well and went away. Or could it be that the missionaries took them away?'[1]

This last wasn't an unreasonable fear: in the general atmosphere where conversion came to represent the worst that could happen to anyone, missionaries were particularly suspect. Like the RSS, they worked in the camps, providing relief, medical care and support. But while the RSS was seen only to be drawing people into the Hindu fold—which seemed more 'acceptable' at the time—the missionaries were seen as 'outsiders' with their own private agenda of conversion to an alien faith, Christianity. And children were particularly vulnerable. Often, children were picked up by gangs and organized cartels and sold into prostitution and begging—many people remembered that there were many more children on the streets of major cities in the north than had been there before. But there are few records that shed any light on this.

All kinds of reasons were put forward for the abduction of children. Although there is no way of confirming this, social workers from India were of the opinion that more Hindu and Sikh children had been picked up by Muslim families than the other way round. If this was true, why should it be so? Damyanti Sahgal provided an explanation:

I was told that there was a nawab in Gujrat who would sit on his throne and abducted girls would be paraded before him and he would choose the pretty ones. The ones who were young, he used to feel them, the older

[1] Anis Kidwai, *Azadi ki Chaon Mein.* Both the above stories are from this book.

ones he would give away. The girls could not do anything—protest, nothing. He would say, give such and such in category no 1, in category no 2, and the best ones, give them in the zenana. Then I heard that two boys, whose parents had been killed, they had been kept also. I heard about this, and I went and asked them to return the boys. They said, no, we will not give these boys back. I said, why, you have a family of your own. She [one of the nawab's wives] said, yes, I have three boys of my own. Then why have you kept these? She said, there is a method behind this. We don't just simply pick up anybody, we don't just take the garbage. We choose who we take. Now these boys, they are studying alongside my boys, they have tuitions (the boys were brought before me and presented to me) and both of them and my children, they are all studying and then I will send them to England because I have money. These children are so intelligent that they will influence my boys, and when they marry, these two boys, their children will be very intelligent . . .

According to Damyanti, and other social workers, the myth about the greater intelligence of Hindus and Sikhs was a commonly held one. It was based, they said, on the economic and intellectual success of Hindus and Sikhs generally, and was the counterpart, I am assuming, of the stereotype of the libidinous and rapacious Muslim. Hindus, according to this stereotype, could then be weak physically, but their mental powers were strong, while the Muslims were the opposite. If it is indeed true that children were abducted for this reason, it is both tragic and ironic that, just as the bodies of women became vehicles for the honour—and dishonour—of the race, so the bodies of children, and in this case male children, became the vehicles for the passage of something as nebulous as intelligence, and a testimony to the insidious way in which stereotypes can take hold of people's consciousness.

If some adults had found it difficult to talk about their experiences as children, there were others who had deliberately silenced them—perhaps because they were too bitter, too difficult to remember, or perhaps because they reminded them of a time best forgotten. In the Gandhi Vanita Ashram at Jalandhar I was told about a successful woman doctor who had, according to ashram workers, been a child of the ashram. Her mother was widowed at Partition, and came into the ashram with her two children, a daughter and a son. The children spent much of their lives in the ashram, but, being of a different class than many of the children there, were at the receiving end of a number of privileges. I was told that it was the ashram that had paid for their education, that had helped the girl, particularly, to win scholarships to study medicine, and that had then provided different forms of support. Married and in a successful medical practice now, the doctor did not wish to remember any of this. She agreed to talk to me, but asked that her name not be mentioned because her children knew nothing of her past, and she did not want them to know. Not, she said, that there was anything to be ashamed of, for, according to her, she was a self-made woman, and although she and her mother had lived in the ashram they had never taken any charity from the authorities. This was, of course, quite a different story from that told by the ashram authorities.

It seemed to me then that part of her fear of being seen as an ashram child also had to do with her identity as a woman. Her mother had come into the ashram after Partition: the doctor was at pains to tell me that the mother had not wanted to do so, that after her husband's death (he was apparently in the army) she had insisted on staying on in Pakistan, but that she had been advised or pushed into doing so by her male relatives. 'She didn't live on ashram largesse,' she said, 'she continued to receive my father's pension.' Ashram largesse, of course, consisted of more than just money — it meant a home, security, work, education for children. But the doctor did not wish to acknowledge any of this. Her desire to distance herself from other ashram children also had to do with this — most of them were children of abducted women ('my mother had nothing to do with *those* women,' she told me), and therefore were somehow tainted, impure. She, on the other hand, was different.

The Indian State mounted a massive and widespread relief operation after Partition. Women who were widowed or rendered single by Partition were taken on by the State as permanent liabilities. Partition children were also provided facilities — education, homes, orphanages, sometimes adoption. But from the vantage point of her successful life today, the doctor did not wish to remember any of this. The denial also seemed to me to be connected with the class to which she belonged: rendered virtually assetless by Partition, she did not want to see herself as anything other than a 'self-made woman' — an image that is important to hundreds of Punjabis. And for that reason, the story of her childhood now did not exist — instead, it was slowly transforming itself into another, a different childhood. Her presence in the ashram could not be denied, but its nature could be transformed. The doctor, Kulwant Singh, Murad, Trilok Singh — there were many kinds of Partition children.

*   *   *

The children of abducted women posed other kinds of problems. In 1954 the governments of India and Pakistan agreed that abducted persons recovered by either country could not be forced to go to the other country. This reversed their earlier decision which has clearly said that no matter what the women said they wanted, they had to go back to their respective countries, defined by their religions. The change came about because most women by now had children, and were reluctant to part with them. And many families were willing to take women back, but not their children.

The definition of abducted persons was broad. In the Indian legislation that was passed (The Abducted Persons Recovery and Restoration Act of 1949) an abducted person could mean 'a male child under the age of sixteen years or a female of whatever age who is, or immediately before the 1st day of March, was missing and who on or after that day and before 1st January 1949, has become separated from his or her family and is found to be living with or under the control of any other individual or family and in the latter case includes a child born to any such female after the said date.' In other words, children picked up by either community at the time of Partition, or in the years following it, women similarly abducted, and children born to such women after Partition, or even women and/or children of one religion found living with members of the other, would be taken as being abducted.

What about those children who were yet to be born? Many abducted women who were recovered were found to be pregnant. A way had to be found to keep them out of public view until such time as the child was born, and then to separate the child from them. Or, if the pregnancy was in the early stages, to 'help' them to decide what to do with the child. Damyanti Sahgal described what was done:

> All those who were recovered, we opened camps for them, in Hoshiarpur, Jalandhar . . . these were young girls, and it had been more than a year that we had begun to recover them. Many of them were expecting [a child]. They were pregnant. This became a real problem. What could we do? We did ask them, and often they'd become very adamant. After all, it [Damyanti is here referring to abortions, though she did not want to use the word] must be done . . . but they were mothers after all, and they would often say, we don't want to do it, this they would say to me afterwards. They said, let me have the child. So for this the government had made Sharda Bhavan [in Allahabad] a place for children.
>
> Children born of Musalmaan fathers, unwanted children . . . Often a woman would say, I want to take the child with me, but I can't keep him/her with me, how will I live? Everyone will say 'thoo, thoo' to me. And then those who were actually pregnant, we'd ask them, do you want to have this child taken away? You know this hospital, Kapoor hospital, we would send the girls there for 'safai' (cleansing)—those who were willing I mean.

Damyanti's sister Kamla corroborated this story: 'It was a government rule,' she said:

> . . . they had this programme. But abortion, it was illegal. So masi [the reference here is to Premvati Thapar, one of the senior officers in charge of the recovery operation] said to them, this is very cruel, these girls are so unhappy, if these children are born, what will they do? She said, what can I do? It is a rule. But this Doctor Kapoor, in Karol Bagh, he was told, if you do this, if you do their abortions, I'll pay you the money, and with that your hospital will be made, and these poor girls, they will be saved. So the girls were all sent to Kapoor hospital and he performed illegal abortions. He could have gone to jail for this . . . There were women who refused to have abortions done also. They would say, on that side we now have no one, here too we will not be accepted, all we have is this child.

While some women agreed to have abortions (and indeed, every social worker I spoke to confirmed these mass abortions, but several said they did not wish to be quoted on the subject: 'you see,' they said, 'abortion was illegal at the time') or more precisely, were coerced into agreeing to have abortions, others went through with having the children, or indeed, by the time they were recovered, had already had children. For them, 'they would hand over their children to the home in Allahabad. With children, it was very difficult. And when women used to want to visit their children, to meet them — if, that is, their relatives would be willing to let the child live with dignity, if they would even look with respect on that child. Otherwise they had to give them up. It was a real problem. Each case was different. The mothers . . . would take time off from us and go there. What they did there, we don't know, how they felt . . . we would give them a ticket and tell them go ahead and meet your children. What kind of future those children had . . . who knows?'[2]

And indeed, no one knows: the 'disappearance' of thousands of such children is one of the many tragedies of Partition history. According to Kamlaben Patel, while most women agreed to a 'medical checkup', older women, those who were above thirty-five or so, were often ashamed at having to do so. They felt they had reached a certain kind of status in their original families and now they were ashamed at having to go back to them after having had an abortion. Equally, if they actually had children from the new relationship, they were not keen to take them with them, for how would they explain their presence to the other children they already had? For younger women, especially first-time mothers, this was not such a dilemma: most of them wanted to keep their children, but here, the problem was a different one — would they actually be allowed to do so? Kamlaben said:

> When the relatives of these women came to see them, they [the women] were reluctant to see them. They felt ashamed of themselves, and some even wept. They knew that if they went back to their parents, they could not take their babies with them, they would not be accepted into their families. And they had to make the difficult decision of whether to leave the babies and go, or to stay on in the camp. Most of them went, weeping at having to leave their babies behind.

[2] Damyanti Sahgal, personal interview.

What happened then, to these children? Kamlaben described how the children were sent by air, gratis, in small baskets, with an accompanying letter giving their particulars.

> There was an air service between Amritsar and Delhi. We asked them if they would agree to take the babies to Delhi. They agreed. Then, we would put each baby in a basket with an envelope containing its history. The basket also had a few clothes and other things. The basket would then be handed over to the air hostess who would hand it over to one of our social workers in Delhi. From Delhi it was sent again by plane to Allahabad. Once there, it would be taken by our social workers to the hospital. I think we sent across some two hundred or so babies in this way.

All sorts of arguments were put forward for why children had been picked up, or indeed, why they could not be released. In May 1948, Mir Inayatullah Khan, a father whose thirteen-year-old daughter had been abducted, appealed to the Pakistan High Commission in India for help in her recovery. As with many cases, he knew where the child was—the abductors were often known to families of abducted persons. In response to Inayatullah's appeal, the Deputy High Commissioner of Pakistan in India wrote to the Chief Secretary, East Punjab:

> 1. I have the honour to say that one Mir Inayatullah Khan has written to say that his daughter, Razia Begum, aged 13 years, has been kept by one Phawa Singh, District Amritsar, son of Jewan Singh of village Bhoma, P.S. Majithia, District Amritsar. In reply to his request for recovery of the girl, Mr Inayatullah was informed by the Indian Military authorites that his daughter did not wish to leave her husband. As you are aware, one of the decisions taken at the Inter-Dominion Conference on 6th December 1947 was that conversions and marriages of persons abducted after 1st March 1947 would not be recognized and all such persons must be returned to their respective Dominion. The wishes of the person concerned are irrelevant.
>
> 2. I should be grateful if arrangements are kindly made for the recovery of the girl so that she may be restored to her father in Lahore. The particulars of the girl are enclosed. An early reply is requested.[3]

[3] *Dawn*, 12 May 1948.

In the altered circumstances of Partition, then, a thirteen-year-old child, defined by the Indian State as a child, and listed thus in State lists of abducted persons, suddenly became capable of making an independent, adult choice about a 'husband', a choice that also implied rejecting a parent.

* * *

Partition children were now joined by another problematic category: 'post-abduction children'. From January 1, 1954 to September 30, 1957, some 860 children were left behind by Muslim women who were 'rescued' and 'restored' to Pakistan, and 410 children were taken with them. On the other side, a 1952 figure of children born to Hindu and Sikh women in Pakistan and brought back along with them stands at 102. Clearly, these numbers only touched the tip of the iceberg. Thus, there were two kinds of post-abduction children: those born to Muslim women who had been abducted in India and then recovered, and those born to Hindu and Sikh women who had been abducted in Pakistan and then recovered. In both cases the children were of mixed blood — where then, did they belong? The problem did not end there: the agreement arrived at between the two countries (and the subsequent legislation) had fixed a cut-off date, finalized after considerable discussion: March 1, 1947. March was fixed because the first disturbance had taken place in Punjab at this time. Any liaisons, marriages or conversions after this date were not recognized as voluntary. Naturally then, the children born of such unions also entered a troubled space, but what kind of date could be put to fix the 'legitimacy' of the children? A child born in, say June or July 1947, and of mixed parentage, had to have been conceived before the cut-off date so he/she entered the ambivalent space of illegitimacy. Or, the mother may have been pregnant when she was abducted and the child in her womb could well have been legitimate, but her arrival in the world after the cut-off date would then brand her as illegitimate.

By this token then, to whom did the child belong, the mother or the father? And accordingly, where should he/she be sent — to the land of the mother or the father? A child born of a Muslim mother and a Hindu father, what was there, asked one member of the Constituent Assembly, where a debate raged on these issues, to guarantee that that child would not be made to live like a 'kaffir' if he/she was sent off to Pakistan? Let us look, he said, at the question 'from the point of view of the abducted woman. The children to her are a sign of the humiliation to which she has been subjected for a year or two. From her point of view, the children are unwanted and if she returns to Pakistan with these children, I think we may be almost certain that they will not be treated as members of their mother's family. In all probability they will be sent to an orphanage.' Why then, the speaker went on to ask, should the children not be kept back in India since 'their father, whatever *his original conduct might have been* (my italics), is prepared to claim them as his own and to bring them up the best way he can . . .'[4]

No matter, then, that the father was an abductor. His claim was stronger than that of the mother. Similar thoughts were expressed at a conference held in Lahore to discuss the fate of post-abduction children. The majority of social workers attending the meeting felt it made more sense to leave children (of abducted women) who were born in Pakistan with their fathers, instead of allowing the women to bring them to India. For in India, the chances were that they would end up in homes and orphanages, presumably because of the purity pollution taboos in Hindu/Sikh society. This view was, however, countered by others who insisted that women should be allowed to take their children with them. Two of the key women involved in recovery work, Rameshwari Nehru and Mridula Sarabhai, also had strong differences of opinion on the subject, with Rameshwari Nehru being more sympathetic to the women. After much discussion a compromise was arrived at by which it was agreed that women could take their children with them to India for fifteen days during which time they could decide whether they wished to keep them or not. The questions that remained shrouded in uncertainty were: what would happen to the child if the woman decided not to keep him/her? Would the child be sent back to Pakistan? Over there, would the police or social workers make an attempt to relocate the father? If they did manage to find the father again—which was doubtful—would he be willing to take the child back? If he was

[4] *Constituent Assembly Debates*, 1949, pp. 708–80. All quotations relating to the debate are from here, unless otherwise stated.

not, who would take responsibility for the child? In actual fact, many women had to leave their children behind—they were more acceptable to families without them, and the children ended up, in all likelihood, in orphanages anyway. In Kamlaben's words:

> The government had passed an ordinance that for women whose babies were born in Pakistan they would have to leave them behind, and children born in India would have to stay in India. A conference was called in Lahore to discuss this but I refused to attend it. I told Mridulaben that I would not attend because if I did, I would be constrained to say what I felt. I said to her, how can it be that a mother, who has already suffered so much, is now told that she can go across but she must leave her child?

'All I wanted to say,' she said, 'was that a mother should not be separated from her child.' Although women had a choice in whether they wanted to keep the child with them, or leave him or her behind, this was hardly a real choice, and most felt forced to leave the children to the care of the camp. 'As each woman left,' said Kamlaben, 'leaving her child behind, she wept, begging the camp authorities to look after the child, to keep her informed. Promises made in good faith by the authorities were often broken—once the woman had left, for them, that was the end of the story. The child's life was another, a different story.'

Within the Constituent Assembly, a significant part of the debate on the Abducted Persons Recovery and Restoration Act was devoted to discussing the difficult question of post-abduction children. Because the Bill/Act being debated had to do with the recovery of Muslim women in India, the question here was whether or not to send their children to Pakistan with them or to keep them in India—the flip side of the question that was discussed at the Lahore conference. Sardar Hukam Singh questioned the assumption that the mother was the person most concerned with the child. 'There may be cases,' he said, 'where the mother might not be willing to take that child to Pakistan and the father may be very much anxious to keep the boy or girl here.' His own concern for them, as indeed that of many others in the Assembly, was, according to him, a humanitarian one. If such children are illegitimate on this side, 'they will be illegitimate on the other side too and I think it would be a matter of shame for the girl to take the child to that place. If such children are taken by the girls *they would be murdered or done away with*' (my italics). Thus it was, he said, from a humanitarian point of view that he was arguing. Such a view dictated that 'these boys and girls be kept in India'. The assumption was that their 'natural fathers' would look after these children. Other members of the Assembly supported this claim. Had the government looked, they asked, at the provisions of the Guardianship Act that was in force in India? Under that, the father had absolute right to custody of the child.

For the government, however, the problem was of another order. Social workers faced a major problem when recovering women: they did not want to leave their children behind. So the Minister was seeking to broaden the definition of an abducted person to take in children, or 'any male under the age of sixteen'. If children became abducted persons too, then, under the provisions of the Inter-Dominion Agreement, they too could be recovered along with their mothers. But, the Minister was asked, was this then to over-ride the law of the land, the law of guardianship which allowed custody to the father? Another member had a different suggestion: why not allow women to keep illegitimate children with them—but if the child was legitimate, the father should have 'absolute control'. Or, said a third, why not think of these children as 'war babies' and put the responsibility for them on the father? The question, of course, was: where were the fathers?

Not everyone subscribed to this view of the father's absolute claim to the child. Gopalswamy Ayyangar, Minister of Transport and Railways, said: 'I do not know about the law of guardianship. It all depends on how you treat the child, whether it is a legitimate child or an illegitimate child and with regard to a child so long as it is a baby, I think the mother should have the first preference as regards the custody, and when she cannot have the custody, her wishes must have the greatest possible consideration.'

Although the minister had his way in expanding the definition of abducted persons as he desired, not everyone in the Assembly agreed with him. Earlier, Hriday Nath Kunzru from UP had suggested that children be kept out of the definition of abducted persons. Could a man, who had abducted a woman, he asked, claim to be father of the offspring of that union? 'It is true Sir,' he said, 'that the conduct of the abductor cannot be commended. He has been guilty of a highly reprehensible conduct, conduct that has put his country to shame. But let us look at the question from the point of view of the abducted woman. The children to her are a sign of the humiliation to which she has been subjected for a year or two. From her point of view, the children are unwanted, and if she returns to Pakistan with these children, I think we feel almost certain that they will not be treated as members of their mother's family. In all probability they will be sent to an orphanage.'

Others supported this stand. Pandit Thakur Das Bhargava, for example, stressed that the children should be kept back in India because 'all those children born in India are citizens of India'. Suppose, he went on to say, that a Hindu man and a Muslim woman had married, who would be the guardian of their children? If a Muslim woman was to take a child born of a Hindu father to Pakistan, 'the child will be considered illegitimate and is liable to be maltreated or killed'. Simply because the Ordinance stipulated that such a child should be sent to Pakistan was no reason why that should be done. Instead, if 'the father insists that he will look after the interests of the child and will see it properly brought up,' he said, 'I do not understand why, by executive action, that child should be given to Pakistan.'

But all members did not speak with one voice. Shri Brajeshwar Prasad (Bihar) felt there was little point in keeping the children in India, for Hindu society was different from Muslim society and had no place for these children, 'illegitimate in the eyes of the law'. Were they to remain in India, such children would remain 'as dogs'.

Were these children, born of Muslim mothers and Hindu fathers then really citizens of India? Were the considerations which made some members of the Constituent Assembly speak out in favour of holding them back in India with their natural-but-abductor fathers considerations of citizenship? Would the same logic have applied to children of Hindu mothers and Muslim fathers? Did citizenship, in other words, devolve through the mothers or through the fathers, through nationality or religion?

In the newly independent, coming-into-its-own State, citizenship itself was a contested question, still in its formative stages and shrouded in considerable ambivalence. The State functioned, for example, as parent-protector and benevolent patriarch towards the millions of refugees who poured into the country. All welfare schemes, all compensation and re-habilitation policies, constructed the refugee as someone needing 'help', 'uplift' and 'welfare'. Punjabi refugees in particular countered this by as-serting their self-sufficiency, their independence, and their refusal to ask the State for charity. But this was as it applied to men. The woman as citizen was a different story altogether. If we go by Hriday Nath Kun-zru's logic that children born of Hindu fathers and Muslim mothers, re-gardless of the fact that the father was/might have been an abductor—in other words, someone who had flouted the laws of the land—were citizens of India, this would mean that Hindu and Sikh men could then assume citizenship for themselves and their children. But for Hindu and Sikh women, on the other hand, there was no such assumption. As mothers, and as citizens of secular India, being reclaimed by the mother country, they nonetheless had to make the difficult choice of whether they could take their children with them or leave them behind. Not only did the children occupy an ambivalent space wherein they belonged to both communities, which therefore complicated the matter of their citizenship, but it would seem that the lesser space occupied by their mothers as citizens also devolved on them.

As the recovery operation for abducted women showed, women's identities continued to be defined in terms of their religious commu-nities, rather than as citizens of one or the other country. They were denied the right—theoretically every citizen's right—to choose where they wished to live. In this, they had no recourse in law beyond the tri-bunal set up to decide disputed cases. They did not even have the right to decide what to do with their children. Clearly, citizenship was not an entirely gender-neutral concept. It is in this context that the attempt to include children in the definition of abducted persons in the Abducted Persons Restoration and Recovery Act becomes important. The Act de-fined an abducted person as: 'a male child under the age of sixteen years or a female of whatever age . . .' Females of any age then, could be ab-ducted persons, but with male children the question of their being ab-ducted ended at age sixteen, the age at which they presumably moved from being minors to majors. Could it be that those drafting the Act felt that after the age of sixteen, a young male was capable of deciding which identity he wanted to adopt, where he wanted to live and belong, and that women—no matter what age—were not similarly capable?

The fate of abducted children threw into question another much discussed and contested subject at the time of Partition: motherhood. I discussed in the previous chapter about how the representation of India as the mother, and the violation of its (her) body through the creation of Pakistan, was mirrored by the violation of the bodies, individually and collectively, of India's women, Hindus and Sikhs who had been raped and abducted by men of the other religion. The mothers of illegitimate children had somehow forsaken their claim to legitimate motherhood. The 'purity' of the mother, her sanctity, and the suppression of her sexuality, were thrown in question by the presence of such children or of their (the mother's) wish to keep them. Just as abducted women had to be brought back into the fold of their religion, their nation, community and family, so also their children had to be separated from them, rendered anonymous, so that the women could once again be reinstated as mothers, and the material proof of their liaisons made less threatening or dangerous by being taken away from the mothers. Perhaps the greatest irony of all was that it was the State that was now defining something as private as motherhood, with, of course, the tacit support of the community and the family.

*　　*　　*

In the end, of course, each case was different. Some women kept their children, others left them, while still others had no choice in the matter. While post-abduction children posed the important problem of legitimacy and illegitimacy, the children of women widowed as a result of Partition could more easily benefit from the welfare policies of the State. These children, and their mothers, became 'permanent liabilities' of the State. Orphanages and homes were run by the government, as well as by voluntary organizations. Financial assistance was provided to students and a special section in the Ministry of Relief and Rehabilitation was devoted to the rehabilitation of displaced unattached women and children. In theory, the Government of India 'accepted the responsibility for the care and maintenance of unattached, destitute displaced women and children.'[5] State governments were authorized to pay a monthly cash allowance of fifteen rupees for one woman plus seven or eight rupees for each of her dependent children to those women who were physically disabled and could not be admitted into homes. Despite the many efforts to rehabilitate destitute children, however, the scale of destitution, and all its attendant problems, was a matter of concern.

In 1954, a former general of the Indian National Army, J. K. Bhonsle, who was also, at the time, deputy minister for Rehabilitation, launched a scheme. His idea was to put in place a training programme which could 'restore the morale of displaced students and impart to them a sense of inflexible discipline joined to physical fitness and perfect allegiance to moral and spiritual values.' In a curious twist of irony, the problem of displaced children, and indeed the problems they faced, came to be seen as one of 'indiscipline' and the solution—if a solution could be found at all—as one of restoring 'moral and spiritual values'. It is not clear exactly which children the scheme was addressing. But its aim was to raise the low morale of students (for indiscipline was seen mainly as a problem of morale) and to produce a 'strong, self-reliant citizen capable of making an enduring contribution to the nation's destiny'. In keeping with this the scheme laid stress on 'India's cultural heritage and traditions, on the life of our heroes and heroines, and on citizenship and patriotism . . .'[6]

To begin with, the National Discipline Scheme was tried out with a small group of orphans and children of widows at the Kasturba Niketan School in Lajpat Nagar in Delhi. It was then extended to other refugee schools covering, eventually, more than 100,000 children, both displaced and otherwise. For the fledgling, beleagured and embattled Indian State, the problem of orphans, deserted and displaced children, or children of abducted women, could not have been an easy one to tackle. A number of relief measures, such as setting up homes and infirmaries, giving educational subsidies, etcetera, were put into operation. But these could only

[5] U. Bhaskar Rao, *The Story of Rehabilitation*, p. 77.
[6] U. Bhaskar Rao, *The Story of Rehabilitation*, p. 77.

be availed of by children who were already in homes, and for whom the government took responsibility. For those who had no home, who were out on the streets, there was no such recourse. And then, relief measures addressed only the tip of the iceberg—no matter how much different schemes focussed on discipline and morale building, these could hardly address the trauma the children had been through, and which, at the time, they could barely have articulated. Several charitable institutions joined the relief effort. These included the Save the Children Committee, the Kasturba Gandhi National Memorial Trust, the Trust for Sindhi Women and Children, the Arya Pradeshik Pratinidhi Sabha, and the Jainendra Gurukul, Panchkula. They worked in collaboration with the Central Advisory Board. We are told that 'ameliorative work was their forte', but there is no way of knowing whether or not they were able to 'ameliorate' the kinds of problems children faced.

*   *   *

There is much that still remains unknown. I have often wondered, for example, how many of the children left behind, abandoned, or killed were girls. Social workers said most of the children abandoned at camps were girl children, and the pressure of work made it difficult to screen potential adopters. Many young girls then ended up as domestic workers or as prostitutes, swelling the numbers of the 'whole generation' of young girls that the writer Krishna Sobti said had been 'sacrificed' to Partition. Homes and educational institutions were set up for both girls and boys: but when it came to the time to leave and make an independent life, it was the boys—young men—who were able to do that more easily than the girls or young women. Some were married off by the ashram authorities and were able to make lives of their own. But for many, Partition changed the shape of their lives.

Concern for the legitimacy or illegitimacy of children needs to be placed in the overall context of Partition: ever since divisions began to surface between the different communities, a concern for the purity of the Hindu and Sikh religions had become important, particularly in the Punjab. Here, the growing strength of the Arya Samaj and the gradual solidification of a Punjabi-Hindu consciousness were the direct result of the fear of conversion by both Muslims and Christians. Loss of the legitimate identity through conversion was, it seemed, the greatest of dangers. With Partition, one part of the body of the nation was forever lost, effectively converted. But, inside the bodies of women and children, the boundaries remained fluid. Hindu and Sikh women were in relationships—apparently forced, but often known to be voluntary—of both love and desire, with Muslim men. But, with some help from the State, they could perhaps be brought back into the Hindu fold, purified. But inside the bodies of children the blood that flowed was intimately mixed. No separation could be made here, no clear lines drawn about where these children should go. No boundaries could be set to their beings. Better, then, to forget about them altogether, perhaps even to pretend that they did not exist.

This we have done with ease. Many parents who lost their children at the time attempted to locate them. They put in applications, filed reports, sent out messages by word of mouth. Some, like Dharam Kaur from village Dhera Dhupsadi in Kurukshetra, were lucky. She lost several relatives, in the violence of Partition. Returning to the site of the violence, Dharam Kaur found the bodies of her relatives, but not that of her daughter, Mohinder Kaur. Unknown to her, Mohinder had been picked up by a good samaritan, a nurse called Grace, and placed in an orphanage where she lived as Anwar Sadeeqa. It was only years later, when Sadeeqa married, that Grace revealed the story of her past to her.

One day, while travelling in a bus with her daughter, Azmat, Sadeeqa found herself sitting next to a Sikh. As children do, the child reached out and touched him, and for some inexplicable reason, called him mamu, uncle. Sadeeqa broke down, and told the old man her story. Niranjan Singh, who had himself just found a long-lost sister, promised to help. On his return to India, he learnt that Lubanwala (where Sadeeqa's family was from) refugees had settled in Kurukshetra, which was near his home. As the story is told:

Niranjan would board a bus every morning and make an announcement: 'I have come from Pakistan where a lady misses her mother very much. If any of you is a Lubanwala Sikh, please stand up.' It worked. Through the word-of-mouth network that lies at the core of many post-Partition reunions, Niranjan learnt that Sadeeqa's parents had survived the Partition violence and settled in Dhera Dhupsadi, a tiny hamlet near Kurukshetra.[7]

Niranjan Singh followed this lead. He arrived, unannounced, one night at Dharam Kaur's house with a note from Sadeeqa which said 'I, Mohinder Kaur, daughter of Javind Singh, am alive.' And, some years later, Sadeeqa was able to come to Dhupsadi, and meet her mother; and her mother travelled to Pakistan to attend the wedding of her granddaughter.

But not everyone had such good fortune. Workers at the Gandhi Vanita Ashram in Jalandhar recount that in 1947 a two-year-old child was brought to the ashram. No one knew who she belonged to or whence she came. Today, at age fifty-two, she still continues to live there, a child of history, without a history.

Not everyone was as lucky as Dharam Kaur and Sadeeqa, however. In August 1956 the Karachi-based newspaper *Dawn* carried an editorial about the different approaches of the two countries to the question of the recovery of abducted women. The editorial referred to a particular case, that of 'a young girl whose distressed father has often told his tale of woe in our correspondence columns.' 'Of what value,' asked the editorial, 'are joint pledges to extend facilities to relatives of abducted women in the pursuit of clues, when a father, now a citizen of Pakistan, who visits his native town to reclaim his daughter, is not only denied legal protection and assistance from executive authority but is actually thrust in jail on flimsy charges and in effect deprived of his right to fight his case.'

The girl's father, Qamaruddin Ahmed, had made several visits to India to find his daughter, a minor who had been abducted by someone from his own village. In 1951, the father was arrested and jailed on charges of being a spy. He spent three years in jail. 'Refusal to restore my child, by the Bharat government,' he said, 'was not surprising, but our own government, in spite of my repeated entreaties, neither provided me any legal help, nor did it assist me in the recovery of my child.' After serving his sentence in India, when Quamruddin came back to Pakistan, he once

---

[7] *India Today*, special issue to mark fifty years of Indian independence, August 1997.

again appealed to the Pakistan authorities for help in recovering his daughter. And was told that 'the Government of Bharat had declined to return my child. Our Government had also dropped the matter.'[8] In 1957, the recovery programme for abducted women was officially closed. And with it, this father's—and that of many other parents'—search for their children.

*　*　*

In the last chapter I spoke of a book that a friend and I had found, that provided a district-by-district listing of Hindu and Sikh abducted women in Pakistan. Entries in the book are classified according to whether the abducted person is a child (usually below sixteen, although sixteen year olds are also sometimes listed as adults) or a woman, or a widow, or—and this is rare—an adult male. In an attempt to look at the dimensions of the problem of the abduction of children, I scanned this list at random, and came up with the following statistics. In Campbell-pur, out of a total of 92 people abducted, 30 were children; in Dera Ghazi Khan this figure was 107 and 23; in Rawalpindi, of 598 abductions, 146 were children; in Gurdaspur, there were 69 children in 188 abductions; in Sheikhupura, of 916 abductions, 318 were children. On an average, male children formed between a third to a half of this figure in most places.

I would like to end this account of children with a sample listing of a very small number of the children who were abducted at the time of Partition (Table 2). The entries here pertain to Sheikhupura district. If this list is to be believed at all, in many cases the rapists and abductors of children were, as is often the case, people from the same village, people who were known to the families whose children disappeared.

*　*　*

What I have attempted above is in the nature of an exploration into a relatively unmapped terrain. Throughout, I have been faced with the question: how do we explore the histories of children? If women are difficult subjects and silences have built up about so much in their lives, how much more difficult it is to look at the lives of children, particu-

[8] *Dawn*, August 1956.

Table 2. Sheikhupura district

R. No.	Particulars of abducted person	Place and date of abduction	Particulars of abductors
QSP/S-13/ U-3C	Angraiz Singh, 4 years, s/o Prakash, Moh. Akandpurian, P.S., P.O. Sayeed Wala, Teh. Nankana Sahib, Sheikhupura	Sheikhupura during riots	He is likely to be in or about Sheikhupura
QSP/B/ N/-4C	Arvel Kaur, 9 years, d/o Magar Singh, P.S. Muridki, Teh. Shahadra, Distt. Sheikhupura	Chak. No. 9 Sheikhupura Sept. 1947	Bakshi Thadola Pind Thadel, Distt. Sheikhupura
QSP/S-2/ N-1C	Amar Kaur, 4.5 years, Vill. Sheikuch P.O. Kathiala Kalan, P.S., Teh. and Distt. Sheikhupura	Vill. Sheikuch, Distt. Sheikhupura Aug. 47	Kathiala Kalan, Teh. and Distt. Sheikhupura
QSP/S-13/ N-3C	Ashok Kumar, 3.5 years, s/o Harbans, Vill. Lal P.O. and P.S. Naranag Mandi, Teh. Shahadara, Distt. Sheikhupura	Narang Mandi Aug. 47	Karim bibi, w/o Jawahar Mosech, Narang Mandi, Distt. Sheikhupura
QSP/S-1/ N3C	Dayal, 3 years, d/o Dharam Singh, Vill. Kalary, Chak 282, Teh. and Distt. Sheikhupura	Kalary No. 282 Sheikhupura	Phallo Isai, Vill. Kallary, Chak No. 282, Distt. Sheikhupura

larly when it is assumed, often with some justification, that they cannot speak on their own behalf. If Partition history has had little to say about children, despite their centrality in it, this lack is not unique to it. For history in general, and particularly Indian history, has not really addressed this important question. In the West, children of holocaust survivors have recently restarted the process begun by Anne Frank many years ago, of looking at their lives at a time when the world seemed to be collapsing around them. Partition was just such a moment: a child may not have been able to understand the violent breakup of family and community, the sudden loss of parents, but he/she could not have remained untouched by it. What, we might ask, has happened to these children? Even as their lives and futures were being decided, many of them remained in ashrams and homes, or were being transported in baskets across the country from one institution to another, most of them lost to history. When and how shall we begin to recover the histories of these children? How shall we insert them into history?

MURAD   *'I would always be out playing . . .'*

Murad, a tonga puller in Lahore, was a child at the time of Partition and lived in India. Like many children, he too did not know what was happening and was forced to move to Pakistan. I have never met Murad: I reproduce his interview here with the permission of the interviewers, Peter Chappell and Satti Khanna, for whose film it was done. I have chosen to include Murad's interview here after much thought and for very specific reasons. It seems to me that Murad's recollection of his childhood experience of dislocation exemplifies many things I have spoken of above. The rather sophisticated, somewhat terse and distant telling of his story is clearly the telling of an adult and Murad was in his fifties when Peter and Satti met him. Yet, according to them, it was the first time he was telling his story in a self-conscious way: if this was so, it made me wonder whether the process of such self-conscious recovery works to lend a coherence and linearity to narratives, such as Murad's seems to have. Another question that this narrative raised for me is whether the 'downplaying' that is so evident in what Murad says — 'we lay there and passed the time' is how he describes an experience that must surely have been full of fear — almost as if the whole thing was a game, is one way of making sense of an experience that may otherwise have been incomprehensible to the child who lived it. It is perhaps because of this that I have been drawn to this interview again and again, for it brings home to me, repeatedly, the question of how a child makes sense of such a traumatic experience and indeed how the adult that child inevitably turns into, remembers and recounts that experience. When Peter Chappell and Satti Khanna spoke to Murad, there was no ambivalence in how he felt about the differences between Hindus and Muslims. Yet in his recollection of his childhood there is an element of nostalgia — and of realism in the last story he tells — for the happy mixing that took place between the two communities. Did Lahore — which became symbolic of the uprooting — and Partition do this to him? Or would a Muslim or a Hindu child — would Murad in other words — have become increasingly Muslim anyway, aware of his identity as someone different from his Hindu neighbour, or was this the result of Partition? And had such awareness come in the normal course, would it have drawn such deep lines through Murad's life as the move to 'Lahore' seemed to have done? These are questions that need to be posed in every instance where one can see a crystallizing of identities around religion after Partition. It is not a question that can be easily answered.

Murad's interview is also important because it is one of the few that provides a perspective from the 'other side'—and it is not surprising to see how similar the experiences are. Minus the geographical location and the name, Murad's narrative could be that of a poor child on either side of the border. More important than the question of location and religion then, are the telling insights Murad offers. To give just one example: 'Landlords go to the landlords and the poor go to the poor,' he says, describing how and where he sought support and solidarity. Class is not so easily dismissed after all.

*　*　*

Murad:

I was a small child. My uncle lived in India. Someone would take me to any of the persons around, but they would refuse to take responsibility for me. People would say that I would bring bad luck. A schoolmaster accepted me and I started living with him. He cared for me. He was more sympathetic to me than my close relatives and looked after my needs. I would take his cattle to the grazing ground. Then the controversy over Pakistan and Hindustan came up.

I would always be out playing . . . My maternal uncles took me to their homes. They thought I would be killed while I was playing out on the streets. One day, we were inside the house. My uncle came in and sat down. Sikhs came! Daughter-fuckers!

First they knocked my uncle down . . . I thought I would also be killed and tried to get out. Sugarcane chaff was piled at the back. I jumped into it and wrapped myself with the stuff. There was another uncle of mine. He came after some time, shook me and said what now? We should run away, I said. They would not spare us even if they killed my uncle. My uncle who had been killed had given a few coins . . . Then we came to a camp nearby. It was miserable there. A man was bringing the sugarcane and another was cutting this into pieces. If they saw a Muslim they would kill him. Somehow, hiding, we reached the camp. Near the camp there was a sugarcane field, no food to be had, we lay on the ground and passed the time.

Both my parents died when I was a child. Wherever I was taken, people refused to take me in saying I would bring ill luck . . . Nobody was ready to keep me. Unwillingly the older uncle took me in. A few Sikhs lived around our village on the main road. People said, 'he plays outside all the time . . . There are bullets flying around, he will get killed.' So they took me back to my village, then some mirasis took care of me. I would graze their horses and eat with them. I got up on the roof, saw the Sikhs come and kill three or four of them. I thought, if they have killed these men, why should they spare me? They will kill me as well. So I jumped into a pile of sugarcane chaff and lay down. I thought they'll think it's sugarcane and go away, they'll get lost. Then we will figure out a way to escape. My uncle came and said, 'they've killed your grandfather as well, let's go away from here.' We headed towards the camp, the Sikhs were in strength all around. A military train came, they said, all those who do not have families to protect them should get into the train. 'We are ready to leave for Pakistan.' We got in. There was a qila near River Beas. The train stopped and we got down. We were three or four boys. They said, let us drink lassi. I said no, I will not drink lassi, they must have poisoned it. We entered the bazaar. All three of them had lassi but I did not. I said, better to drink the river water, the soldiers have checked it. It's free of poison. We came back. All three collapsed and were dead.

Then there were lorries ready to leave for Pakistan. A man said, the Sikhs will slaughter us on the way. I am not going, I said. I will leave only when our soldiers come. I am already lost. Why invite death in this way? The lorries owned by Muslims came. We got in. We got out at Wagah border. Now find your way, they said. Nowhere to go, I thought. I did not know the way. I started following someone from Jalandhar. I would not spend the few coins I had. They would be needed if things got worse. As I reached Sahedra night was falling. There were date trees and shrubs all around. People were miserable and sick with cholera. I left the place and moved towards a village called Attari. I saw an old woman. I said, mother, I want to stay here. 'You can stay here,' she said. 'Where have you come from?' she asked. 'From a well to an abyss,' I replied, 'I have no relatives.' She was kind, she gave me roti to eat. 'If you want to stay we can provide you with a house,' she said. 'What for, dear mother?' I said, 'What can I do with a house? I have no family.' I came out on the road. A truck came. It stopped. Buses were rare in those times. People used to travel in trucks. A man shouted: 'To Jaranwala.' 'Do you dig roots out there?' I said, 'I am already uprooted. Why bother me?' 'Friend, you seem to have suffered a lot,' the driver said, 'come, get in.' I got down at Jaranwala. I roamed about a bit and said, this is the place where they dig the roots out.

I knew no one. A tonga man came shouting, 'Saran di Khoo.' 'What is that?' I asked. 'It's a stop,' he replied. 'Can you take me there?' I asked. 'Why not,' he replied. I was a boy, so he said 'you won't be a burden. You are just a child.' But anyhow, I would lose a bit of money. 'Never mind, I will give you a free ride.' 'You are kind,' I said. He took me to that stop. There was a village nearby. I came into the village. Landlords go to landlords and the poor go to the poor. There were some porters. I went to them, told them my story. 'We are already in a bad shape,' they said. 'It seems you have suffered even more than we did but we can't make both ends meet.' If this is the state, I thought, why not go to the mandi and try my luck there. Can one find work there? 'Yes, you can,' they said. They showed me a hut.

Then I came to Lahore. There was a 'Shawan da Dera' here. I would come to this place regularly. There were cartdrivers who plied tongas. I started looking after the horses. I would get two annas per horse for scrubbing them. The time passed. I said to the chaudhry, 'Can't I ply a tonga?' 'You don't know the roads in Lahore.' 'I will find out. I can ask those who know.' There was a cartdriver who had left his job. His horse was there. No experienced cartdriver was available. So Chaudhry asked me to drive the tonga. I would ask the passengers when to turn, where do you want to get to, which road leads to your place. I tried to hide the fact that I knew nothing. But what a misfortune! My hands and feet started swelling. They became so big. I was out on the street again. I came across an old woman. She offered me a bit of money. I refused and I asked her to pray for me. With God's grace I recovered. There is a 'khangah' of naugaza (nine yards). I started visiting it. There a man asked me, 'Do you have a family?'

A passenger came and asked whether I could take him to Meeran di Khahi. 'How much will you charge?' he asked. 'What is the normal fare in your opinion?' He mentioned an amount. I said, all right. I did not know the way. 'Which way,' I asked him, 'tell me the short cut.' 'Straight to Delhi Gate.' When we reached Delhi Gate, I asked him, 'Which way, sir? Should I turn?' 'No, bugger, go straight.' In my way I tried to be clever so that he could not find out I was not a Lahori. We reached the 'khooli'. I stopped. I got down on the pretence of getting a packet of cigarettes. I went to a shop and asked where this place was. 'It is this very place,' they said. 'How much are tonga charges per passenger from Bhaali to this place?' 'One rupee for a full tonga-load.' He would give twelve annas, I thought. But he gave me a rupee and a half.

There is not much to think about Partition. In our clan marriages used to be arranged as if by 'vatta', a weighing stone. If you have a woman, give us one in return. Give a kilo, get a kilo in return. If you had no woman, you were lost. I was very disturbed. Oh God, I had nothing to fall back upon. Where can you go, if you have nowhere to go? When Id came I felt very sad and I had disturbed nights. You know what happened in India—the riots. First there were elections. Muslim League and Congress appeared on the scene. Lorries came and they asked people to vote. We heard Qaid-e-Azam was our leader. Rumours started spreading. Someone would say you are going over there. Where? I would ask him. Where the hell can we go? I have been living here for centuries. They would say, to your Pakistan. Where will Pakistan be? I would ask. 'Somewhere near Lahore.' But I hadn't seen Lahore.

People would ask, is Lahore a city? I didn't know. I had never been there. No, they would insist you too will go to Lahore. But how? Where I have been born is Lahore for me, but anyhow we were dragged to Lahore.

The root cause of the trouble is this. The English never allowed the men, particularly the Muslim ones, to come up. They never allowed anyone to become strong. The English did not let the Muslims become strong. This is my observation—I have seen this myself. I was a young man when a Hindu Khatri asked an Englishman a question. 'Sir, Muslims can't even find two meals a day. Something should be done to solve this problem.' He said, let them be as they are. They will start killing people the very day their bellies have food . . . now . . . you can smell murder all around. Everywhere you encounter police.

In our village there were two telis, oilpressers, very strong young men. There used to be a very big mela, predominantly a Sikh mela. People would come from far-flung areas to attend it. There would be mahants who managed the gurudwara affairs. Sikhs would carry them on a charpoy. They would sprinkle flour all round and chant *hare ram, hare ram*.

In the past Hindus and Muslims lived like brothers, and looked after each other. Even a big landlord would offer all kinds of help when a poor menial worker was getting married. He would entertain even a very big marriage party. When the party came, they would gather together all the pots and cots. There was a lot of fellow feeling. But when Partition took place, everything got turned upside down. They pierced even infants with their spears. They would carry dead bodies on their spears and one of them would exclaim, 'Oh, I found only one!' . . . So they started hating each other. There was such harmony before this—the poor could enter a rich house and ask for lassi . . .

Now a line has been drawn. Borders have been demarcated. We are here and they are there. If something is sent from Pakistan to India, Indians tax it heavily, and if a thing comes from India, Pakistanis do the same.

7
'MARGINS'

Despite the recent opening up of Partition histories there are many aspects that remain invisible in official, historical accounts of the event. Yet, as one begins to scratch the surface, even of what are seen as 'traditional' sources of history—documents, reports, official letters, newspaper accounts etc.—there is an immediate clamouring of 'voices' that demand to be 'heard', voices that tell of the many histories that lie, still undiscovered, in these pages. Among these are stories of very many people who inhabit a world that is somehow—falsely—seen as peripheral. These histories have remained hidden, to my mind because so much writing on Partition has focused on Hindus and Sikhs and Muslims—or more correctly on Hindu and Sikh and Muslim *men*—that it is as if no other identity existed. More, being Hindu, Muslim or Sikh has been understood only in *religious* terms. Differences of status and class among Hindus or Muslims, or indeed differences of gender or caste, those difficult things that complicate the borders of what we see as identity have, by and large, been glossed over. In its almost exclusive focus on Hindus and Sikhs and Muslims, Partition history has worked to render many others invisible. One such history is that of the scheduled castes, or untouchables. Harijans, Dalits, untouchables, by whatever name you call the protagonists of this history, have remained, in a sense, virtually untouchable even in the writing of this history. In trying to recover these voices I make no claim to have discovered something new. For many years, like others, I too have thought of Partition only in terms of religious identities, and more particularly, the identities of the two opposing communities. It is always difficult to pinpoint when one begins to arrive at a different understanding. For me, I think the process began with my exploration of the histories of women and children. In 1986, Peter Chappell, Sati Khanna and I had spoken to a woman, a sweeper from Batala, about Partition. At the time, I had automatically identified Maya Rani as a woman, assuming that it was from this identity that she would speak. But Maya, when she spoke to us, identified herself differently, as a Harijan, and only then as a woman. Was there then a history of Harijans too at Partition? I realized then that the stories of women and children were not the only ones that lay shrouded in silence. There were others, too, whose lives Partition had touched in unexpected ways, and about whom little was known. Thus it was that I began to look at other stories, other silences.

* * *

When we met her Maya was in her mid-fifties, a sturdy woman working as a sweeper in a school (which she called a college) in Batala. Once school duty was over, Maya did a bit of moonlighting, working in private houses to add to her income. Maya told us the story of her home, Dinanagar. As with many villages in 1947, the fate of hers too had hung in balance for a while. (And indeed, Gurdaspur district, in which Batala falls, was considered one of the 'disputed' districts, neither straightforwardly Muslim nor straightforwardly Hindu/Sikh.) Now there was a rumour that it would go to Pakistan, she said, and suddenly stories would fly that it would go to Hindustan. Each time one of these rumours became rife, people of the other community would abandon their homes and run, leaving everything behind. Maya and her friends watched this helter-skelter flight almost as if it was a game. She laughed as she told this story:

> Weren't we frightened? No, we weren't frightened—everyone tried to scare us, even our parents. But all the children of that area, none of us was scared. Often, we would leave our own roof and climb up onto a neighbour's, just to see. Then we all got together and started to go into people's houses. In some we found rice, in others almonds, sevian . . . we began to collect all these and pile them up in our house. Great big utensils, patilas, parats . . . we collected them all.
>
> Yes, we children did this. Then the city elders, Hindus, they felt this was not a good thing, this kind of looting, and it should be stopped, if possible without any ill feeling. About six or seven of the important ones got together and called us. We were all together, our people. They said, don't do this, you will also be searched later, all your things will be snatched away from you, you shouldn't do this. But we didn't stop, we just went on.

Our father also told us to stop, and each time he said that we'd say, yes, we'll stop. But as soon as the men went away to sit down and talk, we would start again . . . rice, food, all sorts of nice things. From one shop we stole pure ghee and almonds; at other places we found cloth. We collected so many utensils that we filled up a room as large as this one. Once we'd done this, the city elders announced that all copper utensils that were found in anyone's house would be confiscated. People should sell them. They must have wanted to get hold of them. So we sold the whole roomful, at two rupees or two and a half rupees a kilo. Later, people realized that this had all been a trick to snatch away all this cheaply — the shopkeepers took a lot of it . . .

I kept lots of new utensils, hamams, etc., for my wedding. I brought a lot of utensils with me when I got married. I also looted many razais, quilts, some already made and some which I made later with the material we found. There were eleven of us, girls, we all made our dowries with the stuff we collected . . . two of those girls were also married in Batala.

Maya's story seemed amazing to me. How could she and her friends have done this? Didn't anyone try to harm you, we asked. How did you escape the violence? Maya did eventually admit to being somewhat frightened while she and her friends looted their neighbours' houses. But, she said, 'we kept doing this, going from street to street. Our parents were very worried, they kept trying to stop us, saying we would get killed, people would take us for Musalmaans. *But we thought, who's going to take us away, who's going to kill us? We call ourselves Harijans. Hindus, Christians, no one can take us away.* (my italics) And like this, we jumped from roof to roof, not really caring what happened.'

The first time I heard this, it came as a shock to me. Loot and theft are a part of all situations of conflict, and for the economically disadvantaged the chaos of the situation offers opportunities to amass goods and wealth, so it was not that that worried me. But, like all Hindus, somewhere deep down inside me I had assumed that Harijans (Dalits), Gandhi's supposed 'children of God', relegated to the fringes of society, were part of the Hindu community, part of 'us'. Yet, why should they feel this? Was this how they saw themselves? Maya was quite clear that they did not see themselves as Hindus or Christians (or indeed anyone else). Rather, they had their own, distinctive identity. Hard on the heels of this realization came another: in mainstream Hindu society the customary invisibility of the Dalits is based on their status as scheduled castes, untouchables — people whose casteless status somehow places them outside the pale of caste Hindu society. They are the performers of menial, albeit essential, tasks: collecting refuse, cleaning toilets, tasks that must remain unseen, and more, untouched. And precisely for that reason, they remain 'invisible' and 'untouchable'. Here, with Maya, was an ironic twist to this untouchability which, if she was to be believed, actually acted as a protective shield in a fight that was supposed to be between Muslims and Hindus. Further, the fact that Harijans were, to some extent, rendered invisible in Partition violence had led to another kind of invisibility: that of history itself. I realized then that the extreme visibility of Muslims and Hindus and Sikhs in the history of Partition had worked to ensure that those looking at Partition did not 'see' any other identities. Beginning to apprehend this, at first only vaguely, I decided to consciously look for stories that could throw some light on the subject.

And there were many. In January 1948, two social workers, Sushila Nayyar and Anis Kidwai, went to visit Tihar village on the outskirts of Delhi. They had heard that a rich Hindu from Pakistan had left behind huge properties when he had moved, and had therefore, like many people, effected an exchange of property with a rich Muslim in Tihar to whom the land belonged. Each took the other's property. But neither was obliged to carry on with the other's business. The Hindu, therefore, threw out all previously employed workers from his newly acquired piece of property. Most of these were Muslims, but about a third were Harijans. The Muslims made their way to one or the other of the two Muslim camps that had been set up in the city. But for the Harijans, displaced in a war that was basically centred around Hindu and Muslim identities, there was nowhere to go. No camps to help them tide over the difficult time. No recourse to government — all too preoccupied at the moment with looking after the interests of Muslims and Hindus, no help from political leaders whose priorities were different at the time.

Not only were their priorities different, but there was another, more 'political' reason why leaders could not allow themselves to 'see' the

Harijans as separate, or different, from Hindus. In 1932, the colonial State had recognized the Dalits as a distinct group and had awarded them separate electorates. Then, a few months later, this was partially reversed by what came to be known as the Poona Pact. By this, the Congress, which was rapidly coming to be seen by virtue of its opposition to the Muslim League as representing Hindu interests, had drawn Dalits under its umbrella. They were part of the broader nationalist effort in Indian politics — thus while difference was recognized in that the Poona Pact established reservations, Harijans still formed part of the joint electorate. In 1946, this invisibility was further heightened when the Cabinet Mission put forward an interim plan which, it was hoped, would pave the way for a peaceful and planned transfer of power to Indians. The plan suggested the setting up of a Constituent Assembly consisting of Indian representatives in order to enable Indians to devise a Constitution for themselves. But who would be represented on the Constituent Assembly? The Cabinet Mission, in its wisdom, decided that it was 'sufficient to recognise only three main communities in India: General, Muslim and Sikh.' Anyone other than Muslim or Sikh, then, was subsumed under the term General (for which one can read Hindu). Not Sikhs and not Hindus, nor Muslims, but 'general' — how could their different needs then be recognized?

When Anis Kidwai and Sushila Nayyar went to Tihar, they found, on the outskirts of the village, a number of old Harijan men, standing, looking at their old homes, bemoaning their fate. Their village was now being prepared to house the Hindu refugees who would be coming in from Pakistan. 'But what about us,' they said, 'where will we go? Who will look after us?'[1] And indeed there wasn't anyone to look after them, for they did not fit any of the definitions that enabled displaced people to seek help. In December 1947 Ambedkar wrote to Nehru, complaining that scheduled caste evacuees who had come into East Punjab were not able to take shelter in refugee camps established by the Indian government. The reason, he said, was that officers in charge of the camps discriminated between caste Hindus and scheduled caste refugees. Apparently, the Relief and Rehabilitation Department had made a rule that only

---

[1] Anis Kidwai, *Azadi ki Chaon Mein*, pp. 80–82.

those refugees who were staying in relief camps could receive rations, clothing, etc. 'On account of their not staying in the Refugee Camps for the reason mentioned above,' he said, 'the Scheduled Caste refugees are not getting any relief.'[2] So only those who could get into camps were eligible for rations; scheduled castes could not get into camps because camp officers would not allow them in. They were, ostensibly, 'Hindus' living in Hindustan. By and large refugee camps housed two kinds of refugees: those coming in from Pakistan (mostly Hindus), and those waiting to go there (mostly Muslims). The Harijans of Tihar did not fit any of these categories. They were *from* Delhi and needed a place *in* Delhi. Where, then, could they go?

There were further anomalies in this. Not all Dalits were homeless or unable to get into camps. Among those who had managed to come away from Pakistan were large numbers who worked on the land. But for them, the problems were of a different order. According to the administrative rules that had been laid down, compensatory land was made available mainly to those who could be defined as agriculturalists — in other words, to those who owned land. Dalits, however, were not owners. Rather, they were tillers of the land, so they could make no legitimate claim to getting compensatory land. A number of appeals were made to the government suggesting possible remedies for this lacuna — among these was the following letter, dated May 3, 1948, from Rameshwari Nehru, who was, at the time, head of the Harijan Section:

Sir

About 2,50,000 [250,000] Harijans, i.e. 50,000 families of Harijan refugees have migrated from West Punjab and are at present rotting in East Punjab camps. About 90% of them are fine agriculturalists i.e. tillers of the soil and can make a magnificient contribution to the 'Grow More Food' campaign. But they are at present living a life of misery and idleness in refugee camps and are depending for their sustenance on the free but inadequate rations supplied by the Government.

2. The problem of their rehabilitation requires our immediate attention. On a rough calculation even if the Government is spending Re.1/-

[2] Ambedkar to Nehru, December 18, 1947.

per day per refugee, the daily expenses on the relief of these refugees come to Rs 2,80,000 [280,000] which is a huge drain on any Government. Besides signs of gradual demoralization among these refugees living a life of forced idleness are discernible. We must therefore plan their immediate rehabilitation.

3. These Harijans have been life long agriculturalists i.e. tillers of the soil. It will be improper to change their life long avocation and divert them to other channels. They must therefore be settled on land. If possible scientific and improved methods of agriculture must be taught to them.

4. The baffling problem, however, is whence to bring the land? According to a statement made by the Premier of the East Punjab, Dr Gopichand Bhargava, at a Press Conference at Delhi on November 26 1947, Muslims of East Punjab have left behind 33 lac acres of land, whereas the non-Muslims of West Punjab have left behind 61 lac acres of land. It has also been estimated that 12 lac acres of land have been left behind by the Muslims in the 4 states of East Punjab, i.e. Jind, Patiala, Faridkot, Kapurthala. This means that there are 45 lac acres of land available for distribution to immigrants from West Punjab. According to the policy so far announced by the East Punjab Government, the available land in that province will be allotted to land owners as distinguished from mere tillers of the soil as Harijans are. It is humbly suggested that if out of the total of 45 lac acres of land only 5 lac acres are reserved for Harijan refugee agriculturalists and the remaining 40 lac distributed amongst the owners of 60 lac acres of land, we will, without any appreciable cut in the allotment of land to those who had holdings in West Punjab, be taking a bold step for the re-settlement of poor Harijans. Each Harijan family could thus be assigned 10 acres of land with occupancy rights and it should be possible to introduce cooperative farming among them to ensure increased production.

5. It is gratifying to learn that through the intervention of Government of India, the Bikaner State has allotted about one lac acres of land vacated by Muslims in Ganga Nagar colony (Bikaner) to the actual tillers of the soil by granting 16 acres to each agriculturalist family. About 1200 Harijan families i.e. about 6000 Harijans have also been allotted land in that area. In Bharatpur and Alwar States, also, vast tracts of cultivable land have been left by Muslims and Rehabilitation Department of the Gov-

ernment of India have rigidly stuck to the principle of granting land only to the actual tillers of the soil. With a partial application of this principle on a limited scale in East Punjab, the poor tiller of the soil would feel the glow of economic freedom under Congress Raj. He had so far been a mere serf and now in Independent India he would become a peasant proprietor, a free man with some status. He would understand the meaning of swaraj, the significance of Congress Raj. His bonds would be broken and he would consider himself as a free and independent man.

6. It may be remembered that there were only a few Muslim landlords in East Punjab before Partition. The land was mostly distributed amongst small holders of land. [It is recommended] that the tillers of the soil through efforts [be] made to introduce cooperative farming.

7. Another point deserving attention is that allotment of land to those land owners who might look upon trade as their main source of income, holding land only as absentee-landlords, would not be sound agrarian policy. It would be better to allot land to actual cultivators. If this view is accepted Harijan cultivators would be able to settle down on land in common with other agriculturalists.

8. To sum up, therefore, 50,000 families of Harijan agriculturalist refugees from West Punjab demand that in free India they must no more be treated as serfs. As a matter of fact, they are not prepared to accept the position of 'tenants-at-will' which in other words means a life of serfdom. It is therefore respectfully submitted that this matter may be taken up and decided with the East Punjab Government on high level so that the poor tiller may not be deprived of land which is his birth right.[3]

Land—how much was lost and how much recovered in exchange—was a key question at the time of Partition. The irony and tragedy, so evident in Rameshwari Nehru's appeals that the Punjab government follow the pattern set by others and keep the promise of independent India, was that where refugees were concerned, land was seen to belong to only those who owned it, not those who *worked* it. So all compensatory policies and schemes were owner-to-owner—if you lost property, you got property in exchange. But land is surely more than just ownership.

[3] AICC Papers, Relief and Rehabilitation, F. No. 9–26 (II)/1947.

It is, to use an age-old cliche, the product of the labour of those who work it. While relief and rehabilitation policies then had found a way of compensating those who owned the land, there was no way the loss of *labour*, or indeed of the *location* of that labour, could be compensated. For those who were mere labourers, or who lived on the land on which they laboured, once that land went, so did their homes and their work. In a new location, the landowner could hire new labour, or put the land to a different use. Who would make good the other kinds of losses? This was evident with the Harijans in Tihar, as it was in the concerns reflected in Rameshwari Nehru's letter above. Why, one might ask, was no thought put into how the State could compensate for the loss of labour? Could it be that the exigencies of the situation made it difficult for those in power to take account of all contingencies? But then, given the agenda of independence, the promises it held, and the fact that land reform had been ongoing since the thirties, here was the ideal opportunity to change the pattern of land ownership vis-à-vis the Harijans. Why was it not used? Could this, then, the fact that Harijans did not own much in terms of property or goods, have also been a reason for their immunity in the attacks? The seizure of property had, after all, played a fairly significant role in the violence. The Harijans had nothing to be looted, nothing to lose. And there was a bizarre kind of immunity that their work bestowed on them: to put it crudely, if you kill a landlord, another will come up in his place. But if you kill someone who cleans your toilets, it's probably difficult to find a ready replacement.

*   *   *

It struck me that identity is a peculiar thing. My family is half Sikh: my grandfather (my father's father) wore a turban, had a Sikh name, and practised the Sikh religion. Like a good wife, my grandmother, a Hindu, followed suit. Then, as with many mixed Punjabi families, the eldest son is 'given' to Sikhism, while the others have a choice—whether to become Sikh or remain Hindu. My father, being the eldest, thus had Singh attached to his name, while all his brothers had the more Hindu attachment of Chander. But, if the family was religious at all, it was the Sikh religion they practised or, more correctly, remembered to practise on the odd ritual occasion. Even this is not strictly correct: marriages in the family took place according to Hindu custom; death rituals were more Sikh, being followed, usually, by the forty-eight-hour akhand path which involves reading the entire Guru Granth Sahib. And we, my generation, had always grown up with a sort of subliminal awareness of both religions, but also with a distance from the practice of religion. We thought of ourselves as secular beings.

Then, in 1984 Indira Gandhi was killed by her Sikh bodyguards. This was a signal for reprisals on the Sikh community — nearly three thousand Sikhs were killed in and around Delhi alone; and suddenly everyone who had a Sikh name, or looked Sikh, became painfully aware of their vulnerability. By this time, my father no longer wore a turban, and did not have long hair, but we did, and do, have a Sikh name. This was the first time that we — my siblings, our cousins, our Sikh friends — began to get a glimmering of what fear meant, of what our parents and grandparents had gone through. Later, in the relief camps where we worked, I found myself again and again asserting my 'Sikh' identity — somehow I felt it gave me a legitimacy, a closeness with the victims of the riots, that it helped me to understand something of what they had been through. I told myself that as children (and this was the truth, but it somehow became invested with a greater moral force at the time) we had spent a great deal of time in gurudwaras, hardly any at all in Hindu temples; that even in our home, the prayer room (actually a room used more for storage but that was quickly transformed into a prayer room whenever my grandmother came to stay with us) had had a picture of Guru Nanak, not of any of the Hindu gods. Suddenly, many of us, non-religious at the best of times, began to feel Sikh.

By the time, eight years later, when the Babri Masjid was destroyed by right-wing Hindu hordes, my sense of 'Sikhness' had once again become subterranean. Things had, ostensibly, gone back to normal. I did not feel the same need to assert my Sikh identity. But when the mosque fell, I remember — and I was not alone in this — a distinct sense of shame at being *Hindu*. And also a resentment: this was an identity I had not chosen, but one I had been born with, an identity that, until it became necessary to separate 'Sikhness' from, had actually encompassed both. Like many other Hindus at the time, I felt a need to apologize to my Muslim friends; a need to dissociate myself from the communal Hindus who had destroyed the mosque, even a sense of guilt at being 'of the majority community' and, simultaneously, a sense of outrage at myself for this guilt which would not allow me to be critical of Muslim communalism, even though rationally I knew it to be as dangerous as its counterpart, Hindu communalism.

The borders of Hindu and Sikh identities are, of course, more fluid than those that lie between Hindus and Muslims. But, in Punjab at least, while religion may have divided Hindus and Muslims, there was a great deal they shared *culturally* as Punjabis. Even today, when Punjabi Hindus and Muslims meet, there is an immediate sharing of, a reference to, a Punjabi identity. Where then does one draw the borders of religious identity and how are these then transcended and therefore blurred by cultural identity?

And if Partition was not only about Hindus and Sikhs and Muslims, how then had others felt about it and, indeed, how had their lives been affected by it? Christians, for example, occupied a rather ambiguous space. A small community in numbers, they had no special identity in terms of their work, as Harijans had. And because of their supposed 'closeness' to the colonisers, they were not really seen as 'acceptable' figures in the nationalist discourse, because this discourse itself was seen in terms of particular identities. Nonetheless, how had they felt? Was Partition, for them, simply a war between Hindus and Muslims, or was it more? Did they feel involved? In Delhi I spoke to Lakshmi Fenn, widow of an army officer who was involved in keeping law and order in Delhi after the 1947 riots. For her and her husband, the question of being anything other than Indian did not arise and, she added, they were not alone in this. But this was not the expectation people had of them.

She tells a story of two young air force officers (Christians) who were forced to crash land in the Rajasthan desert close to the border. Immediately when they came out of their aircraft they were surrounded by the local people. What are you, they wanted to know? Are you Hindu or Muslim? When they tried to explain that they were neither, that they were, in fact, Christian in terms of religion, and officers of the Indian Air Force otherwise, no one understood what they were talking about. And the two men came very close to being killed. This kind of questioning did not only come from the 'other' community. Jean Simeon, now in her eighties, recalls that as a young woman she felt very involved in the nationalist movement: 'but I was really ostracized within my community for this. What is all this to you, people would say, why don't you leave those Hindus and Muslims to sort out their differences?' When Partition happened, Jean was in Belgaum with her husband, living in a Christian college with an uncle. 'On one side of us was a Muslim mohalla, on the other a Hindu. It was quite frightening.'[4] But seeing them as somehow 'different', people of both communities came to them for help and shelter. Clearly, the expectation was that the violence would somehow not touch them—although violence hardly plays by such rules.

It took Maya Rani's interview to make me realize how much I too had taken for granted about Muslims, Hindus and Sikhs being the primary, indeed the only, identities at Partition. Yet, as even this one interview showed, Partition had also been about many other things—in this case caste, and equally, class. I decided to look deeper into this question, and to go back to Maya's interview. Had she said more about her identity as a Dalit that I had missed? Revisiting the text, I was astonished—and ashamed—at what I had missed. Asked if she or her friends had had any Muslim friends, Maya had responded:

> No, I didn't have any Muslim friends of my own, but my mother had a friend whose condition was so bad that it made me feel very sad. My mother didn't have a sister so this friend was like a sister to her, and she cried for her. We cried too. My mother said: 'your masi's condition is very bad. She had daughers and she pleaded with my mother to keep her daughters. But my mother said, how can we, the police don't allow us to do so. Hindus don't allow us to do so. How can I hide your daughters? My hands are tied.' *You see, the Hindus kept a watch on everyone and if you hid anyone they would come immediately and make you take the people out.* (my italics)

Hindus were powerful enough to ensure that the Dalits did not offer protection to Muslims. It was perhaps this common perception of oppression at the hands of the majority community which made for a greater closeness among the Muslims and the Dalits in Punjab. Maya described a time, some years after Partition, when her mother, concerned

---

[4] Quotations here are from Jean Simeon, personal interview.

for her Muslim friend, went to Pakistan to find her. The roads were opened for a few days. Once there, she met all her Muslim friends who, according to Maya, were happy to see her. Why should they not be, she said, when asked, 'the fighting was between Muslims and Hindus. We didn't fight with the Muslims. It had nothing to do with us.'

Time and again Maya said she and her friends did not feel any danger. Could this be true? I have asked myself this question repeatedly. Yet, Maya was sixteen at the time, not a child. Her sense of non-involvement in the tension came as a real surprise to me. She remembers how scared people were; her memory of the time is graphic, almost visual in its detail. Yet she had no fear herself. Instead, in hindsight, she had a sort of pride of achievement at having amassed so much wealth as a result of being in a situation of conflict. She said:

> . . . there was no danger for us. Because we are Harijans. Whether it had become Pakistan or Hindustan, it made no difference to us. We would stay where we were born. Our elders felt that whatever happened, we wouldn't move from this place. This was our home. If anyone had tried to make us leave, we would have shown our strength. After all, Harijans are not just anybody. We're also a very powerful group. If that had happened, we would have asked for a separate state and they would have had to give it to us. We felt strong in this knowledge.

Feeling strong in the knowledge of your strength, a sense of being a 'powerful group': this was a sense that had been building up among the Dalits for some time. Of the 12.6 million people who comprised the population of East Punjab, some 6.9 percent (approximately 869,400) were Harijans. Since numbers were clearly so important—for they would make a difference in which community would be seen to be in the majority, and which in the minority—in Punjab, this could clearly have been a weapon of strength. Perhaps it was this awareness that led Maya and others to describe themselves as a 'powerful group'.

As I began to look, I found curious paradoxes in these stories—Maya and her friends had not been alone in being 'invisible' or 'untouchable' in the violence in their village. Shortly after the Rawalpindi riots in March 1947, P. N. Rajbhoj, then general secretary of the All India Scheduled Caste Federation, visited the area and said: 'During my tour everywhere I learned with gratification that the scheduled caste people were little affected by the riots. If at any place any man has suffered, it was because he was mistaken for a caste Hindu. Otherwise, when a man told the rioters he was neither Hindu nor a Muslim he was left untouched.'[5] Several questions remained unanswered, however: did this same invisibility/untouchability—despite Maya's experience—prevent Harijan women, and indeed their children, from being raped and abducted? And how could anyone tell the rioters that he was 'neither Hindu nor a Muslim'? If it was indeed true that many Dalits escaped violence because of who they were, it must then follow that the aggressors knew the people they were killing: something that throws out of the window the received wisdom that many scholars of communal conflict cherish—that the aggressors are always outsiders, that they come in and disrupt the world of the victims. And if it is true that the aggressors often knew the people they were attacking and killing, could we then speculate that another source of the Dalits' non-vulnerability could be that they were perhaps seen as too low, indeed too abhorrent to both communities, to be killed in a confrontation which, then, seems to be perceived by both as a contest between social equals? Yet, in many ways, Muslims and Hindus were not social equals, although they were certainly more equal to each other than Dalits were to them. And further, if we are to come back to the question of the rape of Dalit women, why is it then that in this most intimate of contacts, questions of untouchability, of 'lowness', do not arise? Could the answer lie in the fact that rape is a different kind of exercise of power than loot and murder?

There was another side to this invisibility. In most places where communities live, practical arrangements settle into certain kinds of patterns. Different people perform different tasks, all of which go together to make up the business of living, as individuals, families, communities. In western Punjab, as in many other parts of India, lower castes and Dalits provided many of the 'essential services' necessary for daily life. A violent rupture of these life patterns, a tearing apart of the social fabric, such as Partition represented, left many of these 'arrangements' un-

[5] AICC Papers, F. No. G-19 (KW-I), Harijan Sewak Sangh, 1946–48.

settled. People fled, they moved at random, they tried to stay together as communities, but all the systems did not necessarily get replicated in their new homes. In many places Dalits, performers of such essential services, invisible by virtue of their presence, now became visible by virtue of their absence. Where were they? Who would perform all the menial tasks that needed doing—the swabbing, the sweeping, the sanitary services? How would people live? Caste Hindus now began to 'see' Dalits. Dalits acquired an identity.

An identity that, I discovered, had been forming for the Dalits for some considerable time. Gandhi and Ambedkar had both, in their different ways, focussed attention on Dalits and scheduled castes. But the Dalits rejected many of the things Gandhi had campaigned for as mere window dressing—entry into temples, drawing water from the same wells. Instead, what they wanted was political clout, political power and representation, and, most important of all, equal citizenship. On June 10, 1947, shortly after the Partition Plan was announced, H. J. Khandekar, President of the All India Depressed Classes League, sent a representation to Mountbatten asking that adequate representation be given to people of the 'Depressed Classes' in the Boundary Commission for marking boundary lines in the division of Bengal and Punjab, 'in order that the rights and privileges of the scheduled castes may not be crushed or overlooked'. Scheduled castes were a sizeable proportion of the population in Punjab—if other groups were being consulted in the drawing up of boundaries, they too needed to be asked what they felt. He attached the text of a resolution to this letter, a resolution which had been passed by the All India Depressed Classes League at its meeting earlier in the month. It read as follows:

I. This meeting of the All India Depressed Classes League feels that the Depressed Classes of the Bengal and Punjab will be greatly affected by the division of these two provinces and it is feared that there will be forcible conversions of the Depressed Classes in the Muslim Predominating Provinces and to stop this, it is vitally necessary that the boundary commission to be formed under the H.M.G.'s Plan, must include the representatives of the Depressed Classes.

II (a). This committee deplores that due to the absolute lack of representation of the Depressed Classes in the last Punjab Ministry it could not do any constructive work for the Depressed Classes in the province. The Committee appeals to the Congress, Hindu and Sikh Leaders to give accurate representation to the Depressed Classes in the regional ministries, to be formed in the province in the near future.

III. The Committee views with great concern the growing activities of the Muslim, Christian and Sikh missionaries for the conversion of the Depressed Classes to their respective faiths with a view to increasing their number solely for political purpose. These activities, if not checked in time, will not only reduce Depressed Classes to a non-entity but will also affect Hindu Society in general and will create fresh political problems and complications in every province.[6]

In their fear of being used to increase the numbers of this or that community, or their concern at being forcibly converted, the scheduled castes were asserting their difference, and seeking to assert their strength. Scheduled caste groups were not alone in wanting a voice in political power. In November 1948 the Simla Branch of the All Christian Welfare Society expressed concern at 'the manner and the mode in which the Christian interest has been scandalously ignored in the so-called sub-committee for Minorities Rights convened by the Premier and the Speaker of the East Punjab Provincial Assembly.'[7]

A sense of separateness seemed to have become essential to establishing a sense of identity. Thus the fear of conversion at the hands of 'others'—Muslims, Sikhs, Christians. (Among the scheduled castes, there were different groups. The Scheduled Caste Federation was, in some senses, closer to the Muslims while the Depressed Classes League was closer to the Hindus.) Conversion was suspect because it was done, clearly, 'with a view to increasing their number solely for political purpose'. A demand for separate electorates, for proportional political representation, for a presence in the important decision-making bodies, these were some of the broader realities that underlay the sense of dif-

---

[6] All India Depressed Classes League, Karol Bagh, in AICC Papers, F. No. G-19 (KW-I), Harijan Sewak Sangh, 1946–48.

[7] AICC Papers, Punjab, F. No. G-26, 1948.

ference, of separateness that Maya Rani had expressed and that, since my encounter with her, I have heard articulated several times over.

Not all those who belonged to the 'depressed classes' subscribed to this particular sense of separateness, and there were groups who propagated organizing on the basis of 'economic interests' rather than caste. But broadly speaking, a sense of separateness was building up. On the same visit to Punjab mentioned earlier, P. N. Rajbhoj is reported to have said: 'The scheduled castes have nothing in common with caste Hindus. While the Sikhs, on the other hand, are practically the blood and bone of caste Hindus. The number of Scheduled Castes, including the Mazhabi Sikhs, is equal to the Sikhs. Hence if the Punjab is to be partitioned, it must be into three parts, namely the Muslim Punjab, Sikh-cum-Hindu Punjab and the Scheduled Caste Punjab.'[8]

* * *

Here, then, was a parallel text on Partition. While Hindu and Muslim leaders argued and fought over weightage, representation, political power and, later, after Partition, over properties, monies and people (mainly women and children), another community of people—if one can use that term—fought to insert their voices and selves into this battle. Recognize us, they seemed to say, we too are a minority, we too fear for ourselves, we too have our own demands, our own rights and needs, we too want to carve out our own land. And lest this seem like a chimera, they had provided a rationale, and invented a name for this imaginary homeland: Achhutistan, the land of the untouchables. This, then, was what Maya Rani was talking about when she had said: 'we would have asked for a separate state, and they would have had to give it to us.'

The month of November 1946 saw the founding of the All India Achhutistan movement. Mr Beah Lall, its founder, issued the following statement in the same month:

It is justifiable to observe that India was the place of Achhut Masses and it must be handed over to them. The Achhutistan is derived from the

---

[8] AICC Papers, Punjab, F. No. G-26, 1948.

word 'Achhut', the literal meaning of which in India is 'Not impure'. But it was made impure by the mixture of [*sic*] Hindustan, Pakistan and Englishstan. It is *foolishness on the part of Mr. Jinnah* who demands Pakistan only and does not remember Achhutistan. The problem of Achhutistan is the first than that of Hindustan, Pakistan and Englishstan. The latter three Thans have tried and tried their best to crush the people of the former Than, by making their power strong and utilising guns and instruments of fighting . . . What are the conditions of Mehtars, sweepers and Chamars? They are being compelled by the organisations of Municipality and District Boards . . . in the towns, and the Chamars in the villages, to take away their latrines from houses and dead bodies of their animals. Begaris are being taken by the landlords who are generally the people of Hindustan, Pakistan and Englishstan. The existence of power awakens by different organisations of the people of Achhutistan in shape of schedule caste, depressed class and Harijans but their power is always tried to be usurped by the above three powers. The Hindustan people want to emerge [*sic*] them by calling them Harijans, the Pakistan people by calling them schedule caste and converting into Islam and the Englishtan people by making them depressed classes . . .⁹

The concerns voiced above were not uncommon as the following (undated) letter to the Governor of Punjab, in Lahore, shows. This goes a bit further than simply demanding an independent state and actually gives it a geography.

Your Excellency,

The Punjab Provincial Scheduled Castes Federation begs to submit the following 'memorandum' on behalf of the Scheduled Castes of the Province in connection with the proposed partition of Punjab:

1. That the proposed partition of the Punjab is entirely against the interests of the Scheduled Castes who are a separate community from Hindus and an important minority of the province.

2. That the scheduled castes are living in almost all corners of the province and not in one or two particular districts. They will be left entirely at the mercy of other communities if partition is accepted.

⁹ AICC Papers, F. No. G-19 (KW-I), Harijan Sewak Sangh, 1946–48.

3. That the scheduled castes are likely to suffer with the change of population from one area to another and any compulsory change will materially affect the economical social and political life of the Scheduled Castes.

4. That the Scheduled castes are no longer Hindus as has been definitely proved from the recent communal disturbances. The Scheduled Castes cannot expect better treatment from Hindus who being in majority in Eastern Punjab will suppress their voice and injure their noble cause for which they have been struggling hard for the last two decades. The Hindus have already deprived them of their legitimate rights. The proposed partition will further close the doors of uplift of the Scheduled Castes on them.

5. That the Scheduled Castes are already oppressed and aggrieved. The partition of Punjab will divide them into two groups and thus shatter their strength and unity. It is apprehended that the Scheduled Castes will not be able to maintain their honour, civilization and culture under pure majority of other religions in their respective areas.

6. That the scheduled castes of Punjab will prefer death rather than be governed or ruled by any other pure majority of one religion in the divided Punjab. The scheduled castes will not accept or yield to any decision concerning partition which will be forcibly imposed upon them against their wishes.

7. That the British Government should first fulfil her promises with the scheduled castes of the country before power is transferred to Indians and especially the proposed partition of Punjab is accepted.

8. That if at all the partition of Punjab is the only solution at present the following genuine demands of the scheduled castes may not be ignored:

(a) The problem of partition may be decided by the real representatives of all communities of the province in the Punjab Legislative Assembly which can be done in this way that the present assembly may be forthwith dissolved and fresh elections held for the selection of real representatives. The scheduled castes could not elect their real representatives in the last elections on account of joint elections with Hindus. The present Congress 'Harijan' M.L.As are in fact the representatives of Hindus and not the Scheduled Castes for they have been returned to the assembly with the majority of Hindu votes. The Scheduled Castes have no faith in Congress and as such the present congressite Harijan M.L.As can no longer speak on behalf of the Scheduled Castes.

(b) *The Scheduled Castes may be given a separate independent state consisting of Jullundur and Ambala Divisions which are mostly inhabited by the Scheduled Castes people. The Government should bear the expenses for the transmigration of Scheduled Castes people to their 'independent state' from different parts of the province and provide protection, board and lodging till they are satisfactorily established.* (my italics) The Government should also compensate the loss undergone by the Scheduled Castes people during transmigration.[10]

As the time for Partition drew closer, both the Congress and the Muslim League, the two key players in the game, realized the importance of winning the Harijans over to their side—for adding their numbers could help to alter their own. A process of wooing then began. Political alliances are expedient at the best of times, and these were no exception. On March 6, 1947, J. N. Mandal, Law Member of the Interim Government, had said at the UP Scheduled Caste Federation Conference that he had little faith in Gandhi because all Gandhi wanted was to open temples for the scheduled castes. 'I have joined hands with the League,' he said, 'because Muslims and Scheduled Castes are both poor and backward. They are mostly labourers and agriculturists, at least in Bengal, and need immense relief. So no law will be made for the good of Muslims which will not be beneficial to the Scheduled Castes.'[11]

Once again, the lines of difference were being drawn, and once again, they proved intractable and elusive. Where did Harijanness begin and Hinduness end? How were minorities defined? In numeric terms, in which case the Muslims were actually a majority in Punjab? Or in terms of economic and social disadvantage, in which case the Harijans and Christians should have been among the first to be considered? More than anything else, what this revealed for me was how much of the drawing and redrawing of boundaries and borders found an internal reflection in ourselves. Scheduled caste groups, for example, *wanted* to assert

[10] AICC Papers, Punjab, F. No. G-26, 1948.
[11] AICC Papers, F. No. G-19 (KW-I), Harijan Sewak Sangh, 1946–48.

difference. Yet, as with all underprivileged groups, part of the assertion of difference, of otherness, is a wish for parity, equality, sameness— call it what you like—with the majority, or the dominant group. Depending on where history placed them, this group could have claimed allegiance with Hindus or Muslims. Both, therefore, had to be juggled with—attacked, criticized, allied with, opposed—until something was decided, and the opportunity used to put forward one's own demands. Thus Harijan leaders asserted their difference and independence, and yet dealt with both the Congress and the Muslim League, finding ways of rationalizing how they were closer to the religion or culture of one or the other. Knowing the importance of seizing the political moment, Harijan groups played now with one and now with the other.

Dominant groups were not unaware of this either, for they too needed to win the Harijans over, not only for their political presence but for the more basic need of the services they provided. This became especially clear after Partition. Anxious to win Harijans over to its side, the Indian government set up a number of institutions for their rehabilitation—a Harijan housing board was to make loans available to Harijans for building houses. The Harijan Sewak Sangh was to coordinate relief and rehabilitation, 'to look after the interests of displaced Harijans in this country'. The tragic irony that underlay this particular form of attention was that it reinforced the very basis of the discrimination the Harijans were attempting to fight. And yet, while they fought such discrimination at the 'political' level, there was also, at the level of everyday reality and everyday needs, a very real need for relief, for housing, for resettlement. Thus housing, even if based on a differential identity, could not be rejected.

There is another bizarre twist to this tale. For many people, the creation of Pakistan opened up a number of opportunities in terms of jobs. Groups and individuals who did not necessarily have a religious stake in the process of nation-making moved to both countries in search of a better life. Dalits were no exception. In the initial stages, considerable numbers moved from India to Pakistan in the hope of finding a better life there. But for many, this did not happen. While it was still possible to return, hundreds of them attempted to do so. In addition, there were Harijans living in the territories that now came under Pakistan who wished to move to India. India tried to lure them away with offers of relief, housing, loans, jobs, while Pakistan tried to prevent them from going with stories of how difficult things were in India: starving people, food shortages, widespread poverty, skyrocketing prices. Many Harijans were in Sind from where the most convenient mode of departure was by sea. Ships and carriers were in short supply, added to which the government of Sind insisted, for a while at least, that people needed permits to leave, and only a limited number of permits were issued each day. Large numbers of Harijans, then, remained in transit camps, waiting to leave. Their absence resulted in a breakdown of the Karachi's sanitation and cleaning system. Under pressure, the Government of Sind passed a legislation, the Essential Services Maintenance Act (ESMA), which disallowed Harijans from leaving the country. Indian political leaders were enraged by this: there was an uproar in the assembly. What, asked the leaders, was the government doing about this? The government, however, could do little.

They could only negotiate. Perhaps the most moving statement here came from Ambedkar when he said, during an election tour of Punjab in 1952:

> Immediately after Partition, Pakistan Government issued orders prohibiting the Scheduled Caste people from leaving Pakistan for India. Pakistan did not bother so much if the Hindus left, but who would do the dirty work of the scavengers, sweepers, the Bhangis and other despised castes if the untouchables left Pakistan. I requested Pt Nehru to take immediate action and strive for the removal of this ban on their migration. He did not do anything at all. He slept over this issue and did not even casually mention it during the course of various discussions with the Pakistanis. None of the Congress Harijans raised a finger at this persecution of their brethren in Pakistan.[12]

Questions had been raised in the Legislative Assembly about displaced Harijans. Was it true the Minister of State for Rehabilitation, Shri Mo-

---

[12] Bhagwan Das, *Thus Spoke Ambedkar, Selected Speeches,* Vol. II, 1969, Bhim Patrika Publications, Jalandhar, pp. 31–42.

han Lal Saxena, was asked, that the Pakistan government was not allowing Harijans to leave? Yes, he said, some 35,000 were still in Pakistan,
prevented from leaving because of the Essential Services Act. Ambedkar
himself had, since 1947, been fighting consistently to ensure that Harijans were treated fairly. He pointed out to Jawaharlal Nehru in December 1947 that the Pakistan government were preventing 'in every possible
way the evacuation of the Scheduled Castes from their territory.' The
reason, he felt, was that they were needed to do menial jobs and serve as
landless labourers for the landholding population of the country. There
was also a particular desire, he pointed out, to hold on to sweepers who
had been declared as persons belonging to Essential Services.[13] The discrimination was not only at the hands of Pakistan: in Indian refugee
camps, scheduled castes were not being allowed to seek shelter; also,
they did not qualify under the definition of agricultural communities,
because such communities were only those who were declared thus by
the government. In some places scheduled caste communities who had
been living in eastern Punjab were being forced to give up their lands by
rich Sikhs and Jats who wished to take these over. Ambedkar's complaint
to Nehru then was that 'So far, all care and attention has been bestowed
by the Government of India on the problem of Muslims. The problem
of Scheduled Castes has either been supposed not to exist, or deemed
to be so small as not to require special attention.'[14] Ambedkar was right
in this respect, that in the privileging of Hindu-Sikh and Muslim identities, the problems of scheduled castes had been eclipsed. Except, of
course, that the scheduled castes could not be entirely invisibilized —
they performed important, if menial, tasks. The duality was summed up
by a refugee from Lahore writing to the Hindu Mahasabha, endorsing
their vision of an Akhand Hindustan. 'If we scratch an Indian Muslim
(or a Christian),' he said, 'we find that he has got intact his ancient Hindu
castes and sub-castes; it is only the crust of his foreign culture and religion that distinguishes him from a Hindu and the Mahasabha should
seek to remove this crust.' But, he cautioned, 'while we should reclaim
non-Hindus living in India, we should not exterminate them physically

[13] Ambedkar to Nehru, December 14, 1947.
[14] Ambedkar to Nehru, December 14, 1947.

(as Muslims were exterminated in Spain by the Christians) because such *extermination will destroy our community of skilled artisans and thus further accentuate the economic crisis confronting India.'* [15] (my italics) Extermination was perhaps an extreme step, likely to be considered only by someone dyed in the colours of organizations such as the Hindu Mahasabha. But the cautious balancing of scheduled castes—who, after all, were part of the community of skilled artisans—rejecting their personhood but claiming their labour, was what the Congress and Muslim League had both been doing.

* * *

As I listened to these stories, I was reminded of Manto's by now famous story, 'Toba Tek Singh', in which the hero, a mental patient, asked to choose his country on the basis of his religion, chooses to die in the space between the two borders, in No Man's Land. It was almost as if, in the histories of Partition that we know, the twilight world of blurred identities, of the permeability of some communal boundaries, had no place. It had ceased to exist. Your identity was fixed: it could become a stick with which you could be beaten, but equally, it could become a stick which you could use to fight for certain concessions and privileges.

Yet, identities do not easily fall within such boundaries. They are fluid, changing, often expedient. Harijans saw themselves as separate from Hindus and Muslims, but there were times when they felt they were closer, culturally, to one or other of those groups. Hindus, a majority in India, were a minority in Punjab, yet, in relative terms, it was the Sikhs who were, if anything, more of a minority than the Hindus. Hindus from the North West Frontier Province saw themselves further as minorities, beleaguered, surrounded by unfriendly groups, abandoned and deserted by the Congress. Harijans did not see themselves as a religious group, thus they could envisage being under the Hindu fold, or indeed, allying with the Muslims. And these alliances were not on a religous basis but rather on a cultural basis or on the basis of what was seen as a shared oppression.

In the stories that I heard about Partition, and in those from Partition survivors, one of the things that began to fascinate me was what

[15] Hindu Mahasabha Papers, F. No. C-168/1947.

this event had meant to people whom society had marginalized. What, for example, did violence such as the violence of Partition do to such people? The received wisdom on violence and on traumatic events such as Partition is that they are great equalizers. Violence, it is assumed, does not recognize caste and class differences when it is on such a large scale. Equally, the fact that dislocation was an experience common across class seems to suggest that some kind of equalization did take place. In some respects, this is not incorrect. The rape of women, for example, did not, at the time of Partition, seem to have recognized class differences. Nonetheless, inasmuch as the journeys undertaken by upper-class women were often safer (for example, they travelled by air, by car, under escort, seldom on foot like poorer women), in relative terms the majority of those who were subjected to rape were women of the lower classes. Or, where homelessness was concerned, the experience was again a common one across class. But compensation for homes or land left behind or lost had to take account of the original class of the claimant, as we have seen in the case of Harijans who did not qualify for grants of agricultural land.

Unlike women and children, Dalits had a sense of themselves as a group. This is not to say that the grouping was simplistic or homogenous—within Dalit groups there were differences: those who felt closer to the Muslims, those who saw themselves as separate from the Hindus or the Muslims, those who felt closer to the Hindus. All of these differences emerge quite clearly at the time of Partition. But while Christians and Harijans may have had communities and organizations to represent them, to attempt to make their voices heard, for many others this was not possible. Who could have represented the many prisoners who were divided up on the basis of religion, or indeed the real-life mental patients who had to 'choose' or even people who truly live on the borders of society, the eunuchs and lepers? All of them had to declare their religious affiliation, their identity at the time of Partition. And if they were unable to declare it, the choice was made for them.

In many ways the experiences of scheduled castes paralleled those of women. Both groups were marginalized by society, and were yet so essential to its functioning. Their importance lay squarely, but differently, in the material realm. Scheduled castes were essential because of their material location in both the production (i.e., agriculture) and sanitation systems, and indeed in the realm of ritual and custom. Women were equally materially important for the role they played as producers and reproducers of society. But women also inhabited a more nebulous, but equally important, realm: that of honour, of glory, of the protection of the mother and hence the motherland, and thereby of the affirmation of the manhood of their men. Yet, as a group, women had no one to represent them, nor had they been able to collectively mobilize to represent themselves. While the experience of violence and disloca-tion was common, it also remained individual. And more, its very nature ensured that women could not, would not, speak about it. By contrast, because Dalits were organized—even though their organizations may have had differences—they were able at least to *name* their interests. No such avenue was open to women. It is perhaps for this reason that what-ever resistance women were able to muster up remained at an individual level. The individual—and in the case of women, dispersed—voice then could barely be heard and could therefore not insert itself into the offi-cial discourse or into history. This, then, is also why it is relatively easier to locate material on the Dalit experience at Partition—for the histo-rian has access to a rich archive of documents, speeches, representations and so on, which so far have remained relatively untouched—than it is to locate material on women. This is also why much material on the Dalit experience is in the voice of Dalits themselves, individually or through their organizations. Women's voices, on the other hand, are hardly heard in the archive we do have; instead, it is the voices of those who purport to speak for women. Within this broad group are included Dalit women, whose voices are equally absent from the archive of Dalit voices. For women as a group, then, their only collectivity lay in silence.

Paradoxes and complications abound, however. It was difficult to find an easy fit between the democratic agenda and social vision that the new nation had set itself and the way rehabilitation policies were being played out on the ground. Spatial outcastes, Harijans remained second-class citizens even as they were rehabilitated. And while there was little space for them in the new nation's agenda, there was much greater space for women because with them the stakes were different. Thus widows were recognized as being the permanent responsibility of a paternalistic State, homes and ashrams were provided for destitute and raped women, marriage bureaus were set up and the State took upon itself the task of looking after women's 'moral well being'. Despite this, in the shifting geography of citizenship at the time, the norm for the new Indian citizen remained, by and large, the male citizen. And it was this that allowed the State to not only be paternalistic, but also to act as coercive parent where women were concerned. Thus even as they were being assigned rights and privileges as citizens of this country, those very rights were being flouted with impunity through the process of forcible recovery, particularly of those women who did not wish to be recovered.

* * *

I have spoken in this chapter mainly about the experiences of scheduled castes in relation to Hindus, and to the Indian and Pakistani States. I have little information about anything that took place outside of India, but I would like to end this account with two stories which have to do with the experiences of poor, marginalized people, and which relate to the two most important moments of life, birth and death. For me, these stories are moving reminders of the many hidden ways in which Partition touched on the lives of people.

Dais (midwives) perform the task of bringing children into the world, of assisting at their birth. They are usually from the lower castes: the job of birthing is a messy one. It's the dai who deals with the mess: cleaning up the blood, cutting the umbilical cord and so on. Equally important are the people who prepare the dead for burial or cremation: a number of rituals have to be carried out, in both instances the body has to be bathed and dressed. These tasks are performed either by close family members or by those for whom the task is a profession. Anis Kidwai's moving memoir, to which I have returned again and again, more regularly, and with which I have been much more absorbed than I have with any book of conventional history, tells the story of an old man who had no one to perform his last rites.

As I walked through the camp one day, towards the hospital, I found a dead body lying next to a patient on a bed in the hospital tent. This was nothing new: while there was time to tend to the living, there was little time for the dead. Normally, the task of bathing the body and preparing it for burial, putting on the shroud, all these were done by the family or then by the Jamiat. So I didn't think much of this.

Some time later, as Anis Kidwai returned, she found the body had not yet been removed. Is there no one to bury this old man, she asked, where are his relatives? But there were none, except for a girl, probably his daughter, and her young son. The daughter wept the whole time, but was not willing to take on the task of preparing her father's body for burial. Kidwai and her friend, Jamila, then went off to look for somebody. Their first stop was the office of the relief committee. Here the maulvi refused to entertain their request. All the gravediggers and shroud-preparers have left for Pakistan by the last train, he said, and now there is no one to perform these tasks. Despite their entreaties, he refused to help them, saying this is not my business, I have enough on my hands.

Defeated, Kidwai and Jamila tried to recruit the help of students from Jamia, but they too had all left. They tried to persuade the daughter, without luck. Just as they were despairing of ever being able to find someone to take on the task, two old women walked up and offered to do it. 'We've never done it before,' they said, 'but one human body can't be very different from another, and after all, we are all the same before Allah.' And so saying, they began the work while Kidwai, Jamila and some others began digging a grave. Finally, the old man was laid to rest. His daughter did nothing but watch and weep and later, her family responsibilities over, she left for Pakistan.

If the departure of gravediggers created a problem of what to do with the dead, so did that of the midwives, except that in this case the question was what to do with the living. At the age of seventeen or eighteen, Anis Kidwai's daughter, Kishwar Kidwai, found herself inadvertently assisting at the birth of a baby. Impatient to make its entry into the world, the baby was virtually pushing itself out while Kishwar, alone in the 'hospital' at the time, tried desperately to locate a nurse or a midwife. But they had all gone to Pakistan. The doctor who arrived, a Hindu and a male, turned his back to the mother, and gave detailed instructions to Kishwar who followed these nervously but managed to complete all

the tasks assigned to her. Partition dislocated and uprooted people, said
Anis Kidwai, but that did not mean that the round of births and deaths
stopped. Nor, of course, did many of the other things that make up routine and ritual in people's lives. And it was in this that the importance
of people who were otherwise assumed to be marginal becomes clear.

MAYA RANI   *'Blood up to the knees . . .'*

I met Maya Rani in 1985–86 with Peter Chappell and Satti Khanna during the course of their film *A Division of Hearts.* The interview that you
see here was a sort of joint enterprise on all our parts, although the bulk
of the questions were posed by Satti. The transcribing and translation
was done by me. I have chosen to include this interview here for many
reasons. As I mentioned in the above discussion, so much of the discussion on Partition has focused on Muslims, Hindus and Sikhs, that
the experiences of others whose lives were impacted by Partition barely
figure in any telling. From that point of view, Maya's interview is particularly important. Hers is the only telling that directly and squarely
addresses the issue of caste. The importance of the issue only came home
to me gradually, although it was Maya's interview which spurred me on
in the direction of actually looking at caste, and therefore also class, as a
factor in Partition. Had I understood what she was pointing to earlier,
I would perhaps have been able to find more people who could speak
about the issue. As it is, hers is the only such interview, and its place in
this narrative thus is essential.

Maya was in her mid-fifties when we met her, a strong, confident
Punjabi woman who worked hard all day to make a living. Her permanent job in a school gave her a kind of security that was very important for the sense of self-confidence that Maya showed. She talked to
us in her home, pointing to all sorts of objects, reminders of Partition.
These were things she and her friends had looted, taking advantage of
the confusion of the time and the sense of immunity they felt because
they were not part of either of the warring communities. I was struck by
the curious detachment, the almost humorous and somewhat distanced
way in which she told her story. There were no tears here, no nostalgia,
no breaking down. It was as if the violence had happened to someone
else, as indeed it had. As Maya said, they had little sense of fear because
she and her friends were children and the whole thing was something
like a game. There is a point at which she describes the violence, and an

incident of rape. She talks of some young boys who were taking away a woman, and having merely mentioned this, her only comment is: 'and like this nearly two-and-a-half hours passed.' Because Maya's was among the first of the interviews I was involved in, it is important to me also for all the questions we did not ask. Why did we not probe the question of her Harijan identity further? Or try to find out if others too had felt as she did? Eleven or twelve years later, it is little use asking these questions. I have no idea where Maya is now, or whether I would be able to find her again. It is one of my greatest regrets that I did not, at the time, understand the importance of what she was saying, and therefore probe it further.

* * *

Maya Rani:

That day . . . on the way we saw many things—stealing, people killing each other. So we all got up on the roof. The children—they were children then—all the girls from that area, we all went up on the roof to see what was happening. We saw all this and worse, happening. After some time the military came. They shouted to us to come down, otherwise we would be shot at. We weren't frightened even then. We were young then, you see, and not so scared. We just kept looking and looking at what was happening— people were looting and throwing things around. If anyone had any jewellery in their ears, on their neck, they would pull it off, others were hacking and cutting up people . . . for two days dead bodies lay around on the roads, even the dogs did not want them. It was terrible, the death and destruction that happened at the time when Pakistan and Hindustan were created. There was a very rich Muslim lawyer—he had six houses. He said, we're not going to leave whatever happens. We will stay in Dinanagar. We'll stay in the house and only come out when it is safe to do so. There were some old women in that house—they never used to come out. So people thought, well, let them stay. So they did. They stayed inside the house for a whole month. Then, some boys said to them, come, we'll take you, so the family began to fill up trucks with their belongings—but the boys told them, leave all this, we'll reach it to you later. Just take your money and your gold. So they did. But when they'd got a little distance from the house . . . they threw some petrol onto the truck and set it, and everyone inside it, on fire. All of them died.

These are some of the things we saw. Were we frightened? No, we weren't frightened—everyone tried to scare us, even our parents. But all the children of that area, none of us was scared. Often, we would leave our own roof and climb up onto a neighbour's, just to see. Then we all got together and started to go into people's houses. In some we found rice, in others almonds, sevian . . . we began to collect all these and pile them up in our house. Great, big utensils, patilas, parats . . . we collected them all.

Yes, the children did this. Then the city elders, Hindus, they felt that this was not a good thing, this kind of looting, and it should be stopped, if possible without any ill feeling. About six or seven of the important ones got together and called us. We were all together, our people. They said, don't do this, you will also be searched later, all your things will be snatched away from you, you shouldn't do this. But we didn't stop, we just went on.

Our father also told us to stop. And each time he said that we'd say, yes, we'll stop. But as soon as the men went away to sit down and talk, we would start again . . . rice, food, all sorts of nice things. From one shop we stole pure ghee, and almonds, at other places we found cloth, we collected so many utensils that we filled up a room as large as this one. Once we'd done this, the city elders announced that all copper utensils that were found in anyone's house would be confiscated. People should sell them. They must have wanted to get hold of them. So we sold that whole roomful, at two rupees or two and a half rupees a kilo. Later people realized that this had all been a trick to snatch away all this cheaply—the shopkeepers took a lot of it.

We told [our father] that we'd stay close by. You see this house? We used to have Muslim neighbours living as close to us, so we just used to jump down into their house from our roof . . .

I kept lots of new utensils, hamams etc., for my wedding. I brought a lot of utensils with me when I got married. I also looted many razais, quilts, some already made and some which I made later with the material we found. There were eleven of us, girls, we all made our dowries with the stuff we collected . . . two of those girls were also married in Batala.

I didn't have any Muslim friends of my own, but my mother had a friend whose condition was so bad that it made me feel very sad. My mother didn't have a sister so this friend was like a sister to her, and she cried for her. We cried too. My mother said, your masi's condition is very bad. She had daughters and she pleaded with my mother to keep her daughters. But my mother said, how can we, the police doesn't allow us to do so. Hindus don't allow us to do so. How can I hide your daughters? My hands are tied. You see, the Hindus kept a watch on everyone and if you hid anyone they would come immediately and make you take the people out. When things became a bit better we learnt that my mother's Muslim friend had a bad time later as well — the place where she was living was destroyed. Some time after Partition my mother went back to Pakistan — for a while the roads were opened for a few days, eight days. My mother said she must go because she wanted to find out about this friend and to meet her family who were in Lahore. In Pakistan she met many of her Muslim friends and asked them about Fatima, her friend, and learnt that her whole home had been destroyed. But my mother was very happy to meet all her Muslim friends — they too were happy to see her.

Even now when we go to Pakistan we meet all our old friends and everyone is greeted with much affection. The fighting was between Muslims and Hindus. We didn't fight with the Muslims, it had nothing to do with us.

I have never been there. My mother went. And you know that friend of mine, the leader, she went and met my uncle, and they sent lots of things for me and for the children. She's going again soon. She's got herself a permit — she gets a visa from Delhi each time and then both of them go. I met her the other day and she asked me if there was anything I wanted to send for my uncle.

*   *   *

That was a particular kind of time. And we were children so for us the whole thing was almost a sort of game. We had little sense of what its effect could be — that sort of sense only comes when you're older and maturer. How can children have any sense of this? Soon after that I got married and then completely forgot about Pakistan — this was a year or so after Partition and I used all the old stuff for my dowry. A friend of mine, the one who was married in Batala, and I, we were both married together. I had very little gold but she had managed to get a whole lot from some house and she used it to get married. She had a nice wedding. But after getting married we forgot everything about those earlier times.

And now there's no one to tell us anything. If at that time there had been some sensible mature person to guide us, he would have been able to tell us what was happening. After all, what can one person do, you can't think of everything.

The Muslims and Hindus fell at each other because the English divided

them, told them they were different people. They said if you want to be independent, to rule yourselves, you must be separate. Otherwise, why should
we have separated? The first rumour was that Pakistan had been made and
Hindus and Muslims would live there together, and Hindustan had been
made and it would be the same. And this was all good and acceptable. But
then there were people who incited the Hindus and the Muslims by giving
them a negative strength. And they said that to make this area indpendent
there must be, as we say in Punjabi, blood up to the knees. And that was what
happened — there was so much bloodshed that we were knee-deep in blood.
This was the advice of the troublemakers. Become separate, live separately
and don't let this land be at peace. If there is strife here, the English will then
be able to look to another place, knowing they need not worry about this
one. This was the plan of some evil ones.

I don't know any English — I'm just telling you stories from hearsay. There
used to be an old baba, he used to tell us that the people who are behind all
the trouble, they are the ones who want the British to come back. Each time
we used to hear the same things that we were incapable of looking after the
country. So it was good strategy to create strife between us — two killed one
day, three another so that in the end we would give up and say I can't do this,
you do it, you rule this country, it's your work.

Peace? Well, this second time 'round the same thing happened, only it
was between the Hindus and the Sikhs, the same kind of dissensions and
divisions were created as happened at the time of Pakistan. There are evil
people here as well who say we should become separate. It was such people
among the Sikhs who insisted that they wanted to become separate. The
same time is coming, the same kind of time as it was then, some people
dying here, others dying there. The thing that happened at the time of Pakistan and Hindustan, the same feeling as there was at the time was behind it.
But when people came to know what was likely to happen, people in government, they controlled the situation, otherwise things would have been
as bad.

That day, I was sixteen years old. We were on our way to work. I was working in their house, feeding their cow, cleaning her up etc., and cleaning their
house. Just as I finished cleaning my father came. He had a knife this big on
his shoulder. He came and called out, Basant Kaur, and she answered and
said yes, brother, how are you here? He said I've come to fetch my daughter.
She asked why, what's wrong? My father insisted it was nothing, but Basant

Kaur did not believe him. She said, how do you mean, nothing? Normally we don't see anything of you and here you are today, something must be wrong. It was evening. My father said sister, let me tell you one thing, just make your preparations, just get ready to leave. She said why? He said Pakistan has been created. And she cried, Ram, Ram, Ram, Ram what is this that has happened, what is this? Soon everyone from around that area collected and there was all confusion as people asked, what is this that has happened, what is this? Close by there was a Muslim household and the women from there kept saying don't worry, don't worry, we'll continue to live just as we're doing now. Naturally, because they were all friends and had lived together for years. But we went out and kept on walking . . . there they're telling us not to worry and look what is happening here. A little farther there were two bodies and still farther a group of boys, they were Musalmaans, and they were taking away a woman, and like this nearly two-and-a-half hours passed. Then we heard people crying: 'Hindustan, Hindustan', and the Hindus began to feel hopeful again, and now they started to say, don't worry, there's nothing in this Hindu-Muslim business, we'll live together like we have always done. But the troublemakers didn't like this, they were bent upon creating confusion and division. In one house they were getting ready to prepare their meal, but they had to leave and the kneaded flour stayed uncooked in the parat. We went and saw, the fire was still hot. We went into these houses with bated breath, frightened lest the owners were hiding somewhere. We wanted to go in and pick up all their things, steal them, but we were also a bit scared. Suppose they were there . . . ? And we kept doing this, going from street to street. Our parents were very worried, they kept trying to stop us, saying we would get killed, people would take us for Musalmaans. But we thought, who's going to take us away, who's going to kill us. We call ourselves Harijans, Hindus, Christians, no one can take us away. And like this we jumped from roof to roof, not really caring much what happened. Then it was another day, and things got worse. People started carrying things away, the whole Musalmaan mohalla was set on fire. There was fire on all sides, and of course things then became worse. And people thought if the houses of rich people could be burnt down like this, what was there to be frightened of from the poorer ones. And so that too began. In some houses, in one house, there was a small child crying: 'have you seen my mother, have you seen my mother?'

We did wonder what was happening but we had little understanding of it. It was all the big people who seemed to know what was happening. We were just watching most of the time. If the place had gone to Pakistan there was no danger for us. Because we are Harijans, whether it had become Pakistan or Hindustan it made no difference to us. We would stay where we were born. Our elders felt that whatever happened we wouldn't move from this place. This was our home. If anyone had tried to make us leave, we would have shown our strength. After all, Harijans are not just anybody, we're also a very powerful group. If that had happened, we would have asked for a separate state and they would have had to give it to us. We felt strong in this knowledge. Just like now the Sikhs are asking for a separate state, doesn't that then make three countries, Hindustan, Pakistan and Sikhistan, so where's the harm in asking for the fourth country? Even today we feel like this—that time it was only our elders who felt this, but today we too know. Everyone takes power—the Hindus took power, the Sikhs have taken it, at that time the English took it, but where are people like us in the count? Why have we been forgotten? Nobody has bothered about the poorer people, Harijans and Christians, we just don't come into the picture. We have talked with Indira Gandhi and her father, both of them said the same thing, that it is your own country, you are the rulers. My father used to tell us that Nehru had also said this, that this is your country, you are the rulers.

You ask what work my father and grandfather did. My grandfather was a sweeper in the grain market, later my father also worked there, and he had a government job as well. And then my brother also works there along with his government job. The grain market work has been in our family for a long time. I work in the college, and I also work privately in some houses. I start work at eight in the morning, and I'm through by eleven. Then I go to the college, after that to a [private] house, then again to college around two o'clock but sometimes I get there later and they don't really say anything to me if I'm late because they know I don't shirk work. In the other house I wash clothes, dust, clean etc.

My understanding of life tells me one thing: that there can be no end to all this strife and fighting. And even if this can stop, the bad elements in society will not let them end. Right from the age of sixteen, and today I've seen nothing but fighting, nothing but strife. I don't think there's any way this can end. None of us has a recipe for it. Of course if they would stop it would be wonderful. We would have peace in our lands, in our Pakistan, or Hindustan, or in our Punjab, or indeed in the whole world. But the troublemakers will not let this happen. Even in Punjab I don't think we will be allowed to have peace again . . .

We saw a girl killed, cut up and thrown away. They took off her earrings, threw her away, farther on they were dragging a young girl and she, poor thing, fearing for her life, jumped into the canal nearby, she just jumped in. This is what we saw. There was one girl, the daughter of some sheikhs— they had two children, a girl and a boy, the boy was outside so the girl was like a son to them, she used to say she was a boy, everyone used to call her kaka. Some goondas got after her shouting we're going to get hold of kaka, we want kaka, let's see who this kaka is. She jumped off the roof to save her honour, she didn't want to be insulted.

The police weren't interested in anything then. They didn't bother with anyone. The army helped a bit, they provided safe passage to people, helped them to get away. The police were looting as much as anyone else. I think people lost all sense of honour and morals then . . .

In those two-and-a-half hours when we first heard that Dinanagar had become part of Pakistan, the Muslims began to kill the Hindus, and then two-and-a-half hours later there was a phone call which said that no, Dinanagar hadn't gone to Pakistan, it was part of Hindustan. And in this time the tide was reversed and Hindus began to kill Musalmaans . . . shouting slogans they pulled people out, they killed them, they threw them out of their houses, they raped the women, young women . . . The first thing the Hindus said was that we are brothers and sisters, we are together. This is what they said at first. Even if it becomes Pakistan we will live together. After all, how could they leave their lives, their homes and go away? No, they would have stayed together. It was the devil who created this trouble. They wanted to divide us, to show we were incapable of ruling, so that the English would have a chance to come back.

8
MEMORY

Perhaps the most difficult part of an exercise such as this is how to bring it to a close. What can I say about Partition that can adequately serve as a conclusion? That it was an event of major importance? That it touched people's lives in unprecedented, and very deep ways? That its influence on the history of the subcontinent has been profound and far reaching? All of these are correct. But none of these is adequate. There is so much that remains to be learnt about Partition, that an exercise such as the one I have attempted must necessarily only remain a first step in our knowledge of this history.

When I began work on Partition, I had little idea of what I would learn. In many ways I began as an innocent: someone familiar with the 'history' of the event—as many Indians are who have to study 'modern history' at school—and someone who had grown up on stories of it, stories that somehow did not match what we learnt at school, stories that, perhaps because of that, we discounted. When, after 1984, I began to 'hear' these stories, to pay attention to them, my first feeling was of anger. Why had the history of Partition been so lacking in describing how Partition had impacted on the lives of ordinary people, what it had actually meant to them? Why had historians not even attempted to explore what I saw as the 'underside' of this history—the feelings, the emotions, the pain and anguish, the trauma, the sense of loss, the silences in which it lay shrouded? Was this just historiographical neglect or something deeper—a refusal on the part of historians to face up to a trauma so riven with pain and grief that there needed to be some distance before they could confront it?

The tools of history are meant to lead to an objective view of the past: how do you bring objectivity to bear on a situation in which your own family may have been involved? Death, displacement, dislocation, loss of home and family—these were so close to the lives of many historians, particularly from north India, that it was not surprising that the history of Partition had so far been only to a history of the State. 1984 acted as a watershed for many historians. But 1984 had been preceded—and indeed followed—by several equally disturbing developments: the violence in Punjab, the increasing strife in the northeast, the growing influence of the Hindu Right, the destruction, in 1992, of the Babri Mosque by Hindu communalists, the subsequent Hindu-Muslim riots that followed ... People watched, in horror and often helplessly, as the fabric of Indian society began to shred on lines of ethnic and religious identity. Partition came back to revisit many who had been mere spectators and others who had been victims and participants. Stories of 'that time' resurfaced. 1984 was 'like Partition again'. 'We didn't think it would happen to us in our own country' was a feeling expressed by Sikhs and Muslims in 1984 and 1992. It was this increasing polarization of Indian society on the basis of religion, that led, I think, to a re-examination of the history of Partition, a re-examination that was deeply rooted in the concerns of the present. It was this, too, that led me, personally, to understand how and why certain kinds of historical explorations become important at certain times, that particular kinds of explorations of the past are rooted in particular kinds of experiences of the present. It is the present, our involvement in it, our wish to shape it to lead to the kind of future we desire, that leads us to revisit and re-examine the past. This may be nothing new to those engaged in the practice of history, but for me it meant a great deal. It made me realize that the questions that had begun to preoccupy me were not mine alone: others were thinking along similar lines, making similar explorations.

A half century—an arbitrary figure, but perhaps it did have some meaning after all—also seemed to mark other beginnings. Many of those who were victims and survivors of Partition were now in their seventies and eighties: to historians revisiting this history it became important to speak to the survivors, to gather their testimonies while this was still possible. For the survivors themselves, the 'distance' of a half century, the events they had seen in that interim, also worked as a kind of impetus which surfaced memories of the time. While many still found it painful to speak about that time in their lives, there were others who *wanted* their stories to be recorded, they felt that for them the time had come to do so. The conditions seemed to be right for a new exploration of Partition to begin.

When you embark on an excercise that seems, to you, unusual, perhaps unique, you begin by congratulating yourself on having discovered something new, a new approach, new material, a new way of looking at things. And, in the mistaken conviction that yours is the unique perspective, you begin by asserting that no one has looked at things in quite this way before. Yet research is a humbling thing, as I found out. Nothing is really new, other than your interpretation (and sometimes not even that): you simply train a different eye on the past. Quite quickly, then, I learnt not to feel complacent about being the 'first'—many, many others had been there before me. Because I was looking at what I saw as the 'underside' of the history of Partition, I had begun by being sceptical of the tools of conventional history. What could documents, government reports, speeches tell me about what I was trying to look at: feelings, emotions, those indefinable things that make up the sense of an event? Yet, I learnt in the course of my work that even what we see as 'conventional' tools can yield a great deal, for so much depends on the perspective you bring to bear on them. Informed, for example, through women's accounts of the violence they had faced, I was able to trace some of its other dimensions in sources such as documents and reports. Curious about what had happened to children and scheduled castes, I was able to locate material about them, however slight, in speeches, newspaper accounts, parliamentary debates. My debt therefore, to the very 'sources' I was critical of, is great: had it not been for them, I would not have been alerted to many of the things I have written about in this book.

This realization was important to me too as a feminist, and someone interested in history, particularly the history of those who have been marginalized by society, a history which had itself been marginalized in the broader world of history writing. Indeed, a question that I was constantly faced with in the writing of this book was: how do human beings relate to their history? It seemed to me that, at least where Partition history was concerned, there was a contradiction in the history that we knew, that we had learnt, and the history that people remembered. Many historians have spoken of how selective amnesia and memory are at the root of the relationship between human beings and their history, that historiography as a technique attempts to 'dissipate amnesia and cultivate memory'.[1] But in so doing, such an historiography is itself selective in its illumination of certain aspects of the past. It became clear to me as I drew closer to the end of this work, that in any such exploration of the past the aspects we choose to illuminate are determined not only by the present we live in, but the future we wish to work towards. In this book, I have been concerned with looking at what one might call the voices of ordinary people, as well as those on the margins of society. I have consciously chosen to train a particular kind of gaze on the past, for mainstream history has tended to marginalize the experiences of such 'groups' (if one can use that word at all), and my 'hypothesis for the future' would be one in which all such groups, however small, had a voice and a role. I believe too that because of the particular way in which the historiography of Partition has trained its lens on the past, only certain aspects of the past have become visible, and new and different realities will emerge as we begin to re-read the past, bringing different tools of exploration to bear upon the histories we know. Thus it is because I wish to see a society in which women, children and lower castes have an integral role to play that I seek out their histories in the past, that I try to recover what I have defined as their voices.

In doing so, I have found the tools of feminist historiography to be enormously enabling because they allowed me listen to that most unheard of things, silence, and to understand it, to work with it. All too often, histories that attempt to recover hidden voices—and in some ways what I have tried to do in this book is precisely that—make a simple opposition between speech and silence. If something is shrouded in silence, then speech must be good, it must be liberating. There is little doubt that in the history of Partition, the stories of women, children, scheduled castes and many others have been silenced both at the level of the State and at the level of history writing. Yet there is no simple way in which one can march in and attempt to break that silence, irresponsibly and unproblematically. I have referred, throughout this book, to the constant dilemma I faced while writing it. How much of what people spoke about, or of what they did not say, could I put down in

[1] Annarita Buttafucco, 'On "Mothers" and "Sisters": Fragments on Women/Feminism/Historiography', in *Nuovo DWF* (italian), no. 15, 1980.

print? How far could I go in persuading people to speak? For women who had faced abduction and rape how would speaking about it now help? To me, these questions have only become possible through the practice of feminist historiography. In my work, the more I looked at women's voices and found them inserting themselves into the text, the more I realized that the silences did not exist only around women, but also around others, those whose silences have been even less important to society. The search for a history of women, then, was what led me to a search for a history of others. The voices of women, of children, of untouchables to me provide not only a different perspective on the history of Partition, but they also establish this history as a process, a continuing history, which lives on in our lives today in a variety of ways.

I have attempted, throughout this work, to look at 'voices' both in people's narratives and testimonies as well as in letters and documents. The recovery of 'voice' however, is not unproblematic. These are, I know, different kinds of voices: some, which are much more immediate and which reflect the concerns of the here and now, and others, which are more reflective, in some cases more practised for they come after a gap of many years, and perhaps after many tellings. When the history of these voices is written, however, it is almost always written by 'others': how people define their self-identities, and how these identities get represented, are two different things. I am deeply aware that my representations of the experiences of women, children and scheduled castes at Partition are, after all, my representations, selectively illuminated by my concerns and priorities. To me these make for another sort of voice: a voice that reads into, and interprets, other voices. If this is my representation, then the texts of the oral narratives represent, I hope, the way in which the people concerned themselves remember, and reconstruct, events. I have not attempted to make of them more than what they are: one way of remembering, at one time, with one person. It is not my endeavour to place these voices *against* the conventional, factual histories of the time. Rather, I would like to place them *alongside* existing histories: they are the memories of real people, memories of the history of Partition, and for that reason alone, they are important. It is through them that the history of Partition can be seen. There is yet another kind of voice that my work traces: that is the voice of the State, of official discourse, and sometimes, an oppositional voice (such as that of the RSS) but nonetheless a voice of considerable power. Together these different kinds of voices make up the whole that I have attempted to create.

If recovering 'voice' is not unproblematic, it is further complicated by the fact that voices themselves are differentiated. They have a hierarchy. In the process of interviewing people over an extended period of time I found, time and again, how difficult it was to recover women's voices. In joint interviews — and because Partition is so much a part of 'family' histories, and also because families are often fearful of 'letting' their members speak about Partition without the elders, usually the men, being around — it was always the men who spoke. If addressed directly, the women would defer to the men. In separate interviews, whenever those were possible, women would often begin by saying they had nothing to say, nothing, that is, of any importance. Gradually, they would begin to talk, but often they would say only those things they thought you wanted to hear, or those that they thought the men wanted to hear. Over the years of speaking to both men and women I learnt to recognize this as something oral historians have often pointed to. In a perceptive article, Kathryn Anderson and Dana C. Jack point out that a woman speaking about her life may often use two separate, sometimes even conflicting perspectives: 'one framed in concepts and values that reflect men's dominant position in the culture, and one informed by the more immediate realities of a woman's personal experience. Where experience does not "fit" dominant meanings, alternative concepts may not readily be available. Hence, inadvertently, women often mute their own thoughts and feelings when they try to describe their lives in the familiar and publicly acceptable terms of prevailing concepts and conventions. To hear women's perspectives accurately, we have to learn to listen in stereo, receiving both the dominant and muted channels clearly and tuning into them carefully to understand the relationship between them.'[2]

Among women too there were different kinds of voices: it was rela-

---

[2] Kathryn Anderson and Dana C. Jack, 'Learning to Listen: Interview Techniques and Analysis', in Sherna Berger Gluck and Daphne Patai (eds.), *Women's Words: The Feminist Practice of Oral History*, New York, Routledge, 1991, p. 11.

tively easier for me to locate middle-class women to speak to, but far more difficult to find, say, Dalit women—try as I might, I was only able to locate one. And there was virtually no way in which I could speak to women who had been raped and/or abducted. Not only had they very effectively been rendered invisible, but many of them wanted to stay that way, their stories held closely to them. It was as if the memory of the rape, the experience of abduction, was in some way shameful and had therefore to be relegated to the realm of amnesia.

For as long as I can remember, I have called myself a feminist. The political practice of feminism, its deep, personal meanings: these have been to me part of my very being. I have never been more grateful for this than while working on this book, for it was this that alerted me, I think, to the many nuances of the histories and experiences of women. I do not mean by this that the experience of feminism is necessarily essential to understanding the hidden histories of women, but simply that for me it was both essential and enabling. The practice of feminist historiography, too, opened many doors. In a paradoxical kind of way, had it not been for the practice of mainstream—largely male— historiography, and the glaring absence in it of a gendered perspective, feminist historians would perhaps not have known what to look for. There is so much baggage that attaches to the feminist practice of history: in many ways it is seen as being something 'less serious', perhaps 'marginal' and certainly something that seems, by and large, to be the concern of women—which again, in the world of mainstream history, underscores its lack of seriousness. Yet, for those of us who give such historiographical practices the importance that they deserve, feminist history has been enormously enabling—opening up arenas of discussion that would not necessarily become visible otherwise. I cannot, for example, imagine looking at the histories of children if feminism had not opened up this world for me. Nor could I imagine examining the histories of scheduled castes and women comparatively had I not been able to use gender as a category of analysis. Although my book is not 'only' about women, I have come to the conclusion that women, their histories, and where those histories lead us, lie at the core of it.

* * *

Silence and speech. Memory and forgetting. Pain and healing. These are at the heart of my book. At the end of several years of work, I had listened to many stories. Each was unique. In every telling I found a different Partition, in every story a different experience.[3] Each account raised different questions. Perhaps the question that I was most frequently faced with was about the very nature of the exercise: a question that had to do, in the main, with remembering. Why rake all this up again? If people have lived with their experiences, in some ways have made their peace with them, what is to be gained by pushing them to remember, to dredge up the many uncomfortable and unpleasant memories that they may prefer to put away? There is no satisfactory answer to this question. The dilemma remains: is it better to be silent or to speak? Or, for the researcher, is it better to 'allow' silence or to 'force' speech?

As with many other things, it was my encounter with Ranamama, my uncle, that turned my attention to this. When I first began to speak with him there was a tremendous sense of excitement. I was pleased that he seemed to want to tell his story. He had lived too long with his silences. When I asked him how he would feel about my taking his story further, he said, 'Write what you like, my life cannot get any worse.' This was, however, followed by the more sobering realization that I had a moral responsibility not only towards some abstract category called 'the truth' but also—and especially—towards the material realities of Rana's life. Could I be irresponsible enough to make everything he said public? Clearly not—the implications for his life hardly bear thinking about. Yet, was it not wrong then to present only a 'partial' picture? To hold back some of the 'truth' and make available another? This dilemma troubled me, and stayed with me throughout. When Sikh families from Rawalpindi spoke of the attacks and the violence they had seen, I wondered about the right thing to do. Unless I had the 'other' side of the story, would this not mean that I was simply making available material that could be put to dangerous use by the Hindu Right? When the question of rape and abduction of women came up, I asked myself, was it right to try and prise open their silences? Would my search for a historical truth not mean another violation?

[3] See James E. Young, *Writing and Rewriting the Holocaust.*

Many years later, I still have not found a satisfactory answer to this question. How important is it for us to excavate Partition memories? Krishna Sobti, a writer and a Partition refugee, once said that Partition was difficult to forget but dangerous to remember. But does this mean then that we must not remember it? Over the years, despite many uncertainties, I have become increasingly convinced that while it may be dangerous to remember, it is also essential to do so — not only so that we can come to terms with it, but also because unlocking memory and remembering is an essential part of beginning the process of resolving, perhaps even of forgetting. Earlier in this book I spoke of a seventy-year-old professor, a one-time member of the RSS, who broke down while recalling how he had heard a Muslim woman being raped and killed in the nearby market, but had not been able to express his horror or sorrow. Fifty years later, he was able to allow himself to remember, to mourn, and perhaps to begin to forget. Before he could do so, however, he had to be able to *admit* the memory. I think one must, as people inevitably do, exercise some judgment in how far you wish to explore a particular history. I believed quite strongly then, and I do so now, that it is essential for us to confront Partition, to look at its many meanings, if we are to come to terms with its impact in our lives in the subcontinent. Not looking at it, pretending it is not there, will not make it go away. At the same time, however, I believe too that we must approach this kind of exploration with caution: there are instances where silence is more important than speech, times at which it is invasive to force speech, and I think we need to be able to recognize those when we meet them.

During the course of my interviews I became familiar with people's reluctance to speak. What is the use of collecting these stories, they asked, will they help anyone at all? Sometimes, the reluctance was born out of a sense of the pointlessness, for them, of such an exercise. At others it came from a residual sense of fear, a concern that acts of violence from 'that' time could be held against them. I began to understand, gradually, that the silences of Partition are of many kinds. If, at one level, we are faced with a kind of historical silence, at another this is compounded by a familial silence, in which families have colluded in hiding their own histories, sometimes actively as the two brothers I met in Jangpura had done, and sometimes simply through indifference, as had happened, to some extent, in my own family. Sometimes the silence was a form of protest: an abducted woman, forcibly recovered by the Indian State from her Muslim abductor with whom she had built some sort of life, took to silence as a form of protest. A Punjabi refugee who had seen his neighbour's daughters being raped and killed refused to speak at all after this incident. Attia Hosain, a well-known writer, refused to be forced into choosing between India and Pakistan—she did not want a truncated country. In protest, she maintained a silence on writing any more about Partition. For many people there was also a sense of resignation: they had lived through the dislocation and upheaval, at the time they had done all they could to put their lives together again. As several of them said: no one came forward to help at the time, what is the use of doing all this now? Who will benefit from it? Everything went back to the question Manmohan Singh had put to me: what was the use of filling all the tapes I carried with me?

In moments of despair, I tended to agree with this. So much violence, so much pain and grief, often so much dishonesty about the violence—killing women was not violence, it was saving the honour of the community; losing sight of children, abandoning them to who knew what fate was not violence, it was maintaining the purity of the religion; killing people of the other religion was not murder, it was somehow excusable . . . seldom has a process of research I have been engaged in brought me more anger, and more anguish.

For women who had been through rape and abduction the reluctance to speak was of another order altogether. Sometimes these histories were not known even to members of their own families, especially if they were women from ashrams whose marriages had been arranged by the ashram authorities. Or, at other times the histories were known to older members of the family but not to others. Speaking about them, making them public, this not only meant opening up old wounds, but also being prepared to live with the consequences—perhaps another rejection, another trauma. For many women, Partition represented a very fundamental tearing up of the fabric of their lives: the family is, after all, central to the lives of women, its loss was therefore deeply felt. For those who had been taken away from their families through rape and abduction, the loss was even more profound: would they even be able to find the words to articulate their feelings?

And words are, after all, all we have. One of the things that I found in the course of my interviews and research was that people struggled to describe what they had been through at Partition, and often ended by saying what they had seen was indescribable. Ironically, and tragically, in subsequent conflicts and strife, it is Partition that has provided a reference point: to say of a communal situation that it was like Partition again is to invest it with a seriousness, a depth of horror and violence that can, now, immediately be understood. Yet, for those who lived through the violence and dislocation of Partition, the language they had available to them must have seemed particularly lacking to describe what it was they lived through. *Partition:* the word itself is so inadequate. Partition is a simple division, a separation, but surely what happened in 1947 was much more than that. *Batwara,* another name for division, but equally inadequate. *Takseem,* an Urdu/Punjabi word, again signifying division. How can these words take in the myriad meanings of this event? Not only were people separated overnight, and friends became enemies, homes became strange places, strange places now had to be claimed as home, a line was drawn to mark a border, and boundaries began to find reflection in people's lives and minds. Identities had suddenly to be redefined: if you were a Punjabi one day, sharing a cultural space with other Punjabis, you now had to put aside all such markers of identity—cultural, linguistic, geographical, economical—and privilege only one, your religion. You had to partition your mind, and close off all those areas that did not fit the political division around you. Other things rendered the experience indescribable: for many, in the uncertainty created by Partition, violence became one of the few certainties. Ordinary, peaceable people were forced to confront the violence within themselves. Victims became aggressors, aggressors turned into victims, and people began to partition their minds: it was all right to kill if the person you were killing was the 'other'—but in order to obliterate the aggressor in yourself, you had to cast yourself as victim, and so, often you had to live a lie, a pretense that you had not killed. How could a simple word, a word invested with the literalness of geographical division, even approximate the many levels of experience that people had lived through? Where would you find the words that located, that identified the violence not only 'out there' but inside you? And it is perhaps precisely for this reason that in some ways so many people who see themselves as victims are complicit in the violence of Partition, that there is such a reluctance to remember it.

In India, there is no institutional memory of Partition: the State has not seen fit to construct any memorials, to mark any particular places—as has been done, say, in the case of holocaust memorials or memorials for the Vietnam War. There is nothing at the border that marks it as a place where millions of people crossed, no plaque or memorial at any of the sites of the camps, nothing that marks a particular spot as a place where Partition memories are collected. Partition was the dark side of independence: the question then is, how can it be memorialized by the State without the State recognizing its own complicity? It is true that hundreds of thousands of people died as a result of Partition. A half century later, you might well be able to read them as martyrs to the cause of forging a new nation. But alongside there is also the other, inescapable reality that millions of people were killed and in many families where there were deaths there were probably also murders. How do you memorialize such a history? What do you commemorate? For people, for the State, what is at stake in remembering? To what do you have to be true in order to remember? It was not only that people killed those of the 'other' religion, but in hundreds of instances they killed people of their own families; it was not only that men of one religion raped women of the other, but in hundreds of instances men of the same religion raped women of the same religion. What can you do to mark such a history as anything other than a history of shame? No matter how much Indian politicians, members of the Congress, tried to see themselves as reluctant players in the game, they could not escape the knowledge that they accepted Partition as the cost of freedom. Such histories are not easily memorialized.

In many countries in the world today there are memorials to moments of conflict and upheaval. Either with State support or otherwise, scholars have painstakingly built up meticulous archives of people's testimonies, of photographs, letters, documents, memoirs, books in which such historical moments are represented. Very little of this exists for Partition. Until recently, little attempt has been made even to collect people's accounts. Visual representations of Partition—despite the rich archive of photographs that must exist in many newspapers and magazines—remain limited, and while a half century of Indian independence has called for all manner of celebratory events, little has been done to mark this important event in the history of India.

But while there is no public memory of Partition, inside homes and families the memory is kept alive through remembrance rituals and stories that mark particular events. When Mangal Singh and his two brothers came away from their village carrying with them the burden of the death of seventeen of their family members, they built a commemorative plaque with all seventeen names on it, and had it placed in the Golden Temple in Amritsar. An annual forty-eight-hour reading of the Sikh scriptures was held to mark the occasion of their deaths, to commemorate their martyrdom. Till they were alive, Mangal Singh's brothers attended the ritual with him each year. After their deaths he went to it, usually alone, and sometimes accompanied by Trilok Singh, the sole survivor of the family deaths. When I asked Mangal Singh, many years later, how he had lived with these memories, he pointed around him to the fertile fields of Punjab. He said: 'All of us who came from there, Partition refugees, we have put all our forgetting into working this land, into making it prosper.'

A small community of survivors from the Rawalpindi massacres lives in Jangpura in New Delhi. Every year, on March 13, they hold a remembrance ritual for the victims of March 1947. Shahidi Diwas, or Martyrs' Day, is held to commemorate the martyrdom of the many people, mostly women, who 'willingly gave up their lives so that their Sikhi would not get stained'. Each year, survivors of March 1947—the number declines with each passing year—get together to recount tales of the heroism of those who died in the killings. The ritual begins by offering prayers for the dead, paying homage to their memory. Then, their stories are retold—a powerful and moving account of the martyrdom of each person who died. As you listen, the picture of Mata Lajjawanti, who is said to have fearlessly led ninety women to their deaths by jumping into a well full of water, and to have jumped in first herself, rises before your eyes. You see the women, you hear their cries of 'jo bole so nihal' (blessed is he who speaks the word of the guru) as they throw themselves into the well. And as the story ends, a bhajan rises up from a group of singers seated nearby, each year, year after year, the same words:

> sura to pehchaniye
> jo lade din ke het
> purza purza kat mare
> kabhi no chode khet
> know him as the brave one
> who fights against the enemy
> let his body be cut into a hundred pieces
> but never will he give up his faith

The ceremony continues as other tales of death are told, deaths that are valorized, shorn of violence and presented as martyrdom. Over the years as the number of the survivors of Rawalpindi has decreased, the gap between the teller of the stories and the audience has increased: young people and small children now sit in the audience, listening, often rapt, for the stories are told with skill and passion. The women's martyrdom conceals the men's complicity. It was through attending this ritual and listening to the stories of survivors that I learnt that in several villages there had been protracted negotiations with the attackers. Money had changed hands. Weapons had been given up. And through all of this, the women had sat together, sometimes alone, sometimes with the men, plotting their own deaths, their martyrdom.

For the community of survivors, the remembrance ritual works at many levels. It helps keep the memory alive, and at the same time it helps them to forget. They remember, selectively, in order to forget. For what is remembered is what is described as the women's heroism, their bravery. There is no talk of the many who must have refused, who did not wish to thus give up their lives, none of those who were abducted. The two sisters from Thamali, known to have disappeared and, in all likelihood, to have been abducted, find no mention here. Nor do the many other women who figure in the list of missing persons from these villages. With each passing year, a further resolution is put on the hundreds of deaths, the massive loss of life: memory is simultaneously preserved and limited. The community of survivors of the Rawalpindi massacres has chosen to present, in this ritual, their own version of the history of March 1947. They have limited, as have all others, the memory of rape and abduction and have transformed their history into one of valour and heroism.

Once we enter the difficult and troubled terrain of memory then, the history of Partition presents us with different kinds of memories. We have, for example, memories of the State; professional or historical memory; the memories of survivors, whether they are victims or aggressors or both; and the memories that we, as the generation born after Partition, have inherited. How can these be used? Do they, can they, work in tandem or do they have different rhythms? And how do we then reach into those deeper memories, which lie far below the initial layers of silence? For me, this search has only just begun, but in the course of seeking out these stories I have learnt that the exploration of memory can never be separated from the ethics of such an exploration, both for oneself as researcher, and for the subject one is researching. In my work on Partition, I have been constantly aware of this, and although at the end of more than a decade of researching, reading, questioning I am more than ever convinced that it is necessary, and important, to explore Partition memories, I am also convinced that this is not a search that can be taken on without the researcher constantly being faced with questions of its ethicality. It is a search on which the researcher must impose her own boundaries, her own silences but, in the end, it is a search that allows us access to a wealth of information and a different kind of knowledge. When combined with what we already know from the histories that exist, I believe this can only take us further forward in our understanding.

* * *

I would like to end this work, as I began it, with two stories. Throughout my exploration, I have looked, by and large, at stories of loss, violence, division. There was, however, more to Partition than that: there were also innumerable stories of how people had helped each other, stories of friendship and sharing, stories where the borders laid down by the British to keep the two countries apart were crossed time and again, and stories where the trauma and upheaval of Partition actually resulted in opening up opportunities for people to make something of their lives. It is two such stories that I would like to tell.

In 1989 I learnt that in the terminology of the Indian State there was a category of women known as Partition widows. At the time, the People's Union for Democratic Rights (PUDR), a civil rights organization based in Delhi, had commissioned a group of people — of whom I was one — to carry out an investigation into a strike being staged in Delhi. The strike was an unusual one. Not only were all its participants women, but every single one of them was above sixty or sixty-five years in age. Equally unusual was the issue they were striking for: not an increase in wages, for none of them was 'working' in the strict sense of the term, but instead an increase in pensions. As Partition widows these women had been taken on by the State as its 'permanent liability' and had been provided training and work of different kinds so that they could earn a living. The idea was to enable women who had thus been rendered alone by Partition to work, to become economically independent, and to acquire a sense of 'dignity and self worth'. When this group of Partition widows had become too old to work, they retired on a small pension from the State and it was in this that they were now demanding an increase.

The increase was small, and at the end of a few days of protest the State sanctioned the required amount. In actual money terms this amounted to a mere Rs 250,000 a year, and that too for the years of life that remained for these women. But what was significant was the women's determination to place their demands before the State and their strong belief that this was their right: 'I walked all the way from Pakistan. I'll walk here every day if I have to until our demands are met,' said one, while another pointed to the house of the Home Minister and said, 'he is our mai-baap, our parent, and we will place our demands before him.'

There are any number of questions that can be raised about the State's patriarchal, yet benevolent, intervention into the lives of these women, but that is not my intention here. I tell this story merely to point to a lesser-known fact of the trauma and upheaval of Partition, that in many ways out of the tragedy grew a sense of independence and opportunity for many people and particularly for women. If widows learnt to stand on their own feet, other women came into professions such as teaching, nursing, different kinds of business and, importantly, social work. For many middle-class women particularly, social work became a real career option, as well as a way of involving themselves in the making of the new nation, and, as in the case of Anis Kidwai, putting their own grief and sense of loss to rest. Mridula Sarabhai, Kamlaben Patel, Premvati Thapar, Anis Kidwai, Damyanti Sahgal—all women we have met in this book—gave their lives to working with and for the new nation, and for its women. The work was not without its dilemmas: at times the agenda of the State conflicted with the interests of women, but all of them made the best of the opportunity Partition gave them to make something of their own lives, as well as the lives of the women they worked with.

The second story (which appeared in *The News* in Pakistan)[4] I want to tell relates to a different reality. In 1947 twenty-four-year-old Iqbal Begum lost many members of her family in the violence of Partition. Like many others, she too was forced to leave her home in a small village, Kher Dikki, near Amritsar, and move to Pakistan. The horrors of Partition remained with her all her life. Many years later, when her grandson wanted to go on a peace delegation to Amritsar, she advised him against it. 'Don't go to Amritsar,' she said, 'they will kill you.' But while for Iqbal Begum Partition called up stories of violence and loss, her daughter, Kulsoom, had a different experience. She too married into a family from Amritsar: Chaudhry Latif, her father-in-law, was a Partition refugee who had moved across to a house in Islampura (earlier Krishan Nagar) in Lahore. When Chaudhry Latif had moved into the spacious, elegant house in 1947, he had little idea of who the original owner was. One day, he received a letter from Jalandhar addressed simply to 'The Occupant'. Opening it, Chaudhry Latif read in Urdu:

> I write to you as a human being. I hope you will not be put off that a Hindu has written to you. We are human beings first and Hindu and Muslim only after that. I firmly believe you will oblige me by answering this letter in the name of the human bond we have.

---

[4] Arif Shamim, 'Writing Home to a Stranger', *The News*, Lahore, May 4, 1997.

The letter went on to describe how its writer, Harikishan Das Bedi, who had earlier lived in the house Chaudhry Latif now occupied, had had to leave suddenly when Partition became a reality. Bedi, a teacher at the Sanatan Dharam High School in Lahore, had loved nothing more than his books and papers. Forced to move without much notice, Bedi had left behind everything including an incomplete manuscript of a book on geometry that he was writing, which lay on his table at home. Shortly after Partition, in September of 1947, Bedi came back to his home accompanied by the police but he was not allowed to take anything away from there. Later, after Chaudhry Latif moved in, Bedi wrote to him describing in detail where this or that book or paper or document was kept. From across the border, he directed the new owner to his almirahs, his tin trunks, asking if his precious papers and books could be kept carefully. The 'things you don't need, put them in a bag . . .' he said, and established his credentials by telling Chaudhry Latif a little about himself: 'My students included Hindus, Muslims and Sikhs. In my eyes there was no difference between them. You can ask Chaudhry Siraj, my Muslim neighbour, Deena Nath and I guarded his house during the riots. He was not in Krishan Nagar at that time but we did not let anybody harm his house.'

Equally carefully, Chaudhry Latif followed Bedi's instructions. He collected every bit of paper, Bedi's books and documents and, over time, made up small parcels and sent them across to Jalandhar. Chaudhry Latif's son described how his father 'replied to all of Bedi's letters and even sent parcels of his belongings to Jalandhar. They had developed a special relationship.' For many years, the two friends maintained a correspondence across the border, and it was only much later, after Chaudhry Latif had died, that his daughter-in-law, Kulsoom, found all Bedi's letters neatly tied up and kept in one corner of his cupboard. No one knows if Harikishan Das Bedi is alive or dead, but his letters to Chaudhry Latif provide a moving testimony to another side of the history of Partition. In his second letter to Latif, Bedi said:

> I read your letter over and over again and felt that it had been written by a true friend. I also read it out to many of my friends. All agree that had all Hindus and Muslims shared the feelings which you have expressed in your

letter, the bloodbath would never have taken place and we, living in India and Pakistan, would have taken our countries to great heights. But God had other plans. I shudder to think of what Hindus and Muslims have done to their fellow countrymen . . . And the worst part is that it was all perpetrated in the name of religion. No religion allows such bloodletting.

Whether or not Bedi's hopes would have been realized, the correspondence between him and Chaudhry Latif will remain, evidence of the fact that borders can be crossed and friendships built and maintained. When—and if—I come back to Partition, it is this aspect of it that I would like to explore.

GLOSSARY

afim opium

ahimsa nonviolence

akhand path a continuous, 48-hour reading of the Sikh prayer

almirah wardrobe, cupboard

alvida literally 'farewell', but here meant to indicate the farewell prayer of the last Friday of Ramzan the holy month of the Muslims

amma mother; also used to address older women

annas old measure used to describe 1/16th of a rupee

apa elder sister; aunt

ardaas prayer

Arya Samaji member of the Arya Samaj

ashram religious sanctuary or shelter

atta wholewheat flour

aukat boundary (used metaphorically)

azad free, independent

baba old man

badmash bad characters

banyan vest, singlet

barkat blessing

bauji father

begums wives of nawabs

behanji sister

behnoi sister's husband

beri type of berry

beta son

beti daughter

bhapaji elder brother

bhog conclusion of the Sikh prayer

bibaji term of affection, usually for a younger woman

bibi term of respect for a woman; can also mean sister/mother

boris gunny sacks

brahmanvad casteism, the rule of the high castes

bua aunt (father's sister)

chachaji father's younger brother (uncle)

chaddar sheet

chak small hamlet

chamarin woman of the sweeper caste

chamars member of the leather-worker's caste

channas chick peas

chaprasi office helper

charpai string cot

chichar leech

cholas spiced chick peas

chopar game of dice

chowki police post

chowkidar guard

chuaras dates

crore ten million

daan donation

dadi grandmother

dais midwives

dal lentils

dama asthma

danda staff

dangars buffaloes

dargah grave of saint

DAV Dayanand Anglo-Vedic educational institutions set up by the Arya
Samaj

deen dars a particular community

desh bhakti service (also love) of one's country

dharam religion

dharam kanta weighbridge to weigh lorry loads; the balance of the weight
against the weighing stones is here used to signify a moral dilemma

dhoti single-piece garment worn around the legs

didi elder sister

dukhan a type of mourning song

dupatta long scarf

durrie rug

duvanni two annas

fazool kharchi wasteful or unnecessary expenditure

gerua saris saffron-coloured saris

ghee clarified butter

granthi singer of religious songs in a Sikh temple

gujar caste name

gur jaggery

Gurkha inhabitants of northern India and Nepal, usually soldiers

gurudwara Sikh temple

Guru Granth Sahib the holy book of the Sikhs

Haji Hussain ki joru Haji Hussain's wife

halvai cook; one who makes sweetmeats and savouries for roadside eateries, weddings, etc.

hamam here meant to denote a water container

haveli old-style home or house built around a central courtyard

insaniyat humanity

izzat honour

janab-e-ali form of greeting denoting respect, used among men—usually equals or older men

jansanghis members of a Hindu right-wing party called the Jana Sangh

japji sahib bhog end of the japji sahib prayer

japji sahib path sikh prayer

Jat caste name

jatha crowd, a procession

jawan literally 'young', but used also to refer to young soldiers

jeth husband's brother

jethani husband's brother's wife

jungle people forest dwellers

kabristan graveyard

kaddu pumpkin

kaffir unbeliever

kafila a foot-column of people, usually refugees

kaka term of affection for a small boy

kasbah a small township

katori small bowl

kattar strong, almost fundamentalist

kehwa a salt-sweet tea

khangah of naugaza a grave or resting place (see also naugaza)

khatri Punjabi term, used to describe members of the trading caste

khooli (khurli) water trough, usually for animals

khota (also khoti) damaged

kirpan holy dagger or sword of the Sikhs, one of the markers of the Sikh religion

kisans farmers or cultivators

kotha literally 'roof', but also used to signify a house of dancers, usually courtesans

kursi bhakti service of one's 'seat' or political position; lust for power

kurta long shirt worn by men and women

lakh/lac 100,000

lassi buttermilk

Madrasi a term used to describe people from Tamil Nadu

mahants priests; guardians of temples

maharaj generally 'king', used as a term of respect and used here to refer to the Sikh guru, Guru Nanak

maidan courtyard, park, open space

majboor helpless

mala chain, usually of beads, sometimes of flowers

mama (also *mamu, mamuji*) maternal uncle

mami mother's brother's wife

mandi wholesale market

mashki water carrier

masi aunt (mother's sister)

masjid mosque

mataji mother

matlab literally 'meaning', used here in the sense of ulterior motive or reason

matric end-of-school examination

maulvis Muslim priests

maunds weight measure, not used much after metric system established

mehfil session, usually of poetry, music or dance

mehtars caste name for the sweeper caste

mela fair, festival, also used to describe crowds

Mian Ahmed ki joru Mian Ahmed's wife

mirasis travelling singers

mlechcha barbarian, impure

mohalla small residential area

Mohammed ki joru Mohammed's wife

moongphalis peanuts

morcha crowd, procession

mullah Muslim priest

mungphali peanuts

Musalmaans colloquial term for Muslims

nagar place

namaz Muslim prayer

nana maternal grandfather

nanan younger sister-in-law

nani maternal grandmother

napakistan impure Pakistan, as opposed to the land of the pure

naugaza literally 'a place measuring nine yards'; also can relate to the size of a
   grave or the saint buried there

nawab ruler, noble

pagri turban

paisa old measure used to describe a fraction of a rupee

parat wide metal bowl used for kneading flour

path Sikh prayer

pathan inhabitants of north-west Pakistan, a martial race

patila brass or steel casserole-type cooking vessel

pattas land deeds

pethas vegetable similar to squash

pichche se from an earlier time

pies old measure used to describe a fraction of a rupee

pirs saints

potli bundle

purdah seclusion

qila fort

quam race

quwwali group song; usually as an exchange or even competition between two
   parties of singers

raj karega khalsa the Sikh religious cry meaning 'truth will prevail'

ranis queens

razai quilt

roti unleavened bread

RSS Rashtriya Swayamsevak Sangh, a Hindu organization

sabzi mandi wholesale vegetable market

sachche padshah (badshah) literally 'true lord', used as an invocation or a form of
   address for the Sikh

safai (safaya) literally 'cleaning', used here to denote cleansing as in abortion

sala elder brother-in-law

salams salutations
salvar loose, baggy trousers
sant saint
santan da dera a place 'inhabited' by saints
sardar Sikhs, or headmen
sardaran di haveli the home/house of the sardars
seva social service
sevian vermicelli
shahji term of respect
shawan da dera place where shahs (wealthy people) live
Sikhi Sikhism
sindoor vermilion
sloka (shlok) stanza, verse, usually of a prayer or invocation
sudras caste name for the low castes
sukhi ras dry, uncooked food
swaraj self-rule
tahsil administrative division
tahsildar head of a tahsil
tandav nritya dance of destruction
tandoor clay oven
taya (tayaji) father's elder brother
telis oil pressers
thakur used here to signify a personal god, a master
thali brass or steel plate for food
thana police station
thoo thoo spitting, sometimes in disgust
tonga horse-drawn carriage
vaar kita to execute a swing of the kirpan, or holy dagger
vatta weight or measure
veer brave, used mainly for men
watan homeland, country
yaar mate, friend
zait-ul-maniat unclaimed property
zenana women's quarters
zilla administrative division

INDEX

Abducted Persons Recovery and Restoration Act 1949, The, 114, 140, 150, 209, 215, 218

Abducted Persons Recovery and Restoration Ordinance, 114, 217

Achhutistan, 251

Ahmad, Aijaz, 70n, 152n

Ahmed, Qamaruddin, 223

Ahmedabad, 6, 109

Akalis, 70

Akali Sena, 71

Akhand Hindustan, 242

Aligarh, 69

Allahabad, 128, 210, 211

All Christian Welfare Society, 250

All India Achhutistan Movement, 251

All India Congress Committee (AICC), 55, 56n, 60, 250, 250n, 252n, 253n, 254n

All India Depressed Classes League, 249, 250n

All India Radio, 198

All India Scheduled Castes Federation, 247

All Pakistan Women's Association, 128

Ambala (also division), 48, 58, 71, 107, 193, 254

Ambedkar, B. N., 239, 256, 257

Amrita Bazar Patrika, 67

Amritsar, 35, 64, 79, 92, 101, 129, 153, 199, 212, 213, 287, 291, 292

Anand, Som, 103n

Anderson, Kathryn, 280n

Armed Forces Reconstruction Committee, 62

Arya Pradeshik Pratinidhi Sabha, 221

Arya Samaj, 71

Atlee, Clement, 71

Ayesha Bibi, 34

Ayodhya, 6

Ayyangar, Gopalaswamy, 140, 141, 142, 216

Attari, 203, 229

Azadi ki Chaon Mein, 116n, 206n, 239n

Baba Lakhan, 80

Babri Masjid, 6, 244, 275

Baluchistan, 13

Banerji, Purnima, 143

Bangladesh, 40

Barthes, Roland, 15

Batala, 64, 235, 236, 237, 266, 267

Beas River (also Beasa), 92, 94, 229

Bedi, Harkishan Das, 291, 292

Begumpur, 74, 76

Bengal (East, West, and undivided), 17, 57, 65, 67, 71, 142, 143, 249, 254

Bewal, 161

Bhagalpur, 6

Bharat (also Bharatmata, Bharatvarsh), 145, 146, 148, 150, 224

Bharatiya Janata Party (BJP), 6, 174

Bharatpur, 241

Bhargava, Dr Gopichand, 241

Bhargava, Pandit Thakur Das, 141, 142, 144, 217

Bhatt, Maqbool, 185
Bhim Patrika Publications, 256n
Bhonsle, J. K., 220
Bhutto, Zulfikar Ali, 37
Bihar, 56, 58, 60, 155, 217
Bikaner, 241
Bikram, 43, 49
Billo, 48, 49
Bombay, 8, 56, 60, 64, 105
Boundary Commission, 65, 67, 249
Britain, 13, 61
Butalia, Subhadra, 24, 41, 43, 48
Buttafuoco, Annarita, 278n

Cabinet Mission, 239
Calcutta, 191
Cambellpur, 224
Ceasefire Agreement, 141
Central Advisory Board, 221
Central Recovery Operation/Orga-
    nization, 113, 114
Chander, Prabodh, 184
Channel 4 Television, 13
Chappell, Peter, 202, 227, 235, 264
Chaudhry, Rahmat Ali, 69
Chaudhry, Sankho, 55
Chitoor, 145
Choa Village, 161
Congress Party (Indian National
    Congress), 5, 53, 54, 70, 71, 114, 184,
    231, 239, 242, 255, 256, 258, 260, 286
Congress Working Committee, 71
Constituent Assembly (of India), 134,
    140, 146, 217; debates of, 214n

Das, Bhagwan, 256n
Daska, 79, 82
Dawn, 67, 223

Dayawanti, 28, 34, 35
Deena Nath, 295
Dek (river), 79
Delhi, 4, 6, 13, 14, 24, 25, 29, 65n, 68,
    74, 89, 90, 102, 106, 110, 116, 117, 129,
    149, 156, 158, 161, 172, 184, 190, 193,
    199, 201, 202, 240, 241, 245, 267,
    287, 290; Bhogal, 116, 156, 160, 172,
    194, 204; Delhi Gate 230; Gandhi
    Nagar, 78; Jangpura, 13, 19, 156, 172,
    283, 287; Karol Bagh, 210; Lajpat
    Nagar, 220; Okhla, 116
Depalpur Canal, 63
Depressed Classes League, 250
Dera Baba Nanak, 82
Dera Ghazi Khan, 224
Devi Dayal, 111
Dharamsala, 93, 97, 99
Dheer, Gurbaksh Singh, 188
Dheer, Sardar Nand Singh, 163
Dhingra, Kamla Buldoon, 87, 88, 89,
    90, 93, 95, 99
Dhingra, Lina, 87

England, 70, 95, 124, 207
Englishstan, 254
Essential Services Maintenance Act
    (ESMA), 256, 257

Fenn, Lakshmi, 245
Fletcher, A. J., 107

Gandhi, Feroze, 205
Gandhi, Indira, 172, 244, 270
Gandhi, Mohandas Karamchand (M.
    K.), 5, 9, 60, 95, 114, 118, 127, 155, 237,
    249, 254
Gandhi Nagar, 78, 81

Gandhi, Rajiv, 4, 184
Gandhi Vanita Ashram, 128, 129, 170,
    207, 223
Ganga Nagar (Bikaner), 243
Garh Mukteshwar, 58
Ghaziabad, 183
Ghaznafar Ali Khan, Raja, 121
Ghazni, 179, 189
Gluck, Sherna Berger, 280n
Golden Temple, 200, 287
Grand Trunk Road, 64
Gujjar Khan, 175, 182, 189
Gujrat, 108, 121, 124, 206
Gulab Kaur, Sardarni, 164
Gupta, Manohar (Guptaji), 183
Gurdaspur, 68, 224, 236
Gurgaon, 49
Gurudwara Bangla Sahib, 184
Gurudwara Dukh Bhajni, 175
Guru Gobind Singh, 186, 187
Guru Granth Sahib, 184, 244
Guru Nanak, 201, 244

Hall Road, 50
Hardwar, 87, 89, 90, 94
Harijan Sewak Sangh, 235n, 237n, 239,
    240, 248n, 250n, 254n, 255
Haryana, 65n
Heer, 104
Himachal, 65n
Hindu Mahasabha, 257, 258n
Hindustan, 116, 147, 148, 182, 194, 202,
    228, 236, 240, 252, 265, 268, 269,
    271. See also India
Hosain, Atia, 284
Hoshiarpur, 130, 132
Humayun's Tomb, 117
Hyderabad, 47

Ilahi, Zahira, 47, 49
India, 4, 8, 17, 19 passim. See also Hin-
    dustan
India Today, 223
Inter-Dominion Agreement, 121, 122,
    216
Inter-Dominion Conference, 114, 212
Inter-Dominion Treaty of Decem-
    ber 6, 1947, 114
Iqbal, Mohammad, 69
Irwin Hospital, 205
Islampura (Krishan Nagar), 291

Jack, Dana C., 280n
Jainendra Gurukul, 221
Jalandhar (also Jullunder, division
    and city), 48, 64–65, 108, 128, 129,
    130, 133, 170, 207, 211, 223, 229, 254,
    256n, 291, 292
Jamia Milia Islamia University, 205
Jamila Begum, 205
Jamuna River (also Jumna), 4, 94
Jangpura. See Delhi
Jaranwala, 230
Jhelum river, 158, 159, 161, 189
Jind, 241
Jinnah, Muhammad Ali, 5, 9, 68, 69,
    252
J.P. Hospital, 202

Kabul, 189
Kabul Kandhar, 179, 189
Kahuta, 174
Kamlaben, 106, 215
Kandhar, 189
Kangra, 93
Kanshi Ram, 182
Kanya mahavidyalaya, 48

Kapur, Dr, 128

Kapurthala, 241

Karachi, 61, 62, 115, 211, 241

Karnal, 129, 130

Karol Bagh. *See* Delhi

Kashmir, 105, 141

Kasturba Gandhi National Memorial Trust for Sindhi Women and Children (also Kasturba Trust), 206, 220–221

Kasturba Niketan, 206, 220

Katiana village, 80

Kaur, Basant, 35, 157–62 passim

Kaur, Dewan, 187

Kaur, Dharam, 222, 223

Kaur, Harnam, 163, 180

Kaur, Maan, 173, 180

Kaur, Mahinder, 187, 222

Kaur, Sardarni Gulab (Mata Lajjawanti), 169. *See also* Lajjawanti

Khalistan, 186, 194

Khandekar, H. J., 249

Khanna, Satti, 202, 227, 235, 264

Kher Dikki village, 291

Khilji, 145

Khosla, G. D., 127n

Khyber Pass, 96

Kidwai, Anis, 117n, 118, 119, 205, 206, 239, 261, 262, 263, 291

Kidwai, Kishwar, 262

Kidwai, Shafi Ahmed, 118

Koran, the, 32

Kota House, 47

Kotra village, 91, 94, 99

Kripalani, Hoondraj, 148

Kripalani, Shri J. B., 55

Krishan Nagar (Islampura), 291

Kulu Manali, 92, 93

Kunzru, Hriday Nath, Pandit, 141, 216, 218

Kurukshetra (Dhera Dhupsadi village), 222

Labour Party (British), 70

Lahore, 63, 64, 66, 69, 70, 97, 103, 104n, 110, 111, 112, 156, 161, 163, 179, 198, 203, 204, 214, 215, 227, 228, 230, 231, 252, 257, 267, 291, 292; Hira Mandi, 78

Lahore High Court, 44

Lahore Resolution, the, 69

Lajjawanti (Sardarni, Mata), 157, 158, 159, 164, 166–167, 187, 188, 287

Lajpat Rai, Lala, 69

Lall, Beah, 251

Lanka, 148

Latif, Chaudhry, 291, 292

League, Muslim. *See* Muslim League

Liaquat Ali Khan, 9, 121, 122

List of Non Muslim Abducted Women and Children in Pakistan and Pakistan Side of the Ceasefire Line in Jammu and Kashmir State, 107–108, 225

London, 73n

Lubanwala, 222

Lucknow, 205

Lyallpur, 60, 61, 72, 102

Maan Kaur, 163

Madras, 70n, 142

Mahabharata, 141

Mahajan, Justice Meher Chand, 67

Maharaj Nabha, 47

Mahatma Hans Raj, 111

Mahila Devi, 99

Mahiwal, 104

Makhijani, Savitri, 197

Mamu, 32, 33, 37, 38, 41, 42. *See also*
Rana

Mandal, J. N., 254

Mandi, 97

Mann, Simranjit Singh, 184

Manto, Saadat Hasan, 258

Manushi, 105

Mataji, 48. *See also* Dayawanti; Ayesha
Bibi

Mator village, 156, 158

Maulana Azad Medical College, 202

Maya Rani, 235–238, 246–248, 251

Military Evacuation Organization,
60, 139

Ministry of Relief and Rehabilitation, 219; Fact-Finding branch of,
126

Miranda House College, 46

Montgomery, 61, 63, 72, 139, 189, 190,
191

Mool Suta Ukhde (Torn from the
Roots), 105

Mountbatten, Lady Edwina, 110, 131,
197

Mountbatten, Lord, 9, 72, 249

Multan, 60, 72, 91

Murad, 202, 203, 209, 227–232

Muslim League, 5, 70, 231, 254, 255,
258

Mussoorie, 118

Mustwana Sahib, 175

Nabha, 42, 44, 46, 47, 48

Nagar, 93, 96

Nankana Sahib, 66

Nara, 155, 158

Narowar, 82

Nasir Hussain, 58

National Discipline Scheme, 220

Nayyar, Sushila, 116, 117, 239

Nehru, Jawaharlal, 5, 9, 68, 72, 112, 114,
127, 148, 150, 158, 161, 239, 256, 257,
270

Nehru, Rameshwari, 112, 130, 198, 214,
240, 242

Nepal, 63

New York, 280n

Noakhali, 60

North West Frontier Province, 258

Nuovo DWF (Donna, Woman,
Femme), 278n

Organiser, The (journal), 145–149, 150,
151

Pakistan, 3, 17, 19, 28 passim

Pakistan High Commission, 25, 212

Palam (Palam colony), 194

Panchkula, 221

Paragpur, 44

Partition Council, 62, 126

Partition Plan, 55, 57, 59, 65, 249

Pasroor village, 82

Patai, Daphne, 280n

Patel, Kamlaben, 105, 106, 111, 144, 211,
212, 215, 291

Patel, Sardar Vallabhai, 5, 9, 68, 72

Patiala, 58, 65n, 117, 193

People's Union for Democratic
Rights (PUDR), 290

Peshawar, 75, 76, 161, 190

Pindi (Rawalpindi), 162

Poona Pact, 239

Prasad, Brajeshwar, 217

Punj, 125

Punjab (East and West), 3, 17, 39, 55–58, 63–67, 69–72, 97, 99, 102, 106, 109, 114, 146, 155, 156, 177, 184, 185, 212, 213, 221, 245, 246, 251–257, 271, 276, 277
Punjab Legislative Assembly, 253
Punjab Provincial Scheduled Caste Federation, 252
Purana Qila, 75, 112
Purewal, Navtej K., 64n

Quetta, 60

Radcliffe, Sir Cyril, 59, 65–68
Rajasthan, 245
Rajbhoj, P. N., 247, 251
Rajpur Road, 47
Rama (Ram, Shri Ram), 141, 145, 148
Ramayana, 141
Rana (also Ranamama, Mamu), 23, 24, 26–33, 37–39, 41–46, 48–51, 100, 104, 282
Rangabad, 160
Rani Padmini, 145
Ranjha, 104
Rao, U. Bhaskar, 59n, 122
Ravana, 141, 145
Ravi (river), 82
Rawalpindi, 13, 14, 56, 57, 60, 71, 91, 106, 156, 157, 161, 172, 175, 180, 181, 189, 190, 201, 224, 247, 282, 287, 288
Rawat village, 159, 161, 162, 189
Ray, Renuka, 143
Razia Begum, 212
Red Cross, 126
Red Fort, 46
Relief and Rehabilitation Department (Government of India), 239, 241, 242n
Reserve Bank of India, 69
Richada village, 80
RSS (Rashtriya Swayamsevak Sangh), 6, 59, 71, 145, 206, 280, 283
Royal Air Force, 43

Sadda village, 154
Sadeeqa Anwar, 222, 223
Sadiok village, 161
Saharanpur, 44
Sahedra, 229
Sahgal, Damyanti (also Danti), 18, 87–92, 95, 99, 112–113, 116n, 120–126, 128, 130–135 passim
Saintha village, 161, 175, 181
Sajawal Khan, 181, 187
Sanatan Dharam High School, 291
Sarabhai, Mridula, 111, 112, 113, 114, 118, 130, 198, 214, 291
Saran, Raksha, 198
Sargodha, 60
Sarkar, Sumit, 70
Satya (Devi), 120, 121
Save the Children Committee, 221
Saxena, Mohan Lal, 257
Saxena, Professor Shibban Lal, 190
Scheduled Caste Federation, 250
School of Social Work, 198
Selected Works of Jawaharlal Nehru, 127n
Seminar, 152n
SGPC (Shiromani Gurudwara Prabandhak Committee), 172, 185, 186
Shah Nawaz, 158
Shakarpur, 186
Sharda Bhavan, 210

Sheikhupura, 170
Shiv Sena, 6
Shudul, Abdul, 74–77
Sikhistan, 270
Simeon, Jean, 246
Simla, 48, 65, 97, 250
Sind, 55, 60, 148, 256
Singh, Avtar, 179, 193
Singh, Bir Bahadur, 31, 35, 72, 163, 164, 166 passim
Singh, Buta (Jamil Ahmed), 101, 102, 103, 104, 184, 185
Singh, Gulab, 163, 168
Singh, Gurmeet, 162
Singh, Harbans, 158
Singh, Hari, 180–181, 188
Singh, Justice Harnam, 179, 188, 189
Singh, Javind, 223
Singh, Kirpal, 65, 68, 117, 139
Singh, Kulwant, 165, 200, 201, 202, 204, 209
Singh, Maharaja Ranjit, 161
Singh, Mangal, 35, 153, 154, 155, 157, 199, 200, 287
Singh, Manmohan, 76, 78, 284
Singh, Master Tara, 183
Singh, Niranjan, 223
Singh, Pahwa, 212
Singh, Pratap, 189
Singh, Rajinder, 57, 78–80
Singh, Ram, 179
Singh, Sabha, 71
Singh, Sant Attar ji, 173
Singh, Sant Gulab (Sardar Gulab), 179, 188
Singh, Santokh, 99
Singh, Sant Raja (Raja Singha), 157, 163, 164, 175, 179, 188

Singh, Sardar Hukam, 215
Singh, Tara, 156
Singh, Trilok, 199, 200, 201, 209, 287
Singh, Virinder, 184
Siraj, Chaudhry, 292
Sita, 141, 145
Sobti, Krishna, 89, 221, 283
Spain, 258
State Bank of Pakistan, 69
State High School (Nabha), 42
Statesman, The, 155, 162, 165
Steedman, Carolyn, 73
Stern Reckoning, 127n
Story of Rehabilitation, The, 220n
Surat, 6
Swaminathan, Shrimati Ammu, 142
Syed, Sir Ahmed, 4

Thamali village, 156, 158, 160, 161–162, 187, 192, 288
Thapar, P. N., 91, 111
Thapar, Premvati (Auntie, Masi, Premi), 85, 89, 111, 112, 133, 210
Thoa Khalsa, 35, 155, 157, 161, 163, 166, 167, 168, 170, 173, 175, 178, 181, 182, 184, 187
Thus Spoke Ambedkar: Selected Speeches, 256n
Tihai village, 161
Tihar village, 238, 239, 243
Tiwana, Khizir Hayat Khan, 70
'Toba Tek Singh,' 258
Tyagi, Shri Mahavir, 143

Unionist Party, 70
Union of Indian Sovereign Democratic Republic, 145

United Council of Relief and Welfare, 197
Upper Bari Doab Canal, 63
UP (Uttar Pradesh, United Provinces), 56, 111, 183, 216
UP Scheduled Caste Federation Conference, 254

Vaid, Sudesh, 19, 78, 87, 107, 172
Vietnam, 286

Vikram, 34. *See also* Bikram
Vishwa Hindu Parishad, 6
Vohra, Dr Devi Chand, 92, 93

Wagah, 39, 64, 229
Wah camp, 189

Young, James E., 7n, 9, 11n, 282n

Zainab, 101, 102, 103, 104

Urvashi Butalia is the Co-Founder of Kali for Women, India's first feminist publishing house. She is coeditor of *Making a Difference: Feminist Publishing in the South* and *In Other Words: New Writing by Indian Women*.